THE DHOFAR WAR

THE DHOFAR WAR

British Covert Campaigning in Arabia
1965–1975

Stephen James Quick

UNIVERSITY
of
EXETER
PRESS

First published in 2024 by
University of Exeter Press
Reed Hall, Streatham Drive
Exeter EX4 4QR
UK

www.exeterpress.co.uk

Copyright © 2024 Stephen James Quick

The right of Stephen James Quick to be identified as author of this work has been asserted by him in accordance with the Copyright, Designs and Patents Act 1988.

Paperback edition published 2025.

All rights reserved. Apart from short excerpts for use in research or for reviews, no part of this document may be printed or reproduced, stored in a retrieval system, or transmitted in any form or by any means, electronic, mechanical, photocopying, recording, now known or hereafter invented or otherwise without prior permission from the publisher.

https://doi.org/10.47788/QBOS3439

British Library Cataloguing in Publication Data
A catalogue record for this book is available from the British Library

ISBN 978-1-80413-098-8 Hardback
ISBN 978-1-80413-207-4 Paperback
ISBN 978-1-80413-099-5 ePub
ISBN 978-1-80413-100-8 PDF

Cover image: RAF Wessex helicopter (painted with SOAF markings) supplying Royal Engineers (2 Troop, 48 Field Sqn. (Ripon)) on the Hornbeam Line.
© Sid Pass 1974

Every effort has been made to trace copyright holders and obtain permission to reproduce the material included in this book. Please get in touch with any enquiries or information relating to an image or the rights holder.

Typeset in Adobe Caslon Pro by S4Carlisle Publishing Services, Chennai, India

In gratitude to my parents, Mr R. Quick and Mrs K. Quick, and some return on the investment of surrounding me with books from an early age.

Contents

	Figures and Tables	viii
	Glossary and Abbreviations	x
	Preface and Acknowledgements	xiii
	Maps	xv
1	Introduction: A Rare Cold War Success	1
2	The Dhofar War: Origins, Players, and Timeline	16
3	Politics and Diplomacy	29
4	Military Strategy	69
5	Military Operations and Tactics	97
6	Non-Kinetic Military and Informal Support	142
7	Conclusion: 'Cut from a Different Cloth'	184
	Notes	196
	Bibliography	224
	Index	231

Figures and Tables

Figures

Figure 2.1. Western Dhofari Jebel covered in 'Khareef' monsoon mists.

Figure 2.2. Landscape in central Jebel.

Figure 2.3. British soldiers outside their 'sangars' (protected living quarters) at 'Reef Base' on the Hornbeam Line.

Figure 2.4. Interior of a three-man sangar on the Hornbeam Line with life's essentials (weapons, ammunition, medical pack, water canteen, shaving and 'brew' kits).

Figure 4.1. Cross-section of barbed-wire construction of the Hornbeam Line (soldiers of the SAF's Northern Frontier Regiment can be observed providing guard duties in the foreground).

Figure 4.2. British-produced SAF propaganda leaflet. Source: TNA—DEFE 25/186—'Muscat and Oman General'. ACDS (Ops) 76/3, VODS 'Psyops in Oman and Dhofar—Updating Sitrep', 19 March 1971.

Figure 5.1. Mirbat Fort, view from the Wali's Fort.

Figure 5.2: Mirbat Fort showing the gun pit where the 25-pounder artillery piece was fired at point blank range at the advancing Adoo by the SAS.

Figure 5.3. British soldiers returning to base on foot (Jebel area, west of Salalah).

Figure 6.1. British soldiers being transported by an RAF Wessex helicopter on the Jebel (the Mughsayl coastline can be seen in the far distance).

Tables

Table 1.1. 'Sliding scale of influence' war phases
Table 2.1. Key Dhofar War events timeline
Table 3.1. Key British–Omani treaties and agreements
Table 4.1. COIN and warfare experience of CSAFs
Table 5.1. Key wartime operational-level contribution and influence
Table 6.1. Key Dhofar campaign non-kinetic and informal UK support contributions
Table 6.2. Key British persons of influence in Oman during Dhofar War
Table 6.3. Arms exports to Sultanate of Oman during Dhofar War (sipri tivs—millions)

Glossary and Abbreviations

ADDF	Abu Dhabi Defence Force
Adoo	Anglicized Arabic word for 'enemy'—widely used to describe the Dhofari insurgents
Artesh	Iranian Army
Askari(s)	Native soldier(s) (non-SAF)
BATT	British Army Training Team
BBC	British Broadcasting Corporation
BBME	British Bank of the Middle East
BF	Batinah Force
BoE	Bank of England
CASEVAC	Casualty Evacuation
CAT	Civil Aid Team
CBFG	Commander British Forces Gulf
CDS	Chief of Defence Staff
CENTO	The Central Treaty Organization (formerly Baghdad Pact)
CIGS	Chief of the Imperial General Staff
CO	Commanding Officer
COIN	Counterinsurgency
CSAF	Commander Sultan's Armed Forces
DCA	Dhurfari Charitable Association
DF	Dhofar Force
DFC	Distinguished Flying Cross

GLOSSARY AND ABBREVIATIONS

DLF	Dhofar Liberation Front
DR	Desert Regiment
DSO	Dhurfari Soldiers Association
FO/FCO	Foreign Office/Foreign and Commonwealth Office
FST	Field Surgical Team
GCHQ	(UK) Government Communications Headquarters
GOC	General Officer Commanding
IC	Intelligence Corps
IIBG	Imperial Iranian Battle Group
IMF	International Monetary Fund
IO	Intelligence Officer
Jebali(s)	Inhabitant(s) of the Jebel
Jebel	Mountain/mountain range
JR	Jebel Regiment
LFA	Land Freedom Army
LPD	Landing Platform Dock
LSP	Loan Service Personnel
MAF	Muscat Armed Forces
MAN	Movement of Arab Nationalists
MBE	Member of the Most Excellent Order of the British Empire (award)
MI	Muscat Infantry
MOD	Ministry of Defence
MOFF	Muscat and Oman Field Force
MR	Muscat Regiment
NATO	North Atlantic Treaty Organization
NDFLOAG	National Democratic Front for the Liberation of Oman and the Arabian Gulf—affiliate movement of PFLOAG
NFR	Northern Frontier Regiment
NLF	National Liberation Front
OG	Oman Gendarmerie
OIS	Oman Intelligence Service
OLA	Oman Liberation Army
OR	Oman Regiment
ORD	Oman Research Department

PD(O)	Petroleum Development (Oman)
PDRY	People's Democratic Republic of Yemen (from Dec 1970)
PFLO	Popular Front for the Liberation of Oman
PFLOAG	Popular Front for the Liberation of the Occupied Arabian Gulf
PRPG	Political Resident Persian Gulf
PRSY	People's Republic of Southern Yemen (initial state entity formed after UK withdrawal from Aden/South Arabia in Nov 1967)
RA	Royal Artillery
RAF	Royal Air Force
RAFO	Royal Air Force of Oman
RCT	Royal Corps of Transport
RE	Royal Engineers
RFA	Royal Fleet Auxiliary
RPG	Rocket-propelled grenade
RM	Royal Marines
ROP	Royal Oman Police
RN	(British) Royal Navy
SAF	Sultan's Armed Forces
SAM	Surface-to-air missile
SAS	Special Air Service Regiment
SB	Special Branch (Police)
SEP	Surrendered Enemy Personnel
SIS	Secret Intelligence Service
SOAF	Sultan of Oman's Air Force
SOE	Special Operations Executive
SON	Sultan of Oman's Navy
TOS	Trucial Oman Scouts
UAE	United Arab Emirates
UAR	United Arab Republic
VE	Victory in Europe (Day)

Preface and Acknowledgements

The decade-long war in Oman's Dhofar province (1965–1975) has been largely overshadowed in both the British and wider counterinsurgency (COIN) literature as well as in the public imagination by higher-profile campaigns. These include the campaigns in Palestine (1944–1948), Malaya (1948–1960), Kenya (1952–1960), Cyprus (1955–1959), Aden (1963–1967), and in Northern Ireland over a thirty-year period from the late 1960s. This is due in part to the fact that the Dhofar War was largely conducted away from the full glare of international publicity in a little-known corner of the Arabian Peninsula by secretive and largely covert means. It was, however, one of the few successful COIN campaigns carried out against Marxist-inspired insurgents during the Cold War, making it a significant historical episode.

This book presents a comprehensive survey of the Dhofar War and the associated British role in order to bolster its rightful place within the wider COIN literature and the public imagination. Significantly, it also serves to reinterpret a divided scholarly narrative, therefore presenting a more balanced and considered verdict of the history of the war and the role of the UK in realizing the defeat of the Dhofari insurgents in 1975. In short, the book establishes that although the Dhofar War was not a directly UK-fought campaign to the extent of its other post-World War Two COIN undertakings, it was, however, a decisively British-enabled win.

This book was made possible through the support of a number of key individuals, chiefly Dr Walter Ladwig and Dr Simon Anglim of King's College London, and the advice and guidance provided by colleagues based in the United Arab Emirates. Special thanks are also due to Gp. Capt. (Ret'd) Ray Goodall and to the late Lt. Col. (Ret'd) David Neild for their valuable first-hand insights into, and recollections of, past events. The helpfulness of the many archivists encountered during the research for this book should also be acknowledged (especially Ms Debbie Usher at the Middle East Archive at St Anthony's College, Oxford), and, in addition, that of the military staff at the Sultan's Armed Forces Museum in Muscat, who were most gracious in their assistance. Further, the completion of the book was only possible due to the cheerful patience of my wife throughout, and the kind proof-reading assistance of friends, colleagues, and family members alike (they know who they are). Last, but not least, I would like to express my gratitude to the publishing team at the University of Exeter Press, for both seeing the potential of this book, and their support in seeing it through to publication.

Finally, it should be mentioned that the responsibility for any mistakes, errors, or misrepresentations made in the text of this book is mine alone.

The opinions expressed in this book are those of the author and do not reflect the views of Rabdan Academy, or the United Arab Emirates government.

MAPS

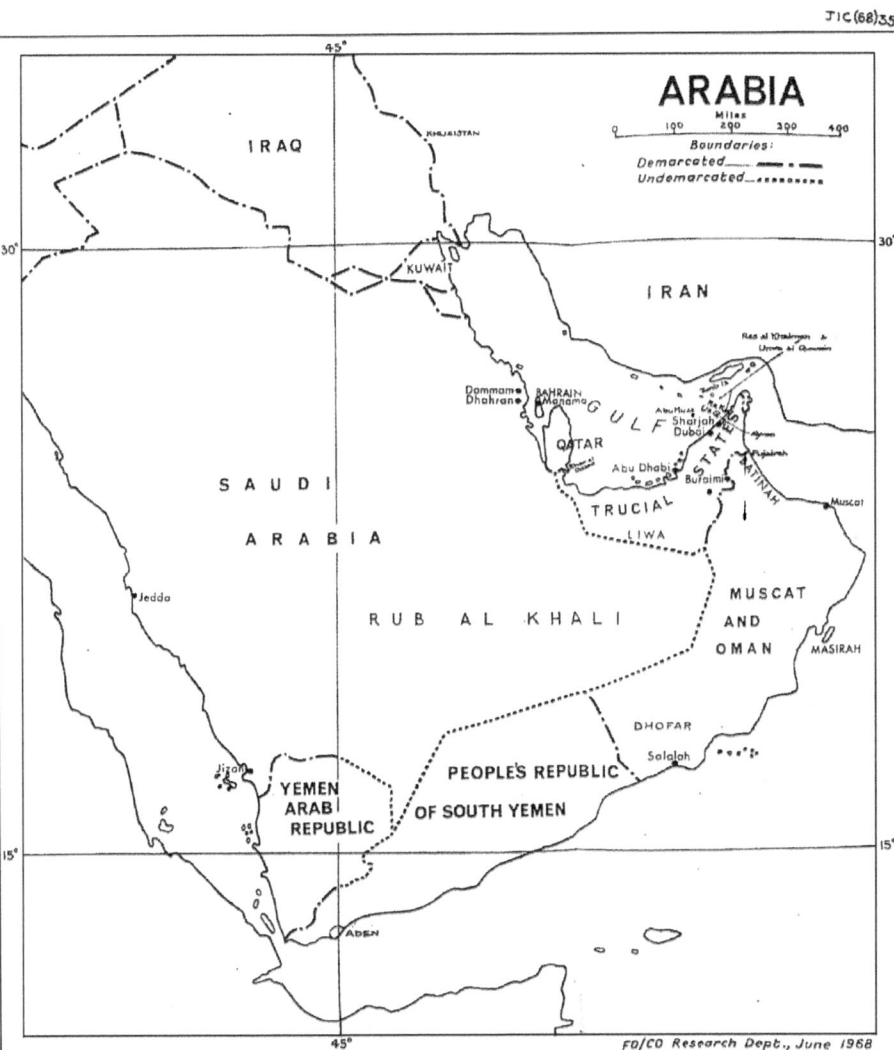

Map 1. Oman and Gulf region (pre-1970 coup).
SOURCE: TNA—CAB 158/70—'Cabinet Joint Intelligence Committee (A): Likely Developments in the Gulf and their Probable Effects for British Interests', 7 June 1968. © The National Archives

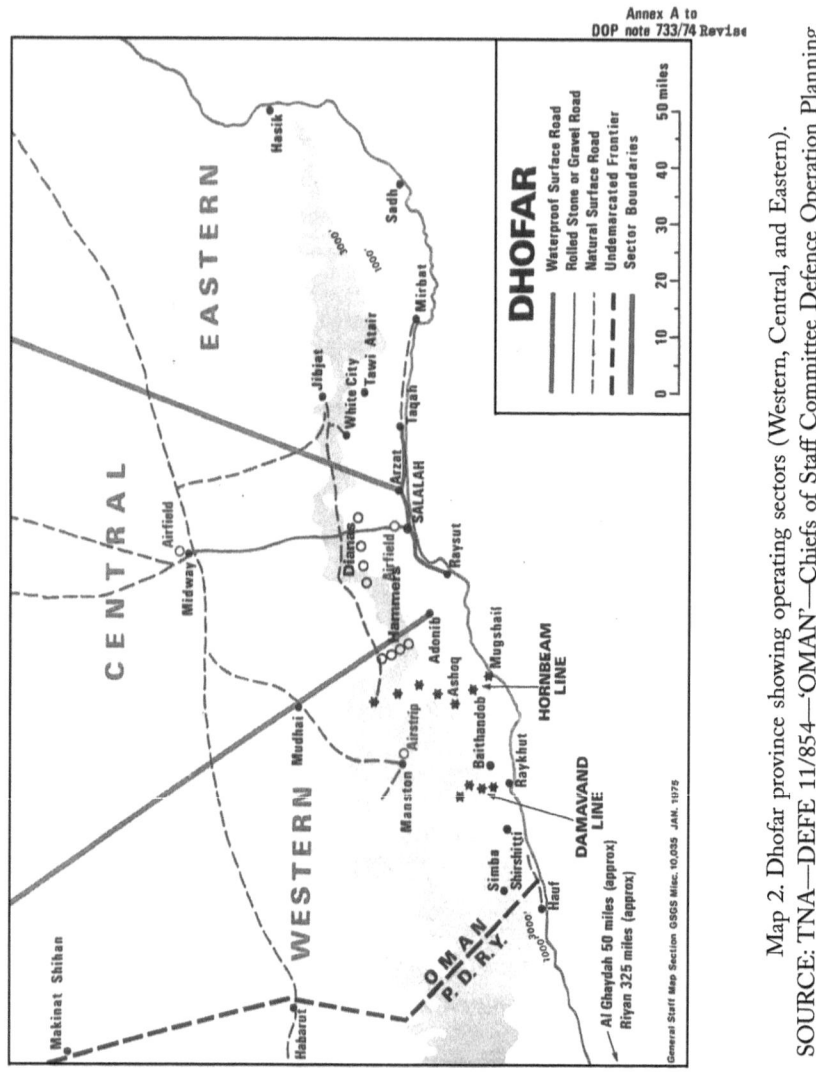

Map 2. Dhofar province showing operating sectors (Western, Central, and Eastern).
SOURCE: TNA—DEFE 11/854—'OMAN'—Chiefs of Staff Committee Defence Operation Planning Staff: The Progress of Operations in Oman Report by DOP Staff—Annex A to DOP Note 733/74 (Revised), 26 February 1975. © The National Archives

1 Introduction: A Rare Cold War Success

Oman's Dhofar War was one of the few successful counterinsurgency (COIN) campaigns undertaken during the Cold War period. Engineered through largely secretive and covert assistance to the Sultanate from the government of the United Kingdom (UK), the ultimately successful Dhofar COIN campaign arguably prevented the loss of both Dhofar province and greater Oman to a well-backed and executed Marxist insurgency. The Dhofar COIN win further helped to halt the spread of Communism and likewise combined Chinese or Soviet great-power influence in the Arabian Gulf in the ideologically polarized Cold War period.[1] The campaign also enabled the UK to support a historical ally and helped facilitate an orderly implementation of its military withdrawal East of Suez in 1971, in marked contrast to the rushed and untidy exit from Aden in 1967.[2] The outcome of the Dhofar COIN campaign also contributed directly to the maintenance of world economic stability by securing continued access to vital Gulf oil supplies via the Strait of Hormuz.[3] The Dhofar campaign may not have been a flawless anti-insurgency undertaking at an operational level, but it was a model for attaining war outcomes whilst successfully limiting involvement and cost for the sponsoring COIN partner. In short, the COIN win in Dhofar was a rare occurrence in the Cold War era and, alongside the British role in its achievement, should be lauded as such.

Literature concerning the Dhofar War to date is largely both politicized and polarized, and the relatively limited body of work that does exist can be broadly divided into three main narrative groupings. Firstly, the orthodox historical view contends that the war was essentially an ideal or 'model' British counterinsurgency campaign, and includes many of the original biographical materials from those who served in the conflict and from earlier scholars of the subject.[4] Within this narrative, the Dhofar COIN campaign has even been described as the best ever conducted by the UK since the victory in the Malayan Emergency of the 1940s and 1950s.[5] Secondly, revisionist scholars, often armed with archival documentation not available to the original writers on the war, have argued that the campaign was not particularly 'British', nor indeed successful, and that it lasted longer and was more costly than it should have been.[6] As a subset of the revisionist school, the Omani 'official narrative' purports that it was not Britain, but actually the Sultan of Oman who guided his own armed forces to victory—primarily through his own skills and leadership abilities.[7] Thirdly, the general left-leaning view quite rightly puts a balancing emphasis on the war from the insurgent perspective. It also backs up the revisionist stance, largely viewing the Dhofar campaign (like the overall UK COIN record) as not particularly successful, and that it was, moreover, a throwback to previous exploitative British colonial campaigns and associated Imperial attitudes and outlook.[8] This particular view also, however, acts to endorse the orthodox perspective by reinforcing the overwhelming British influence on the war, albeit for different and more pervasive reasons of intent. Fourthly, these main literature narratives also feed into divergent perspectives on specific war-related phenomena which require clarification. These include the importance of the 1970 coup that brought Sultan Qaboos to power and whether it can be considered the war's turning point, and differing pre- and post-1970 campaign perceptions of success.

The historical reality of the Dhofar War is more complex and nuanced than the explanations provided by any such entrenched perspectives, and in addition to the different narrative groupings, there is also the issue of emphasis. There are several publications dedicated largely to the military aspects of the Dhofar War. Key amongst these are, for instance, Tony Jeapes's *SAS Operation Oman* (1980), John Akehurst's *We Won a War: The Campaign in Oman 1965–75* (1982), and J.E. Peterson's *Oman's Insurgencies: The Sultanate's Struggle for Supremacy* (2007).[9] These publications are all excellent in their own right, but in going beyond their primary focus—which understandably involves delving into detailed operational and often tactical minutiae—this book will rather demonstrate the full extent of both the wider UK military and non-martial role in the Dhofar War and its subsequent contribution towards securing the defeat of the Dhofari insurgents. Is this respect, this study adds to the more varied

INTRODUCTION: A RARE COLD WAR SUCCESS

and broad approach towards the subject as seen in publications such as James Worrall's *Statebuilding and Counterinsurgency in Oman: Political, Military and Diplomatic Relations at the End of Empire*, and Abdel Takriti's *Monsoon Revolution: Republicans, Sultans, and Empires in Oman, 1965–1976*, albeit with a markedly different emphasis.[10]

With such diverse narratives and emphases within an already limited literature base, this book serves three main purposes. Firstly, this study seeks to respectfully redress some of the overall shortfalls of the existing literature. It does this by underlining and reinforcing the paramount role played by Britain in achieving the Dhofar War victory, as well as highlighting the true breadth and extent of this role, which extended much further than military assistance alone. In this, the second factor acts to reinforce the first, through acknowledging the non-UK contribution by others such as Sultan Qaboos, the Sultan's Armed Forces (SAF) soldiery, and foreign forces like the Iranians, but by also reinforcing the key argument that no other party had the same level of impact. Hence, one of the yardsticks utilized throughout the study to underscore the primacy of the British role is the level of success in the war from the UK perspective. Secondly, this study aims to enhance or add to the existing literature primarily through the introduction of the 'sliding scale of influence' framework narrative, which emphasizes the evolving nature of the British role throughout the war. Explained in more detail later in this chapter, instead of an often binary 'British' or 'not British' influence-related debate apparent in the existing literature, the framework shows that the UK role changed from near protagonist to a more 'hands-off' role whilst still retaining the key levers of influence over Oman and the war. This situation existed alongside most related efforts being veiled in a shroud of discretion—and often secrecy—throughout the war, largely being out of the view of the general public and on occasion even from the British Parliament.[11] Thirdly, this study aims to raise the profile of the Dhofar War in academic circles as well as in the public consciousness. The importance of the war, its outcome, and the British role has, to date, been undersold academically. In addition, despite its very limited size, there are also lessons that could and should be drawn from the Dhofar example which are discussed in more detail in the concluding chapter. Finally, the war has also never had its deserved place in terms of public interest, primarily because of its largely secret nature, and limited impact on British society (for instance with no Vietnam draft equivalent), and very limited UK casualties. It has been overshadowed in both history books and popular culture by other campaigns such as Vietnam and Northern Ireland. The Dhofar War case is also not only of academic interest but is also a remarkable story in itself. The events of the war read like a film script or elements of a great novel with exotic locations, Sultans, princes, coups, Special Forces, fortitude, heroism (on both sides), impending defeat, then ultimate victory—but also treachery, betrayal, and intrigue in equal measures. For all these reasons, the Dhofar War should be afforded the status, prominence, and significance it deserves.

In order to address its main themes, and to set both the tone and context of this book, brief explanations of some key dates, names, and terms are necessary. The book primarily covers the period from 1965 to 1975. This is due to 9 June 1965 being the first attack by the newly formed Dhofar Liberation Front (DLF), and the official announcement of victory by Sultan Qaboos taking place in December 1975. There was, however, insurgent activity from 1963, and even after the official announcement of the war's end, all the way up to 1980.[12] Related to this qualification is reference to the insurgents themselves. The official name of the insurgent group fighting in Dhofar changed over time. The DLF was formed in 1965; this changed to the Popular Front for the Liberation of the Occupied Arabian Gulf (PFLOAG) in 1968. The name was modified again to the Popular Front for the Liberation of Oman and the Arabian Gulf (PFLOAG) in 1971, and finally to the Popular Front for the Liberation of Oman (PFLO) in 1974. For clarity, this book largely refers to such organizations interchangeably as the 'insurgents' or as the 'Adoo', which is an anglicized version of the Arabic word for enemy.

With regard to insurgency, as far back in history as the writings of Sun Tzu, guerrilla warfare was seen in terms of military conflict and the tactics employed by the 'weak' over the 'strong'.[13] Ian Beckett describes the development of such irregular modes of warfare into revolutionary guerrilla warfare encompassing subversion, propaganda, and military action into a concerted effort to seek power and overthrow the status quo, stating: 'More properly, therefore, modern revolutionary guerrilla warfare might be termed insurgency.'[14] As such, insurgency can be seen as a combined politico-military campaign

INTRODUCTION: A RARE COLD WAR SUCCESS

which seeks to control the population and overthrow the incumbent political authority of a territory or government of a state.[15] Following this, in its simplest form, counterinsurgency therefore 'is an umbrella term that describes the complete range of measures that governments take to defeat insurgencies'.[16] More specifically it is the 'range of military, political and socio-economic measures adopted by security forces in response to the outbreak of revolutionary guerrilla warfare or insurgency'.[17] COIN can, therefore, be seen primarily as a response to insurgent actions, and where conventional warfare concentrates largely on controlling territory, anti-insurgent activities are geared to controlling populations.

The modern use of the term 'hearts and minds' stems from its use by Field Marshal Sir Gerald Templer relating to UK actions in the Malayan campaign (1948–1960). Although such a concept is not universally accepted with regard to post-war UK COIN, 'The phrase "hearts and minds" is generally associated with a less coercive approach to counterinsurgency which emphasises the importance of "minimum force" in order to win the "hearts and minds" of the people' by addressing socio-economic or political grievances.[18] Whilst not always less coercive, the definition lies between this position and the 'firm smack of government' or a more conventional 'annihilation of the enemy [approach]' spectrum end, or more iron fist than velvet glove, and this was largely the case in Dhofar as elsewhere.[19] Essentially the phrase means acknowledging that insurgents can rarely be defeated by force alone due to the political element of insurgency, and the need for the governing status quo to gain the population's support to win.

The concept of strategy is applicable to varying contexts but essentially revolves around the plan to achieve policy goals and the relationship between 'ends' and the available 'means'.[20] In the military context of this book, strategy is defined as: 'The link between military means and political ends, the scheme for how to make one produce the other', and more specifically the means of achieving the overarching policy goals of the British government and its institutions via military support to Oman.[21] Following the established levels of warfare, in the context of this book, operations refer to large-scale and complex manoeuvres or missions by civilian security agencies or, more commonly, military actions at unit size or above at the campaign level designed to achieve strategic aims. During the Dhofar War, this would usually mean military procedures of company or larger size and complexity, often involving land, air, and sometimes sea-borne military assets to achieve an objective. Whilst often challenging to precisely differentiate between the operational and tactical levels of warfare in a small war such as that which took place in Oman's Dhofar province, tactics then are generally the physical ways by which operations are carried out and therefore how strategy is executed. This pertains to the Clausewitzian separation between tactics as the employment of military forces in any type of engagement (or operation) and the higher-level use of such to achieve the aim of the war or the strategic end.[22] For the purposes of this book, tactics translates into the methods utilized by military units at the 'fighting' level, usually from regimental level and below, to achieve their military aims within operations.

Finally, in this book's narrative, the term 'British' refers to the governmental apparatus, state or private organizations of Britain, or UK state employees or private citizens, as specified. UK historical influence within Oman and resultantly in the Dhofar War was cumulatively all-encompassing but cannot be explained purely in terms of state actions, as both public state and private actors had key roles in achieving victory. Although the UK state-centric perspective is the main focus in the subject literature, non-state influence is clearly highlighted also.[23] British influence in this book is thus primarily described in terms of state actors, but the secondary-level sway brought by private organizations or individuals is also addressed.

In terms of general organization, this book has a defined structure and logical flow between chapters. Whilst the introduction establishes its overall purpose, scope, its structure and approach, the remainder of the work is organized in a thematic basis. Chapter 2 provides an essential physical and historical contextual setting for the reader both in terms of Dhofar itself, and the key events, progression, and outcome of the ten-year conflict. It also highlights the main international state 'players' in the war, as well as the key individual characters involved. Chapter 3 examines the level of Britain's political and diplomatic influence on the Dhofar War, analysing the UK's overarching and regional strategic goals relating to the war, as well as those aimed more specifically at the Omani state level and whether these were achieved, as well as the key aspects of related British influence. Via the 'sliding scale of influence', Chapter 3 establishes that even though Britain's political and diplomatic

INTRODUCTION: A RARE COLD WAR SUCCESS

influence diminished during the war, it still played a central role in the campaign win. Chapter 4 then moves the focus to analysing the influence of Britain on the Dhofar War from a military strategy perspective. It establishes that such influence, unlike in other areas, did not diminish over the duration of the war and remained firmly in British hands throughout. As a result, the strategic-level aims of the UK were largely eventually achieved, and Britain retained the principal strategic influence over the Dhofar War, largely through its senior seconded military personnel. Moving down the levels of warfare, Chapter 5 covers Britain's influence and success at the operational and tactical levels. Although ultimately strategically successful, notions of success in the Dhofar War are more nuanced, with elements of failure apparent, and this is addressed from an operational perspective. Issues such as control and influence over operations in general are covered, as well as specific key operational episodes. The chapter evaluates the extent of the 'sliding scale of influence' with regard to operations, especially concerning the contribution of non-UK military forces, including those from Iran and Jordan. It then highlights the key control of tactics at unit level and below via UK personnel which enabled the SAF, SOAF, and SON to operate effectively during the war. Chapter 6 then addresses the influence of Britain in the sphere of non-kinetic military and informal support for the Dhofar COIN campaign, which includes economic and financial provision aspects, in addition to that pertaining to the supply and impact of personnel and of British military training, technical military support, and the provision of war materials. The chapter highlights that although influence in certain areas of 'non-kinetic and informal' support waned during the war, in other key aspects, it remained constant, which reinforced the British role in achieving the eventual victory. The book's conclusion (Chapter 7) acts primarily to reinforce the utility of the 'sliding scale of influence' framework in clarifying the prime UK role in the overall Dhofar War victory. The practical implications of the book's findings are also highlighted, including the potential relevance of lessons learned in the Dhofar campaign to COIN policy and doctrine going forward, both from a UK and a wider standpoint.

In terms of general approach, two main themes are utilized throughout this study to fulfil its highlighted purposes. The first is ascertaining how successful the Dhofar War was from a British perspective, and secondly how the UK role changed over the course of the war, utilizing the 'sliding scale of influence' framework. The UK involved itself in the Dhofar War for several reasons ranging from pure self-interest to genuine altruism, and worked towards achieving a set of aims or goals from the strategic level downwards, and in multiple areas, as per this study's thematic chapter structure.[24] These were, in the main, achieved, but Britain can be judged not to have solely conducted the Dhofari COIN campaign, in contrast to its previous COIN actions. Additionally, from a pre-eminent position on political, diplomatic, military, as well as economic fronts, Britain's influence over Oman and the war declined in many ways throughout its duration. In the most important areas, however, of military strategy, operational command and control, tactics, and key support functions, Britain's influence and importance remained firm throughout and were, collectively, the primary reason for the insurgent defeat. Britain set the required end-states for the war through its goals and was the main driver in achieving them. The Dhofar War can therefore be considered not so much a wholly UK COIN campaign as in the cases of the Malayan or Kenyan (Mau Mau Revolt) Emergencies, where Britain was the colonial power in charge of all arms of the state, but was, nonetheless, very much a British-inspired and facilitated win.

This idea of changing levels of influence is central to the 'sliding scale of influence' framework introduced by this study, which presents an original way of viewing British sway over, and role in, the eventual victory. As such, it highlights the clear distinction between fading influence in many areas but also comprehensive and near-total continued control in others. What started out effectively as a purely British-led and implemented campaign from the early forays into Dhofar by the SAF under the Commander Sultan's Armed Forces (CSAF) Col. Tony Lewis, in the mid-1960s, evolved.[25] The early UK-dominated campaign later changed significantly into an international coalition involving substantial forces from both Jordan and Iran.[26] Whilst some areas of UK influence declined over time, in others, however, it was fully maintained. This situation was leveraged to enable the overall UK-engineered war-winning strategy to be implemented, the final campaign offensives in the Western Area of Dhofar to be successfully conducted, and victory declared in 1975.

The 'sliding scale of influence' framework divides the Dhofar War into three broad phases. Unlike later periods, the Dhofar COIN campaign can be

INTRODUCTION: A RARE COLD WAR SUCCESS

considered an almost wholly British-run affair in Phase 1. This is due in part to a situation of inertia from the circumstances inherited from the Jebel Akhdar campaign and the 'Exchange of Letters', which formalized large-scale UK military assistance to Oman from 1958. Alongside the general level of cooperation and influence by Britain over Oman gained through centuries of interaction and at times intervention, the 'Exchange of Letters' represented the moment Britain's official role in Oman was enacted. For the first time, serving members of the UK armed forces assumed the mantle of establishing, running, and the ongoing development of the military forces of Oman. A commitment was made to provide British taxpayers' money on an ongoing and substantial basis to equip, train, and organize the newly designated SAF. When the Dhofar insurgency first developed, it was the SAF with a seconded UK officer in charge that was despatched to Dhofar in 1964 to quell the then localized and small-scale nationalist-oriented uprising.[27] In addition, although ordered by the Sultan, the SAF organizational and fighting ability was directly influenced by the British government. Oman did not have the independent means or experienced leaders to initiate such a task without external assistance. With the Sultan having moved from his Muscat base and permanently relocating to Salalah in 1958, both the day-to-day business of Muscat-based governance and the strategic and operational aspects of the COIN campaign were left primarily to a small group of key, and largely British, national advisors within the bounds of the incumbent Sultan Said's preferred generally coercive approach towards the insurgents and populace.[28]

During Phase 2 of the war, when Sultan Said's negative influence on the campaign, and lack of cooperation or heeding of advice, reached crisis point by 1970, it was the UK government that both supported and facilitated the July 1970 Salalah coup to help salvage the war.[29] The UK government then formed the Interim Advisory Council (IAC) to keep the vital branches of government working in Muscat, firstly so that the fledgling administration of the new Sultan Qaboos could survive, secondly to keep up the prosecution of the war, and in effect to temporarily run the country. This continued until the arrival of Qaboos's uncle Tariq from self-imposed exile abroad to take over the role of Prime Minister, a month after the coup. The UK-facilitated coup was one of the main contributors to success in the Dhofar War because it fundamentally changed the parameters of the conflict. In terms of governance

Table 1.1: 'Sliding scale of influence' war phases

PERIOD	DATES	CSAF TENURE	KEY FEATURES/EVENTS
PHASE 1: Pre-1970 coup Virtual British monopoly	1964–early 1970	Col. Tony Lewis Brig. Corran Purdon	Sultan indebted to UK for assistance in Jebel Akhdar campaign Sultan retired to Salalah. Operations from Muscat controlled largely by UK civilian and military advisors Exchange of Letters (and later upgrade) instigated SAF reforming under a British LSP CSAF plus provision of LSP staff and regimental officers Almost complete autonomy for British LSP CSAF to conduct initial Dhofar expedition in 1964 and for remainder of campaign UK exerts main external influence on Oman/Dhofar campaign
PHASE 2: Post-1970 coup (to 1972) High point of influence then transition to decline	1970–mid-1972	Brig. John Graham	UK government instigation of 1970 coup to depose Sultan Said Post-coup 'high point' of British influence: • IAC British formed and controlled (invites Tariq bin Taimur to take PM role) • Increase in British aid and military support (inc. regular UK units e.g. SAS) • 'Hearts and minds' campaign instigated (UK control) • Successful British-led military operations in 1972 including Sarfait, Op. AQOOBA (Hauf raids) and Battle of Mirbat (July 1972)—high point of British military contribution to the Dhofar COIN campaign Phase 2 also reflected decline of UK influence in Oman/on Dhofar War: • Arrival of Tariq bin Taimur (brother of Sultan Said)—increased Omani control over government decision-making and initial Omanization efforts

INTRODUCTION: A RARE COLD WAR SUCCESS

PERIOD	DATES	CSAF TENURE	KEY FEATURES/EVENTS
			• Diversification of Sultan's advisors ('Muscat Mafia') • More assertive Sultan on military matters e.g. Operation AQOOBA (May 1972)—primarily Sultan-initiated SOAF attacks in PDRY territory • Expansion of embassies in Muscat and first Omani embassies abroad • Oman admitted to Arab League and UN • First SAF officer training programme for Omanis
PHASE 3: Accelerated decline (late 1972 onwards) of general British influence post-1972	Late 1972–1975	Maj-Gen. Tim Creasey Maj-Gen. Ken Perkins	More assertive Sultan—gradual decline in UK diplomatic and advisor influence on economic, social development and military procurement issues Arrival of Jordanian and Iranian troops and equipment. British troops outnumbered 4:1 by Jordanians/Iranians Iranians placed under CSAF operational command but reported to Shah direct: • Sep/Nov 1972—first Iranian helicopters and SF troops arrive in Dhofar* • Dec 1973—Imperial Iranian Battle Group (IIBG) committed to Dhofar* (SF battalion later in Mar 1975) • Apr 1974—First Jordanian troops arrive* (SF battalion later in Mar 1975) • Dec 1974—IIBG increased to brigade size (c.3,000 personnel)* By 1975, c.10,000 Omani/Baluchi troops, 1,200 Firqa, 3,000 Iranians, some 800 Jordanians and just c.1,000 UK troops** Several offensive operations in western theatre spearheaded by Artesh troops backed up by Iranian air and sea assets, and weight of numbers/logistical backup provided greatly supports operations UK's military strategic and operational control maintained, however (and tactical also), via SAF chain of command, and key theatre military assets remain British (e.g. SAS)

* J.E. Peterson, *Oman's Insurgencies: The Sultanate's Struggle for Supremacy* (Lebanon: Saqi, 2007), pp. 482–85.

** M. DeVore, 'The United Kingdom's Last Hot War of the Cold War: Oman 1963–75', *Cold War History*, 1–31 (2011), 20.

W. Ladwig, 'Supporting Allies in Counterinsurgency: Britain and the Dhofar Rebellion', *Small Wars & Insurgencies*, 19, 1 (2008), 72.

and in areas of policy which set the conditions for success, it was key. Post-coup, British advice was heeded by the new Sultan for the implementation of a concerted civil development programme, and although this remained relatively limited and slow to implement until later in the war due to lack of funding and interest from the Sultan and his ministries, it was a start to show the Jebalis the government was interested in their wellbeing.[30] This step, allied to an expansion of the SAF to reclaim the campaign momentum and incorporate many elements of a British-style 'hearts and minds' approach, helped prove to the Jebalis and the British government paymasters that Qaboos and the Omani COIN effort was a 'horse worth backing'.[31] Although 'to destroy' the enemy by inflicting 'maximum kills' was always the primary aim, the hearts and minds element was important in a sticks and carrots approach towards the insurgents and Jebali population.[32] This was achieved primarily through the deployment of the UK's elite Special Air Service (SAS) Regiment to Dhofar as well as utilizing formations of other regular British military units such as the Royal Engineers (RE), Royal Artillery (RA), and Royal Air Force (RAF) Regiment, collectively accounting for over 700 personnel.[33] The SAS-led 'hearts and minds' approach was born of similar initiatives in previous British campaigns to either win over or coerce the population back to the government side, often utilizing a combination of both elements. As Col. Mike Harvey, Dhofar Forces Commander, put it: 'The war is for the minds of men. The [objective of the] war is to win and control the people.'[34] Coercive measures such as food denial—effectively attempting to reduce the food supply to starve the enemy into submission or ensure they had to carry food instead of weapons or ammunition—were utilized both in Sultan Said and Qaboos's reigns with full British support.[35] Full food controls were in place and imposed at the exit points of Salalah town, and those of the smaller coastal settlements of Taqa and Mirbat by early 1972.[36]

The 1970 coup and its immediate aftermath represent the high point of overall British influence on the Dhofar campaign. This is observed through the facilitation of regime change, strong initial political and military leverage over the inexperienced new Sultan through the UK-imposed IAC, and the reliance on both seconded and regular British military personnel and units to change the approach and increase the intensity of COIN operations in Dhofar. Once Sultan Qaboos, however, gained more experience and consolidated his

INTRODUCTION: A RARE COLD WAR SUCCESS

position, the control (or at one point overarching influence) of the UK in Oman and the Dhofar campaign began to diminish. This is perhaps best illustrated by the airstrikes against the PDRY in retaliation for the Habrut Fort incident (Operation AQOOBA) in 1972. The SOAF air strikes were insisted upon by Qaboos (and backed by his CSAF, Brig. John Graham) despite UK governmental fears of the potential to spark open inter-state warfare in Southern Arabia, and illustrated the Sultan's growing authority at Britain's expense.[37] Despite this operational-level input, the general British influence and control over theatre strategy and other key elements of the war remained as strong as ever.

Phase 3 saw an accelerated decline in British influence in Oman and with relative speed from military, political, as well as economic perspectives. Although the number of UK military personnel was eventually substantially increased to upwards of 1,000, and while the CSAF and key SAF officers remained British, the UK's overall influence was to decrease.[38] The British aim was to limit assistance (including the deployment of the SAS in increased 65-plus-man squadron strength, or some quarter of total regimental numbers) and that it be short term and of minimum cost, so few further assets were committed to the campaign after the swift initial post-coup expansion.[39] Without the hoped-for quick victory stemming from the SAF's first major post-expansion offensive in 1971 (named Operation JAGUAR), UK diplomatic efforts were concentrated on the broadening of war support. British-only support morphed into a broad international coalition, and Qaboos also broadened the diversity of his advisors which, together, resulted in a relatively reduced UK contribution and level of influence.[40] In conjunction with Sultan Qaboos's input, substantial financial aid was also garnered from across the Gulf region, with military assistance additionally supplied primarily by Jordan and Iran, which—combined—represented quadruple the UK contribution in the latter stages of the war.[41]

This situation also facilitated a shift in influence in terms of dictating military achievements on the ground. Despite their often poor performance in the field, the sheer weight of Iranian troop numbers and firepower, as well as available air assets, proved an important contribution towards achieving the eventual 1975 victory.[42] This was a significant shift from the situation of only British-funded, supported, and officered forces engaging with the insurgents in the early stages of the war. The situation represented a reduction in UK general operational influence, despite a serving British army CSAF remaining in overall command of the war effort.

Initially highly dependent on UK advice and security, as the new Sultan gained in confidence and started exercising the power afforded to him, he actively pursued a policy of offsetting British influence over his administration.[43] Sultan Qaboos continued to diversify the counsel he took to involve Arab as well as American advisors, as part of what the UK Ambassador to Oman, (later Sir) Donald Hawley, referred to as 'a certain palace clique'.[44] The Sultan also began to assert his authority over aspects of the country's economic, infrastructure, and social development. This extended to the Dhofar COIN campaign, in which the Sultan was increasingly forceful in both procurement and operational issues; sometimes to the chagrin of British officials.[45] In diplomatic terms, Sultan Said effectively subcontracted the running of much of his affairs to the UK government, including the representation of Oman's interests in the UN up until 1971, when, under Qaboos, Oman eventually took its own seat.[46] Oman was also admitted to the Arab League and its first diplomatic missions were set up abroad, which served to enhance Oman's independent image and diminished UK influence over its affairs, including the war. Likewise, from an economic standpoint, whereas Sultan Said was largely dependent on British funding to run his administration (especially for the Dhofar War), Qaboos enjoyed increased oil revenues which resulted in an approximately fourfold increase in state income in 1973.[47] Qaboos chose to spend this income windfall as he saw fit, raising British advisors' eyebrows with conspicuous consumption such as the building of luxurious new palaces, including the remodelling of Muscat's Al Alam Palace and the 'grander, [and even] more opulent' Bait Al Barka outside the capital.[48] In the later stages of the war, the Sultan also chose to go against sound British military advice on military procurement, including his insistence on the purchase of the UK-built Rapier air defence system and Anglo-French Jaguar ground attack aircraft, which senior UK personnel deemed too expensive, unnecessary, and not a priority to facilitate a win in Dhofar.[49]

Alongside the highlighted areas of decline, the 'sliding scale of influence' framework importantly also emphasizes the areas where British influence was maintained, or indeed where control remained virtually complete. In spheres

INTRODUCTION: A RARE COLD WAR SUCCESS

such as the control of war strategy, operational control, and tactical design and implementation, as well as several non-kinetic and informal support functions, Britain's level of influence never reduced, and control was maintained due to the central importance of UK personnel in running the Dhofar War from multiple aspects. Despite an incremental relative decline in influence in areas such as political, diplomatic, and economic sway, and military forces on the ground, in the key areas that facilitated the execution of the Dhofar campaign and achieved the eventual war win, it can be seen that Britain's influence remained effectively undiluted.

In short, this book offers significant new interpretations of the Dhofar War from the perspective of the British role and influence, and consequently, therefore, also on the ultimate achievement of the insurgent defeat and overall victory. Although included in some detail, what it does not do is offer a comprehensive summary exclusively of the operational and tactical military aspects of the war. Firstly, several other publications already fulfil this role admirably, but the primary reason is that the remit of this study is much wider. As such, it devotes much of its inquiry to the non-martial aspects of the war, from political, diplomatic, and economic aspects to non-kinetic elements of support. As such, the overall aim of this book is therefore to steer the debate, augment the existing literature, add new perspectives on the British role, as well as to raise the profile of the Dhofar War and associated COIN campaign case to the level it deserves in both academia and in terms of broader public interest and appreciation.

2 The Dhofar War: Origins, Players, and Timeline

To fully appreciate the context and development of the Dhofar War, an associated survey of relevant aspects of geography, climate, politics, and history is necessary. Located on the edge of the Southern Arabian Peninsula, Dhofar has a geography distinct from the rest of Oman. The Indian Ocean meets Dhofar on a narrow flat coastal belt of up to a mile in depth before the land elevation rises abruptly to over 4,000 feet to form the Qamar, Qara, and Samhan mountain ranges. The only exception to this terrain is the 50 miles of coastline surrounding the Salalah plain, where the land extends up to 6 miles inland before finally transforming into Jebel highland.[1] This extends some 18 miles inland before flattening out to become the sandy Negd plain, which evolves into the Rub Al Khali desert, extending for hundreds of miles into Saudi Arabia.

Dhofar is also unique in both Oman and the Arabian Peninsula, for when much of the region is subjected to extreme summer temperatures, between June and September, a large proportion of the province is covered in a cooling Khareef monsoon mist from sea level up to approximately 2,000 feet, in effect creating a unique rainy season. During the insurgency, the Sultan of Oman's Air Force (SOAF) was often unable either to fly or observe ground movements in such weather, the wet and muddy conditions often prevented infantry manoeuvres on the Jebel, and the large monsoon-induced waves on the coast usually prevented close-in naval support or supply operations. The SAF was, therefore, generally hampered both in terms of logistics and manoeuvrability, whereas the insurgents could move more freely and transport their supplies under such cover, often via camel train. The mists cleared annually by October to reveal the resultant lush greenery 'as verdant and fertile as Somerset', also providing the insurgents with plentiful cover and a strong tactical advantage.[2]

ORIGINS, PLAYERS, AND TIMELINE

Figure 2.1: Western Dhofari Jebel covered in 'Khareef' monsoon mists.
© Stephen Quick 2022

In addition, the approximately 30,000 residents of Dhofar at the time of the insurgency were both culturally and ethnically distinct from the rest of Oman, largely speaking pre-Arabic South Arabian dialects.[3] Alongside the general distinction between northern Oman and the province in terms of the distribution of adherents to the Ibadi and Sunni schools of Islam, this cultural and ethnic differentiation, in conjunction with Dhofar's independence until 1879, geographical separation from the rest of Omani territory, and harsh topographical and climatic conditions, all had a significant bearing on both the development and longevity of the insurgency.

War Origins

Britain's extensive support for Sultan Said bin Taimur of Oman helped him to maintain his power and rule as he saw fit from 1932, when he succeeded his father. He oversaw a conservative regime in which he 'could be persuasively defined as a tyrant … [and] could certainly be described as a despot'.[4] Through the policies of this 'charming tyrant', Omanis were largely prevented from travelling abroad, and access to the trappings of the modern world including public music, radios, books, and even newspapers was systematically withheld.[5] Even when oil revenues started in 1967, limited funds were directed to economic or social progress. By the mid-1960s, Oman existed in a primitive, almost feudal state of development, with only three primary schools and a literacy rate of 5%, as well as just a single hospital and an infant mortality rate of 75%.[6] Although inheriting significant debt from his father's rule, with the UK's £1.5 million contribution per year (via the Canning Award/Zanzibar Subsidy), the Zakat tax on agricultural produce, and through austerity policies, Sultan Said had managed to rebalance the country's finances.[7] With sale of Gwadur port to the Pakistani state in 1958 (for £3 million) and oil revenues of £8 million in 1967 (rising to over £40 million in 1970), such austerity was increasingly hard to justify to both his subjects and loyal UK advisors alike.[8] Sultan Said's rule also engendered discontent in the country's north, which had previously facilitated the tribally oriented Imamate versus Sultanate power struggle of the 1950s. This culminated in the Djebel War and decisive defeat for the rebels on the Djebel Akhdar in January 1959 as led by Suleiman bin Himyar al Nabhani and Talib bin Ali al Hinai, the contemporary Imam's brother.[9]

The Sultan moved permanently from Muscat to his palace in Salalah in 1958 and continued to run the country via his contracted and seconded British advisors based over 500 miles away in the capital. Abdel Takriti states: 'Dhufar [*sic*] was accordingly treated as a private estate, heavily exploited by its ruler.'[10] The level of development was also even lower in the province than the rest of the country, with just a single primary school, zero public medical facilities, and no electricity or running water.[11] Stunted development, highly restricted movement in and out of the country, allied to oppressive taxation and judicial systems all contributed to simmering unrest.[12] Additionally, although married to a local woman from one of the more powerful local tribes, Sultan Said did not hold Dhofaris in high regard.[13] Former CSAF Brig. Corran Purdon recalled the Sultan's comment: 'If you are out walking and meet a Dhofari and a snake, tread on the Dhofari'; and former SAF officer John McKeown further highlights a comment made to a later CSAF (Brig. John Graham) that his Dhofari subjects were 'evil and dangerous men—I want you to destroy them'.[14]

The roots of the Jebel Akhdar rebellion (1957–1959) stemmed primarily from the issue of authority and control over the hinterland vis à vis the

ORIGINS, PLAYERS, AND TIMELINE

Imamate. With Oman's stunted developmental status, one of the primary catalysts for the Dhofar insurgency was the experience gained by workers who had left Oman (especially Dhofar) to find employment in the booming oil industries or armed and police forces of other Gulf countries, including Kuwait and the Trucial states.[15] With realization of the comparative disadvantage of their countrymen and inspired by the Movement of Arab Nationalists (MAN) and the discourse of Nasserism, organizations such as the Oman Revolutionary Movement (ORM), and several Dhofar-specific nationalist-oriented dissident groups such as the Dhufar Benevolent Society (DBS), Dhufari Charitable Association (DCA), and Dhufar Soldiers Association (DSO) were established in the early 1960s.[16] As a result, the road from resentment to physical unrest was soon to follow. The DSO included Dhofaris serving in other British-run Gulf militaries who were well-trained, and therefore possessed skills useful for insurgency-related activities and who '[strongly] desired the overthrow of the Sultan'.[17] The key facilitator of the insurgency was Musallam bin Nufl, a minor Sheikh of one of the houses of the influential Bait Kathir tribe, who started agitating after being dismissed from the Sultan's service in 1963.[18] Bin Nufl facilitated the merging of the various dissident groups into the Dhofar Liberation Front (DLF) in mid-1965, which became the primary group instigating the insurgency.

The Insurgency Begins

The SAF was formed primarily as a result of the 1958 'Exchange of Letters' agreements between the Sultan of Muscat and Oman and the UK government. The existing Omani military units, formed or developed in the early 1950s largely through British efforts with Colin Maxwell and Pat Waterfield as early COs (future Deputy CSAF and Oman's Military Secretary, respectively), including the Muscat and Oman Field Force (MOFF), Batinah Force (BF), and Muscat Infantry (MI), were renamed and re-formed into the SAF alongside the addition of a small air force capability.[19] British personnel commanded all such units and provided most regimental officers, supplied by the UK as Loan Service Personnel (LSP), including the CSAF as professional head of the Omani military. Col. David Smiley was the first LSP CSAF (1958–1961), followed by Col. Hugh Oldman (1961–1964). Taking up his post in March

THE DHOFAR WAR

1964, Col. Tony Lewis was the CSAF who led the SAF into the Dhofar insurgency and, subsequently, to war.

In November 1964, Col. Lewis despatched a company of the Northern Frontier Regiment (NFR) to Dhofar province by road to counter the regional alarm caused by Bin Nufl's activities, which included mine-laying and attacking oil company resources from 1963 using Saudi Arabian-sourced weaponry.[20] This action represented the first time the SAF had ever officially operated in Dhofar. After an uneventful month-long tour and no insurgent contact, the NFR returned north. This operation was followed by six months of relative quiet in Dhofar, then by a deployment of two companies of the Muscat Regiment (MR) in May 1965. Several incidents then took place to escalate the situation. Firstly, in May 1965 the Iranian Navy captured a dhow off the Iraqi coast which contained both Dhofari dissidents and substantial military supplies. Following their interrogation and review of seized documents, it was surmised that 'WE [sic] had a nationalist rebellion on our hands which was supported by Saudi Arabia and Iraq.'[21] Secondly, the DLF was formally established at its First Congress meeting on 9 June 1965 to 'take up arms and engage in its struggle against imperialism and its mercenary troops', and on the same day undertook its first official operation, which resulted in the killing of a driver of an oil company lorry on the Midway Road.[22] This date is described as being regarded by Bin Nufl's DLF as the official start of the Dhofar insurgency, and, along with SOAF being called into action against the insurgent forces for the first time, consequently why this book specifically begins its war timeframe from 1965 also.[23] Unlike the NFR's uneventful previous tour, the MR actually engaged with the Adoo and also suffered the SAF's first casualty in the widening insurgency.[24]

By October 1965, the growing capability and confidence of the insurgents was apparent through the execution of their first offensive operations against the SAF and the civilian Midway camp. Further evidence also became apparent of significant external support being channelled via Saudi territory.[25] In early 1966, the situation escalated when the first SAF British officer was also killed in Dhofar and Sultan Said narrowly survived an assassination attempt by insurgent sympathizers at a camp inspection of the resident Dhofar Force (DF) in Rayzut, a military unit not under SAF command.[26] By this time, the SAF had lost control over most of the Jebel, and only maintained domination over the Salalah plain and the northern deserts. The insurgents, drawn largely from the resident 'tribes of strange non-Arab peoples ... speaking languages of their own and maintaining their own obscure manners and customs' who knew the terrain intimately, unlike the Sultan's effectively 'foreign' forces, were able to progressively consolidate their control over the Jebel.[27] In all, the SAF's and therefore the Sultan's response to the initial insurgent threat proved both 'weak and ineffective'.[28]

The British withdrawal from Aden in November 1967 and resulting formation of the Marxist People's Republic of Southern Yemen (PRSY), subsequently named the People's Democratic Republic of Yemen (PDRY) from late 1970, proved to be the catalyst for a significant growth in the conflict's scale and evolving ideological focus.[29] By September 1968, as a result of the Front's Second Congress held at the Wadi Himrin, the DLF had morphed into the newly named PFLOAG.[30] This later resulted in a purging of the original nationalist leadership element, leaving a core of highly

Table 2.1: Key Dhofar War events timeline

DATES	CSAF	EVENT
Nov 1964	Col. Tony Lewis	Deployment of SAF (NFR) to Dhofar for first time
May 1965	Col. Tony Lewis	MR deployed to Dhofar and seizure of insurgent dhow off Iraq
9 Jun 1965	Col. Tony Lewis	Initial DLF offensive action. Official start of Dhofar Insurgency
Apr 1966	Col. Tony Lewis	Assassination attempt on Sultan Said by subverted DF soldiers
Sep 1968	Brig. Corran Purdon	DLF leadership displaced by Marxists and renamed PFLOAG
May–Aug 1969	Brig. Corran Purdon	Failed SAF operation against Sherishitti complex. Last SAF-controlled area in western Dhofar lost to insurgents (Rakhyut)
Jul 1970	Brig. John Graham	Coup launched which brings Sultan Qaboos to power
Aug 1970	Brig. John Graham	SAS Regiment deployed and start of 'hearts and minds' campaign

(*continued*)

THE DHOFAR WAR

Table 2.1: Key Dhofar War events timeline (*continued*)

DATES	CSAF	EVENT
Feb 1971	Brig. John Graham	Establishment of HQ Dhofar under Col. Mike Harvey
Oct/Nov 1971	Brig. John Graham	Operations JAGUAR and LEOPARD (combined SAF, UK, and Firqa forces) result in first permanent SAF position on Jebel by May 1972)
Apr 1972	Brig. John Graham	Operation SIMBA secures Sarfait position in western Dhofar
May 1972	Brig. John Graham	Operation AQOOBA airstrikes in reprisal for Habrut Fort attack
July 1972	Brig. John Graham	COIN force win at Battle of Mirbat
Sep 1972	Maj. Gen. Tim Creasey	Operation HORNBEAM initiated (leading to construction of first permanent Jebel blocking line to hinder Adoo supply lines)
Nov 1972	Maj. Gen. Tim Creasey	First Iranian forces (SF) arrive in Sultanate
Dec 1972	Maj. Gen. Tim Creasey	Operation JASON—second front in northern Oman by NDFLOAG thwarted—upwards of 80 insurgents/sympathizers captured
Dec 1973	Maj. Gen. Tim Creasey	Midway Road permanently reopened by Iranian Forces
Apr 1974	Maj. Gen. Tim Creasey	First Jordanian Forces (engineers) arrive in Sultanate
Jun 1974	Maj. Gen. Tim Creasey	Hornbeam Line completed
Jan 1975	Maj. Gen. Tim Creasey	Rakhyut re-taken by Iranians. Damavand Line construction begins
Oct/Nov 1975	Maj. Gen. Ken Perkins	Operation HADAF launched, Sherishitti Caves captured and Darra Ridge cleared (Operation HILWAH)
Dec 1975	Maj. Gen. Ken Perkins	Dhalqut entered on 2 Dec. CSAF notifies Sultan Dhofar secure for civil development. National declaration of victory on 11 Dec

indoctrinated Marxist insurgent leaders, including Mohammed Al Ghassani, in charge by 1970. The PFLOAG subsequently regained a secure base access at Hauf in Yemeni territory and supplies and training from the PRSY/PDRY, Chinese and Soviet advisors, and other members of the Communist bloc, alongside countries such as Cuba and North Korea, as well as support from Egypt, Saudi Arabia, and Iraq.[31] Allied to these developments, by 1966, each of the three SAF infantry regiments deployed to Dhofar on rotating six- to nine-month tours regularly employed what would now be considered highly repressive measures by Sultan Said's directive, including mass detentions, well-capping, crop-burning, and food denial, which had the effect of turning many neutral Dhofaris against the ruling status quo.[32] The Sultan's refusal to heed British advice to employ an insurgent amnesty programme, coupled with a lack of significant social and economic development, only made the situation worse.[33]

Due largely to Sultan Said's instinctive frugality, the SAF also had insufficient basic supplies including uniforms, and poor equipment such as bolt-action rifles, whilst the Chinese insurgent sponsors provided plentiful automatic rifles and machine guns to their protegees.[34] The SAF also lacked helicopter support, which hampered Jebel operations and especially casualty evacuation, and the growing insurgent military capability added to such problems; an example being the failed May 1969 operation against PFLOAG's Sherishitti Caves base (Operation LANCE), which was repulsed with multiple SAF casualties.[35] August 1969 then witnessed the Adoo's capture of the town of Rakhyut, which consolidated insurgent control of western Dhofar, and by the time Brig. Graham assumed command as CSAF in April 1970, the insurgents controlled the only overland route to Muscat, the entire Jebel mountain area, and effectively the whole province, bar the Salalah plain.[36] The situation had deteriorated so much that by 1970 it was considered in some UK quarters that the COIN campaign could actually be lost by 1971.[37] In addition, to raise the alarm levels further, in June 1970 the PFLOAG's sister organization, the National Democratic Front for the Liberation of Oman and the Arabian Gulf (NDFLOAG), attacked military outposts in northern Oman, which meant revolutionary activity on two simultaneous fronts within the Sultanate.[38]

Figure 2.2: Landscape in central Jebel. © Stephen Quick 2022

Enter Qaboos

The July 1970 coup arose from such circumstances and was one of the key events of the Dhofar War. The coup resulted in Sultan Said being supplanted by his son, Qaboos, and had widespread ramifications for the COIN campaign. Aside from the general reformist social and economic approach taken by Qaboos, which contributed towards alleviating key population-related grievances, from a military perspective one of the key campaign developments was the formal deployment of the UK's SAS Regiment to Oman with his agreement. The elite Special Forces unit then implemented a new plan to win the war, devised shortly before the coup by the regimental commander, Lt. Col. John Watts. A key element of the Watts-authored 'Five-Point Plan' which ensued was the implementation of a 'hearts and minds'-type campaign. This encapsulated many elements employed successfully in previous UK COIN operations including civil medical assistance, training of the government security forces and local militia (Firqa), and the development of an effective intelligence-gathering and utilization capability. It was, as described by Col. Mike Harvey,

ORIGINS, PLAYERS, AND TIMELINE

Commander Dhofar Brigade from 1971, the need to 'adopt the well known two-handed posture of the closed fist of the military force and the open hand of friendship, judiciously balanced by a clear political Aim [*sic*]'.[39]

Following the 1970 coup, the deployment of the SAS and elements of other regular UK military units such as the RE, RA, and RAF enabled Brig. Graham to plan for and then execute offensive operations. These were aimed to establish a permanent Sultanate military presence on the Jebel and take the fight to the insurgents. The long-awaited offensive operations (Operations LEOPARD and JAGUAR) were launched in 1971 and fortified blocking lines were subsequently built, bisecting the Jebel to hinder insurgent supply lines. With newly acquired helicopter support, the Leopard Line was constructed from late 1971, and evolved into the more effective Hornbeam Line to the west of the Salalah plain by 1974.

During 1971, Oman's international standing was also reinforced through membership of the Arab League and the United Nations (UN). Bolstered by such diplomatic developments, further offensive operations were undertaken in 1972 with the seizure of Sarfait on the western border of Dhofar (Operation SIMBA) in April. The insurgents' destruction of Oman's Habrut Fort in

Figure 2.3: British soldiers outside their 'sangars' (protected living quarters) at 'Reef Base' on the Hornbeam Line. © Sid Pass 1974

THE DHOFAR WAR

Figure 2.4: Interior of a three-man sangar on the Hornbeam Line with life's essentials (weapons, ammunition, medical pack, water canteen, shaving and 'brew' kits).
© Sid Pass 1974

ORIGINS, PLAYERS, AND TIMELINE

May resulted in overt Omani cross-border reprisals carried out via SOAF airstrikes against the insurgent base areas at Hauf in the PDRY (Operation AQOOBA). Due largely to the gathering success of the 'block, clear and hold' strategy of SAF commanders, the insurgents then launched a rare, large-scale conventional attack on the coastal town of Mirbat, some 40 miles east of Salalah. The attack was repulsed by forces spearheaded by the embedded SAS 'British Army Training Team' (BATT), reinforced by a further regimental detachment at a critical stage of the battle and the intervention of SOAF fighter jets during a fortuitous break in poor flying weather. The failed attack resulted in dozens of fighters killed and what Brig. Graham not only called a 'bloody nose' for the insurgents or 'the bloodiest nose ever suffered by [the adoo]' from a military perspective but was also a significant psychological blow to the wider insurgent organization and caused significant infighting within PFLOAG ranks.[40]

The win at Mirbat heralded a new era of success for Omani COIN forces, which were further reinforced by the addition of increasing numbers of, firstly, Iranian war supplies and then military units from late 1972, culminating in the deployment of a full Artesh brigade in November 1974. In early 1974, Jordanian engineers were also attached to the SAF and by the year's end, such troops were involved in several high-profile operations and collectively accounted for almost 4,000 of the approximately 15,000 military personnel fielded by Omani COIN forces.[41] With the highly effective minefield-fortified blocking asset in the form of the 50 km-long Hornbeam Line largely completed and operational in 1974, the emphasis increasingly moved towards operations further to the west in Dhofar province.[42] With operations to maintain the security of the Midway Road involving the newly deployed Jordanian SF units underway by early 1975 [a 6-month only tasking before handing back to Omani troops), the Iranian contingent also recaptured Rakhyut and constructed the Damavand Line, a further key fortified line, to block insurgent supply lines.[43] From August 1975, the momentum of SAF operations continued to build steadily, culminating in the seizure of positions south of Sarfait, enabling a final push on the Sherishitti Caves complex and the final remaining insurgent stronghold of Dhalqut. Unlike the SAF military setbacks at Sherishitti in 1969 and later in January 1975, the Omani COIN forces took the objective with relative ease and, following the Darra Ridge clearance from the

THE DHOFAR WAR

Iranian-held position of Rakhyut, all meaningful resistance ceased. The incumbent CSAF, Maj-Gen. Ken Perkins, via Dhofar Brigade Commander Brig. John Akehurst, was then able to report to Sultan Qaboos on 4 December that Dhofar: 'is now secure for civil development', accomplishing the Brigade's mission aim penned by the latter some fifteen months previously.[44]

Sultan Qaboos was subsequently able to officially declare victory on 11 December 1975. The COIN campaign had lasted a decade and resulted in thousands of casualties. The war had also consumed up to 50% of Oman's GDP, bringing it close to economic collapse, requiring the pooled additional resources of Britain, Iran, Jordan, and several Gulf nations in order to prevail.[45] The Omani status quo had, however, survived, and Communist expansion in the Arabian Peninsula was halted. As a result, the vital Strait of Hormuz remained free from Communist control, therefore maintaining its position as the primary thoroughfare for Gulf oil supply exports to the outside world.

3 Politics and Diplomacy

From the period covering 1965 to 1971 in the Dhofar War, the legacy of Britain's continued historic political and diplomatic commitment to Oman was key to avoiding defeat at the hands of the Dhofar insurgents. This aspect of British support was later to prove pivotal, firstly to the turnaround in the COIN campaign's fortunes, and secondly to the eventual SAF victory over the Adoo in 1975. As a result of the insurgent defeat, the UK's state-centric political and diplomatic goals relating to Oman and the Dhofar War were also achieved.

British aims can be grouped together broadly as overarching and regional UK strategic goals and objectives aimed more specifically at the Omani state level. The latter were centred around building up the Sultanate's institutional and governance-related capacity to operate more self-sufficiently as an independent nation in prosecuting a COIN campaign on its own soil. Britain's main political aim was, therefore, to help attain stability in Oman to safeguard its own regional strategic interests at the least possible cost. As illustrated by previous in-country interventions, as well as being a long-time ally, Britain considered Oman a vital buffer to competing regional interests. Contemporary political and financial realities, and the lingering effects of 'economic *force majeure*', however, meant the UK was only willing to provide limited assistance to Oman throughout the war and there was no 'blank cheque' available.[1]

At the start of the Dhofar War in 1965, Britain was the dominant external power in Oman, holding considerable political and almost exclusive diplomatic influence over the Sultan and the wider country. This situation continued up until the July 1970 coup, which saw the accession of Sultan Qaboos. From a period of almost total control over the country's affairs with a new, young (only twenty-nine years old), and inexperienced Sultan on the throne, Britain experienced a progressive loss of influence. As Qaboos matured and settled into his role and through the expansion of his increasingly non-British inner advisory circle, the situation changed markedly.[2] Finally, from being the only country bar India with a consulate and diplomatic presence in Oman and being solely responsible for the Sultanate's external affairs, Britain's almost exclusive influence over Omani diplomatic affairs declined significantly. Following the Sultanate taking up its new seats in the Arab League and the UN in 1971, more countries opened diplomatic missions in Muscat and the Omanis reciprocated in several capital cities around the world.

Despite Britain experiencing a relative loss of political and diplomatic influence over the duration of the Dhofar insurgency and the UK's contribution to the war effort being more costly than desired, continuing UK efforts and sway in these spheres remained vital to the overall war effort. Resultingly, they were a key factor in achieving final victory in 1975 and Britain's regional, Oman-specific, and domestic-related aims. Without such efforts, the war would likely at least have lasted longer and may even have been lost by COIN forces as late as 1971, or a full six years into hostilities.

Overarching and Regional Strategic Aims: From Oil to International Reputation

Britain's regional, political, and diplomatic aims were wider than those pertaining merely to Oman and the war itself. Success in the Dhofar War was essential to be able to achieve such wider regional strategic aims. These aims were rooted in multiple factors relating to Gulf oil supplies; regional stability, to enable a smooth UK regional withdrawal; countering further Communist encroachment in the Gulf; maintaining a strategic military presence, as well as political and economic influence; and upholding the UK's international status and reputation, both in the region and further afield.[3] Britain's regional strategic aims must also be viewed in context, and access to Gulf oil supplies was a key issue for the UK and the Western economies within the overall Cold War geopolitical situation.[4] Britain was experiencing worsening economic issues in the 1960s which continued throughout the decade of the Dhofar War, with the UK's struggling post-Imperial economy being highly dependent on imported oil. Over two-thirds of the UK and the West's oil supplies were Gulf-sourced, and supplies had to be shipped primarily through the narrow (approximately 21-mile width at the narrowest point) Strait of Hormuz.[5] With Oman's strategic position at the entrance of the Gulf and controlling the lower half of the Strait, the continued governance of a Western-friendly regime in Oman was considered a strategic imperative. The scenario of a hostile and revolutionary regime taking over governance in Dhofar, then Oman, and therefore being able to potentially throttle the flow of oil from the Gulf to the West (and to Britain itself), with the resultant scale of negative [political and] economic impacts, was deemed a situation to be avoided at nearly all costs.[6]

With the withdrawal of forces in Aden in 1967 and the resulting loss of Britain's largest military base area outside the UK, both the scale and gravity of the Dhofar insurgency increased and therefore also the scale of the challenge presented to planners. Firstly, the PDRY regime, which emerged in Aden and the Southern Protectorates in 1970, was Marxist, which represented a fundamental Cold War threat to UK interests. It offered sanctuary and a functional base area for its fellow Oman-focused revolutionaries at Hauf in PDRY territory. Secondly, because of its departure, Britain lacked sufficient in situ military forces to counter such threats.

Britain's politically driven and increased involvement in the Dhofar COIN campaign (especially from 1970 onwards) aimed to boost the capability and resilience of Oman itself but, more importantly, to enhance the capability of the Sultanate's military forces to enable the insurgent threat to be firstly countered, and later beaten. Britain never committed large military forces to the Dhofar campaign. This was in direct contrast to the approximately 40,000 UK-commanded troops deployed in the Malayan or 10,000 in the Kenyan emergencies, for example.[7] UK regular forces serving in Oman at their peak consisted of up to 1,000 personnel only, and hailed mainly from the Army and RAF.[8] These largely consisted, however, of military leaders from high-ranking staff personnel through to junior officers and some non-commissioned officers (NCOs) to provide the organizational backbone to the SAF. Such leadership was undoubtedly a major factor in Oman's eventual COIN campaign win. Britain also provided vital political and diplomatic support as well as government-sanctioned financial assistance, all of which directly affected the war's outcome.

THE DHOFAR WAR

Although actively limited for much of the Dhofar War timeline, Britain's political-related assistance provided to Oman ultimately made a key contribution to the insurgent defeat by 1975. As such, this support not only prevented a Marxist insurgency success in Dhofar, but it also averted a potential further loss of the whole of Oman, or even wider Gulf area to likely hostile regimes as per the case in Aden. As a result of the COIN win, the vital flow of oil to the world's advanced economies, including Britain's, was also safeguarded and fears of an 'Eastern domino theory' were laid to rest.[9]

Britain desired stability in the Gulf region per se, but also to be able to withdraw East of Suez in 1971 as planned.[10] With the USA preoccupied by its expanding commitment in Vietnam, the UK was still having to act in its traditional regional power role. This is illustrated with FCO officials stating in 1971: 'The defeat of the rebels in Dhofar would encourage others in the Gulf and elsewhere who are opposed to communist infiltration. Stability in Oman is important for stability in the rest of the Arabian Peninsula.'[11] The UK's first Ambassador to Oman, (later Sir) Donald Hawley also wrote: 'The Domino theory would almost certainly apply and revolutionary success in so traditionally conservative an area could breed further success. This is the danger.'[12]

Britain's economic problems in the 1960s were significant. The pivotal year of 1967 saw a run on the pound, the requirement to approach the International Monetary Fund (IMF) for an emergency loan, and a devaluation of sterling by the end of the year under Prime Minister Harold Wilson's Labour government.[13] This contributed to a reassessment of the large defence budget vis à vis commitments by the incumbent government. This resulted in the 1968 Wilson government's Defence White Paper and the policy intent to withdraw British forces East of the Suez Canal by 1971. With the chaotic Aden withdrawal in the context of the Cold War still fresh in the minds of officials, steps were taken to promote stability in the Gulf area to enable as smooth an exit as possible by 1971. As part of this process, steps were taken to federate the small UK monarchical protectorates in the Gulf such as the Trucial States, thereby reducing their dependence on Britain for protection. As one of the most strategically situated of Gulf territories in a state of (by then) Marxist-inspired insurgency, Oman could not be allowed to share Aden's fate. Resultingly, the UK government decided to substantially increase its assistance (especially from 1970) and efforts towards boosting the general resilience of the Sultanate in the face of a growing insurgent threat.

As a direct result of British political intervention and the resultant increased assistance, Omani COIN forces in Dhofar avoided outright defeat; they held the line on the Salalah plain and were in a position to proceed to the military offensive in late 1971 via Operations JAGUAR and LEOPARD. This regionally stabilizing effect also had the result of securing the continued viability and sovereign status of not just Oman but also of the recently independent Gulf Sheikhdoms such as Bahrain and Qatar, and the newly established Federation of Trucial States named the United Arab Emirates (UAE) as part of Britain's East of Suez withdrawal strategy. With regional stability enforced, Britain was therefore also able to conduct its high-profile and geopolitically significant withdrawal East of Suez in December 1971, whilst maintaining the important staging post and communication facilities at RAF Masirah, located off the Omani mainland. The 1971 withdrawal process was also achieved in an orderly manner, and therefore in stark contrast to the Aden experience and hasty British exit just four years earlier.[14]

A further key reason for British intervention in Oman and Dhofar was to prevent Communist encroachment on the Arabian Peninsula against the backdrop of the Cold War.[15] The logic was similar to that applied to the Malayan Emergency, where it was perceived that Communist insurgents were attempting to destabilize the country and region as part of a worldwide Communist conspiracy orchestrated by both the Kremlin and the new regime (from 1949) in China.[16] Through the UK's political and diplomatic influence and support, this curtailment of the major Communist powers' regional intervention was largely achieved.

The Dhofar conflict was being fought within the environment of numerous overt, covert, and proxy Cold War campaigns underway across the world initiated by the Communist powers as well as the nations of the capitalist West. With large-scale resources of both soft and hard power being invested in the conflict chessboard, issues of power, prestige, and influence meant no territory would, or could, be given up easily, and Oman was no different. Its strategic position within the Gulf and larger Middle Eastern region made control of Omani territory a high priority for all protagonists. The British withdrawal from Aden in 1967 and the subsequent emergence of the Chinese, then USSR-backed Marxist PDRY regime meant that the regional stakes had increased. With the evolution of the original Omani nationalist DLF insurgents into the Marxist-oriented, and later firmly PDRY-backed PFLOAG in 1968, the gravity of the situation facilitated the political decision in Whitehall to continue to politically and diplomatically back and later (post-1970) to substantially increase support to Oman in the Dhofar War.

As the USA, the leader of the non-Communist bloc in the Cold War, was becoming ever more focused on the escalating conflict in Vietnam, the UK continued to act in its traditional Gulf region policeman role, with the USA 'content to leave Gulf affairs to Britain'.[17] As a result, Britain took the lead in countering the threat of Communist ideology and potential resultant regime change in Oman. At the same time, the UK promoted regional stability through active wider political measures such as strongly encouraging the Federation of the Trucial States, which helped to bolster resilience against Communist encroachment. In terms of support to Oman and in the Dhofar War specifically, the methods are discussed in more detail in subsequent chapters but consisted of various forms of help, such as economic and military assistance. The key takeaway is that such support methods were all politically sanctioned by sitting UK governments and implemented effectively through diplomatic channels.

Britain also achieved key objectives whilst avoiding a potential inter-state war with the PDRY. Had such a conflict transpired, with the backing of the PDRY by the key global Communist powers, this scenario would have increased the likelihood of further Marxist-backed territorial gains in Dhofar, greater Omani and potentially wider Gulf territory, and risked potential 'hot' interactions between Britain and the Communist PDRY sponsors. Britain's political and diplomatic counsel (or compromise) in the guise of advisors such as the CSAF and regional or in-country UK diplomats reined in or tempered the wishes of a sometimes over-enthusiastic Sultan Qaboos on certain matters. This included cross-border issues such as the SOAF attacks on Hauf and those of the SAS-trained Mahra tribesmen, which both represented infringements on sovereign PDRY territory.[18] As Geraint Hughes states: 'His [Qaboos's] support for cross-border reprisal raids against the PDRY put him at odds with the CSAF and officials in Whitehall, who were determined to avoid a wider war in Southern Arabia.'[19] Britain therefore balanced the delicate

POLITICS AND DIPLOMACY

situation of achieving strategic objectives and winning the war militarily, whilst conducting the campaign in accordance with established diplomatic protocols to avoid the very real potential for escalation.

Due largely to British politically sanctioned assistance to Oman, the Dhofari insurgents were defeated, an inter-state conflict with the PDRY was avoided, and the Communist threat to the Sultanate was negated. Britain therefore avoided a melt-down in the general stability of the region upon its East of Suez withdrawal as would have been the case if a Communist takeover in Oman had allowed the Gulf monarchies to also be undermined and potentially overthrown. Despite the volatility associated with the 1967 and 1973 Arab–Israeli Wars, in the greater Cold War proxy power game the British-facilitated COIN win in Dhofar helped to achieve a level of stability for the whole region. The Dhofar War victory achieved this by limiting the spread of Communist influence, proxy war, or physical regime change, and should, therefore, be considered a political and diplomatic success in terms of achieving UK interests.

The retention of strategic access to territory (bases) was also a key aim for the UK in the Dhofar War, primarily through the offshore RAF base located on the Omani island of Masirah.[20] Had the Dhofar War been lost, the likelihood of a Communist takeover of Oman proper would have risen, which in turn would have resulted in the loss of RAF Salalah, and potentially also the Masirah base. The UK commitment to the Central Treaty Organization (CENTO) and the strategic requirement of RAF Masirah for servicing this purpose, and as a historically important staging post for personnel and aircraft to service both the Gulf region and East of Suez commitments, was a key consideration.[21] Additionally, the extra RAF presence was key to potentially countering both the overt and covert Communist threat to the Middle Eastern region. In Palestine or in Cyprus, for example, Britain had failed to win COIN campaigns and was forced to cede control of territory in strategically significant areas of the world to insurgent forces. This was especially acute in the case of Aden, where the departure and ceding of all territory and Britain's largest overseas base was described as a humiliating 'scuttle'.[22] In Palestine, Britain exited in failure after conceding it could not control the situation between the protagonists anymore, and in Cyprus, for example, Britain prevented Enosis, the attempted political union of Cyprus and Greece, and retained the sovereign base areas (in perpetuity) but ceded control of the remainder of the strategically important Mediterranean island due to its inability to defeat the insurgents.[23]

Ad hoc facilities had been utilized by the RAF on Masirah Island since the early 1930s.[24] Arrangements were formalized as a result of the 1958 'Exchange of Letters', and the base area was held by Britain on a ninety-nine-year lease with the base, at its peak, housing over 500 military and approximately 200 additional civilian personnel as opposed to the much fewer personnel (approximately 250) based at RAF Salalah to provide 'minimum facilities' for the operation of SOAF.[25] Despite Britain's planned withdrawal East of Suez in 1971, the UK still wished to be able to project power over the Middle Eastern region and more widely across the world. With the military withdrawal from base facilities at Bahrain and Singapore complete by late 1971, the relatively small RAF base on Masirah Island only increased in its overall strategic value. Because of the limited SOAF contingent and inadequate RAF facilities and force protection personnel based at RAF Salalah, the larger RAF Masirah was used as a base for strategic Hawker Hunter, Victor V-Bombers, and Nimrod nuclear submarine hunter assets.[26] Strategically important as a staging post for forces necessary to service Britain's CENTO obligations, post-East of Suez withdrawal RAF Masirah was also then the main forward air position from which to launch British military aircraft in defence of Hong Kong or elsewhere as required.[27] In addition, the base hosted an important British Broadcasting Corporation (BBC) relay station. This, however, also operated a listening post and hosted other intelligence assets for the Government Communications Headquarters (GCHQ) as part of Britain's MI6 Secret Intelligence Service (SIS); both part of the larger FCO organization.[28]

Through Britain's assistance to Oman, the threat of a Communist takeover in Dhofar province and potentially the whole of Oman was negated. The political desire to maintain the RAF facilities on Masirah Island and their strategic utility was successfully achieved. Despite this, with a changing view of strategic priorities by the mid-1970s, RAF Masirah was subsequently abandoned in 1977, only two years after the end of the Dhofar War, and similarly to HMS *Jufair* in Bahrain during the East of Suez withdrawal, the facilities were duly taken over by US forces.[29]

Britain had been the most politically and economically influential country in Oman for two centuries prior to the Dhofar War. Despite a deliberately considered policy of state-building in Oman and helping to both increase and reinforce the perception of Omani independence at the expense of its dominant historical position in the country, Britain still wished to retain its influence in Oman on all fronts, albeit at a diminished level.[30] Success in the Dhofar COIN campaign was key to achieving this objective and guided the political commitment to the war. Britain had previously experienced ignominious withdrawals from Palestine and Aden coupled with the resulting loss of international prestige.[31] Preceded by the debacle of Suez in 1956, the hasty and humiliating Aden exit in 1967 occurred during the Dhofar War and led to the formation of another hostile Marxist state during the ideologically divided Cold War period. As a result, the maintenance of Britain's reputation as a world power and the perception of its prestige was also a key Dhofar campaign factor. This was especially the case after 1970, when the low-profile, indeed largely undisclosed role of the UK in Oman, bar the continued top-secret role of the SAS, became more widely known due in part to proactive 'narrative-forming' British government media briefings.[32] Britain wished to maintain what remained of its diminished influence and prestige in the Middle East, whilst at the same time shedding 'at least some of its colonial baggage' and related negative connotations, seen as anachronistic in the post-Empire era.[33] Britain's international standing and reputation was also subject to regular bruising from the annual protest from 1965 until 1969 in the UN General Assembly via the 'Question of Oman' issue. Led by newly independent nations and enthusiastically supported by the Communist bloc, the Assembly debated the issue of colonial control and oppression of Oman, and demanded the UK desist in its colonial-like presence in the country.[34] Closely related to this, due to the key requirement of not damaging the external perception of legitimacy of Oman after the 1970 coup, the UK accepted a reduction in political influence in Oman. With Britain's help and in a short period of time, Oman achieved full Arab League and UN membership in 1971 and completed an internationally profile-raising round of foreign embassy openings in Muscat and of its own diplomatic outposts abroad. This was a long way from Britain having previously been effectively handed near full responsibility by Sultan Said for controlling the Sultanate's external affairs.[35] Over time, Qaboos also diversified his counsel to include several key non-British advisors including the Libyan businessmen Omer Barouni and Yahya Omer and the influential

Saudi Shaker brothers.[36] These individuals became trusted confidants of the Sultan. With official influence both in and outside the country, they displaced much of the even-handed advice of the previous predominantly British advisors and were viewed with a level of suspicion by UK officials with even some hints of Central Intelligence Agency (CIA) interest or involvement in this traditionally solely British-influenced strategic territory.[37] This situation also had the effect of reducing Britain's overall influence at court and on Omani affairs in general. Through its diplomatic and political efforts with regard to the Dhofar War, Britain was, however, able to maintain certain key aspects of influence despite the active attempts of the Sultan's new advisors to cut its influence and steer contracts away from UK firms.[38]

Due largely to the assistance rendered by Britain to Oman in the Dhofar War, this earned the deep and lasting gratitude of the new Sultan. This situation was evident not only during the war but endured after the conflict and throughout his reign. Despite the eventual departure of the long-standing influential figures of PRPG and resident Consul-General, from both Oman-based RAF stations by 1977 and the meteoric rise of Qaboos's 'shadowy cabinet', the UK's general influence (including economic) in Oman remained strong.[39] Cooperative, professional, and friendly relations with Oman continued post-conflict. Such links have continued up to the modern day, with strong economic and military links including British seconded and contract personnel continuing to be attached to the Omani armed forces.[40] This situation is reminiscent of the earlier Malayan, Kenyan, and Cypriot campaigns, where economic, military, and diplomatic ties flourished after COIN conflicts. Military bases remained, for example, in Cyprus post-COIN campaign. This situation was even the case in Aden, where, after a COIN loss and withdrawal after a bitterly fought insurgency, cordial links with the new regime remained, with pilots and maintenance services provided to the new PSRY (and later PDRY) air force via the British company Airwork Ltd.[41]

Largely because of loss of political influence, tangible economic effects can be illustrated through the Sultan's purchase of military equipment from non-British sources. These included the USA and the Netherlands, as well as negotiating weapons and equipment purchases or donations from Iran, Jordan, Abu Dhabi, Qatar, and Saudi Arabia, and civil development contracts awarded to West German and US firms.[42] Despite this, continuing and expanding links

POLITICS AND DIPLOMACY

with Oman were illustrated by the tangible economic influence and benefits gained from the gratitude and goodwill of the Sultan, primarily 'for military and other services rendered to Oman by the United Kingdom', by way of a *quid pro quo*.[43] This can be seen for instance via large-scale exports and civilian and military procurement contracts, which benefitted both British companies themselves and therefore, indirectly, the UK Exchequer. An example of this is the 90% increase in British exports to Oman (to £81.9 million) during the period from January to October 1975 over the entire 1974 figure.[44] Through key UK state representatives such as the CSAF and Amb. Hawley, Britain retained its place as Oman's primary trading partner or supplier throughout the war period and beyond.[45] Though debatable whether the influence of the British Secretary for Development (attached to the Prime Minister's office) played any part, the significant post-coup contracts awarded to Taylor Woodrow and Cable & Wireless were notable, as were the sale of Rapier missile defence systems to Oman in 1974, Jaguar jets in both 1974 and 1981, and as subsequent sales of Scorpion and Chieftain Tanks in the 1980s.[46]

Of key importance also to the UK's overall influence in Oman was the continued sway of seconded serving, then retired, British military personnel in high-ranking government or military positions. This was to an extent unique even compared to the transitional security arrangements involving UK military personnel in countries post-COIN campaign (or post-independence) of even the more successful British COIN campaigns such as in Malaya or Kenya. This ensured significant and continuing leverage for the UK on a fully independent and sovereign Sultanate's policy in these spheres with Omanization of the SAF, for example, only starting in earnest by 1982, some seven years after the war's end.[47] An example of this is the later appointment of Brig. Peter Thwaites as the Omani Chairman of the Joint Staff in 1976, following his earlier employment as a wartime LSP CO of the Muscat Regiment under Sultan Said. He, in turn, was replaced by Maj. Gen. Tim Creasey as the re-titled Chief of the Defence Staff from 1981 up until his death in 1986; his second tour in charge of the Armed Forces of Oman as a seconded officer.[48] A key instance of this continuance of top-level military influence, despite the almost complete Omanization of the SAF by the 1980s, was LSP Air Marshal Sir Erik Bennett holding the position of Commander, SOAF all the way up until the change in service title in 1990 to the newly designated Royal Air

THE DHOFAR WAR

Force of Oman (RAFO).[49] This ensured direct or indirect British influence at the highest levels of the military of Oman, not just during the entire Dhofar War itself, via the CSAF and other LSP officers and contract officer personnel, but for well over a decade after the Dhofar COIN campaign was won.

Although conducted in a low-key and largely secret manner, especially until 1970, the campaign win in Dhofar helped later to bolster Britain's credibility to allies and enemies alike in the region and wider world by facilitating a rare Cold War COIN win 'to add to their renowned victory in Malaya'.[50] This was especially the case after the reputational legacy of the Aden COIN campaign and the subsequent humiliating withdrawal, and the more distant hangover of the lamentable exit from Palestine some two decades earlier in 1948. Despite the largely hidden extent of the UK's Dhofar campaign involvement, those that needed to know—from the Cold War superpowers and proxies to the fragile new states of the Gulf formerly under British protection—were able to observe UK resolve and capability to maintain the status quo and fight to do so if necessary. Dhofar was a successful example of how to counter Communist insurgency and proved that such forces could be beaten if tackled in the correct manner.[51]

Britain finished World War Two on the winning side and cemented its place in the contemporaneous world order via a permanent seat on the UN Security Council. Despite also developing a strategic nuclear weapons capability in the 1950s, its world power standing, however, receded substantially during that decade. In a bipolar Cold War world, Britain was no longer the hegemon or superpower as it had once been, and despite the wartime victory was effectively bankrupt whilst still having superpower outlay in terms of military expenditure. The extensive costs of military operations did not end on Victory in Europe (VE) Day, with large-scale actions undertaken from 1945 to 1946 to re-establish European control in Asia, including in Indonesia, Indochina, and Malaya.[52] The extent of such undertakings can be illustrated by the large-scale military (COIN) operations undertaken in Palestine up to 1948 and then in Malaya for a full twelve years up until 1960. Concurrently with the Malayan Emergency, campaigns were carried out in both Kenya and Cyprus, as well as the military intervention in Oman to thwart the Imamate Rebellion in the late 1950s. Britain later also intervened in Borneo (including Brunei) from 1963 to 1966 and was fighting an insurgency in Aden up until

POLITICS AND DIPLOMACY

1967, as well as smaller operations in the Caribbean, for example. The loss of Cyprus, Kenya, and Aden caused significant internal and external reputational challenges for the UK. With a win in Oman in 1975, despite not being an overtly or publicly UK-fought campaign, it enabled Britain to enjoy a rare Cold War reputational boost to those who mattered, be they friends or enemies alike.[53]

In terms of boosting a flagging international reputation, despite being highly limited in size and scope compared to other Cold War-era COIN campaigns, Britain had managed to achieve a COIN win in Oman against (Communist) insurgents that other Imperial or world power nations had largely failed to achieve.[54] Despite the campaign's limited size it was, nonetheless, not only a rare military success against Communist insurgents but therefore also an important political and diplomatic win for Britain. Additionally, due to its discreet and unmatched national-level efforts to build up Omani institutional development and robustness, as well as successfully cultivating the external perception (reflecting the reality of Oman as an independent nation acting in its own interests), the embarrassment of the annual UN 'Question of Oman' which was used by the Communist bloc as a 'stick with which to beat Britain' was finally ended in 1971.[55] This achievement was largely a result of British-instigated post-coup political and diplomatic developments involving Gulf nations and background lobbying of member-state delegations within the UN itself. This was a positive development in a (by then) generally anti-colonial international community and reduced such negative connotations for Britain's international image. Notwithstanding a relative loss of influence due in part to British desire not to affect its stage-managed outward pretence of developing legitimacy for Oman, through the UK's political and often discreet diplomatic assistance to Oman, the defeat of the insurgents in Dhofar was achieved. As a result, the maintenance of British economic and political influence in Oman through a grateful Sultan, and of the UK's international reputation and status, was successfully achieved via a historic COIN victory.

In terms, therefore, of the UK's overarching and regional strategic aims, most were achieved. Success in the Dhofar War, born of UK political and military influence and assistance, was critical in achieving its wider regional strategic aims pertaining to Gulf oil supplies, regional stability, and thwarting Communist encroachment. This was achieved in addition to maintaining a

UK strategic military presence, political and economic influence in Oman and the wider Middle East, and boosting its international status and reputation.

Oman-centric and British-related Aims: Stability, Status Quo, and State-building

More directly Sultanate-related in nature than the previously covered overarching and regional strategic goals, such Oman-specific and British aims consisted of multiple factors. These included Omani stability and maintenance of governance status quo, the build-up of Omani state capacity and internal development, keeping the UK's engagement limited, and to keep UK assistance to the Sultanate in the Dhofar War 'as discreet as possible'.[56] Such largely Omani-specific aims importantly also, in turn, contributed to achieving the UK's overarching and regional strategic aims. Britain certainly acted in self-interest in all cases, but Oman was a special case that the UK supported through a mixture of strategic necessity and paternalistic obligation over a period of nearly two centuries and is a position which differs from the general exploitation narrative set forth in certain elements of the historical subject literature.[57]

In a similar fashion to its other previous post-war COIN campaigns, Britain's principal aims revolved around national stability and maintenance of the Omani status quo, through countering the threat imposed by the Dhofar War.[58] This was achieved via the goal of making—through concerted state building efforts—Oman more resilient and able to respond to security challenges with minimal UK help, unlike the expansive ongoing support supplied in previous British COIN campaigns.[59] There is significant cross-relevance to these goals, and maintaining Omani stability and the governing status quo was effectively achieved in a number of different ways. This was secured firstly by continuing and capitalizing on Britain's historical influence in both sponsoring and protecting the Sultanate, secondly through the political will in the UK to support Oman in the Dhofar War, and thirdly via key specific British political and diplomatic interventions.

For over two hundred years prior to the Dhofar War, Britain had been the guarantor of Omani stability. Always with self-interest a key consideration, the arrangement both guaranteed Omani freedom from non-British outside interference and the ruling Al Said dynasty's survival. Such influence ranged from cooperation to intervention when deemed necessary, as well as the historical financial and military assistance provided by the British Indian colonial administration and latterly directly by the UK government. Historical British political and economic influence in Omani affairs had an inertial impact on the scale and bearing of the UK's subsequent influence on the Dhofar COIN campaign. Diplomatic and treaty relations between Britain and Oman were initiated by the East India Company for the purpose of regulating trade in the 1640s and 1650s.[60] Initially pre-union English, then later British influence proper, increased steadily through growth in diplomatic interaction to formal treaty arrangements. This activity was undertaken largely for the purpose of limiting French influence in the Gulf region and within Oman specifically at a time of increasing Franco-British rivalry.[61] An important intervention by British Political Agents in 1871 as the brokers between competing Sultanic power claims thus helped set the stage for later UK assistance to the Sultans of Oman, including key military interventions in 1913 and further in 1915, and through the British-brokered Treaty of Sib in 1920. The latter established primacy for the Sultan on the Muscat and Omani coast, whilst the tribes and the Imamate were given effective control over the country's interior. Britain once again came to the Sultan's aid in the 1950s, firstly by ejecting Saudi forces from the Buraimi Oasis in 1955, utilizing the Trucial Oman Scouts (TOS), followed by military assistance during the Imamate-instigated rebellion, which lasted until 1959.[62] Under the command of the British Political Resident Persian Gulf (PRPG) based in Bahrain, UK support included personnel or units from the TOS from the neighbouring Trucial States, as well as additional assistance in the form of (seconded and contract) UK officers of the Sultan's military forces, and for the first time regular 'home' British military units including the Cameronians regiment.[63] The Imamate Rebellion leaders retreated to the summit of the Jebel Akhdar or 'Green Mountain' in late 1957, and were only eventually dislodged by large-scale RAF bombing and a final assault by two squadrons of the SAS alongside regular British (including the Foreign Office-controlled TOS) and Omani troops in 1959.[64] The insurgent leaders escaped to Dammam in Saudi Arabia, and the rebellion was effectively over. As a result, stability was returned to the Sultanate and the Sultan was unchallenged for supremacy over the whole of the Muscat and Omani territory until the advent of the Dhofar insurgency in 1965.

Table 3.1: Key British–Omani treaties and agreements

TREATY NAME	AGREEMENT DETAILS
1646 and 1659 Rainsford Treaties	Earliest written agreements between Omani officials and the East India Company.
1798 Treaty (and 1800 reaffirmation)	Agreement between the Sultan of Muscat and the East India Company.
	The first major treaty signed between representatives of the two entities
	Confirmed British influence over that of the French in the region.
	1800—Statement that friendship between the company and Muscat's Sultan should: 'endure till the end of time or the sun and moon cease in their revolving careers'.*
1839 Treaty of Commerce	General agreement including articles for the suppression of the slave trade in Omani territories (inc. East African possessions).
1861 Canning Award (Zanzibar Subsidy)	After split of Omani territories after their father's death, agreement held that resultant Sultan of Zanzibar pay annual compensation to his brother, the Sultan of Muscat. Payments taken over by the British Indian government in 1883, then transferred to the British government on India's Independence in 1947. Payments terminated in late 1960s due to the onset of commercial-level oil income for the Sultan.
1891, 1939, and 1951 Treaties of Friendship, Commerce and Navigation	All direct descendants/revisions of the original 1798 Treaty.
1920 Treaty of Sib (or Seeb)	British-brokered agreement which recognized the autonomy of the Imamate regime in Omani interior and sovereignty of the Sultan's authority over Oman's extensive coastal areas.
1958 Exchange of Letters	Provided for British assistance and funding to create and give ongoing support the SAF and to set up Oman's Air Force and funding for civil development projects.
	Formalized RAF Salalah and Masirah base leases.
	Pledge of 24 seconded British officers to serve in SAF (including the CSAF).**

TREATY NAME	AGREEMENT DETAILS
1960 Exchange of Letters 'upgrade'	Up to £1 million annual support from UK to the SAF.
	Sultan's Air Force fully funded by UK and increase in numbers of seconded officers to include 15 junior officers for regimental duties.
	Agreement for UK to pay for majority of set-up and running of expanded civil development programme (£280k capital/set-up and £165k per annum).***

* Donald Hawley, *Oman & Its Renaissance* (London: Stacey International, 1995), p. 59.
** J.E. Peterson, *Oman's Insurgencies: The Sultanate's Struggle for Supremacy* (Lebanon: Saqi, 2007), p. 102.
*** Ibid., p. 148.

Relations with Britain were further formalized at this time after visits of the British Under-Secretary for War, Julian Amery, in 1957, followed by the Chief of the Imperial General Staff (CIGS), General Sir Gerald Templar. After initial negotiations led by Amery in January 1958, the result was the 'Exchange of Letters' between the Government of the UK and the Sultan of Muscat and Oman, dated 25 July 1958, and concluded in London during the Sultan's extensive annual UK visit.[65] As part of the agreement, the British government agreed to pay a large annual stipend towards not only the running, but also the reorganization, modernization, and expansion of the existing Muscat Armed Forces into the newly designated SAF.[66] Britain also agreed to supply seconded (loan) officers to the newly formed SAF. These included the highly experienced World War Two veteran Col. David Smiley as the first designated CSAF, along with twenty-two other UK officers in an arrangement which was further expanded some two years later.[67] As part of the 1958 agreements, Britain also extended the lease for Masirah Island's offshore RAF facilities and future management arrangements put in place for RAF Salalah in Dhofar. All these arrangements meant Oman's national stability was essentially politically backed, bankrolled, and guaranteed by the UK, with, by signing the agreement, the Sultan also effectively handing over 'de facto control over the newly designated Sultan's Armed Forces' to Britain.[68]

Although of secondary importance, another historical factor of significance for guaranteeing Omani stability was the strong influence Britain exerted over the development and succession of Oman's rulers. The young Sultan Said was encouraged by UK officials to attend one of the top private schools in British India as part of a strategic mentoring process. When his father, Taimur, was permitted to abdicate by British officials in 1932, the UK ensured that 'its man', the then young Crown Prince Said, continued the ruling Al Said dynasty. Under such arrangements, Oman remained stable, if economically backward, and fulfilled Britain's wider strategic needs. In a similar manner, and as for many other princes or hereditary leaders in British-influenced territories, Crown Prince Qaboos, the only son of Sultan Said, was sent to the UK to be educated. With Said's agreement, Qaboos arrived in the UK in the late 1950s in an arrangement brokered by the Sultan's trusted British advisor (ex-Consul-General) Maj. Leslie Chauncy. Chauncy liaised with the British Foreign Office to find a suitable family for the young Crown Prince to lodge with and be tutored by. The Romans family from the village of Felsham near Bury St Edmunds was subsequently chosen to discreetly and in a 'protective' manner, considering the nature and standing of their charge, prepare Qaboos academically and socially to attend the Royal Military Academy, Sandhurst, which he entered in 1960.[69] Here, he successfully completed the standard British army officer commissioning course; and where he was a contemporary of Timothy Landon, whose significance to both him and Oman would become clear a decade later.[70] After Sandhurst, which was said to have 'left its mark on Qaboos', he served for several months in Germany as a regular British officer in the Cameronians Regiment, a line infantry regiment of the Scottish Division.[71] After this period of military experience, and a three-month-long worldwide Grand Tour chaperoned by the ever-reliable and discreet Maj. Chauncy, he was posted to local (county-level) government departments in the UK in a glorified intern capacity to learn the intricacies of regional state governance.[72]

Although supported by Sultan Said, this process was primarily a calculated British initiative which was to reap dividends post-1970. With Qaboos having received the bulk of his formal education in Britain and with service in its military, he was considered both an Anglophile and more likely to share the general British outlook on how to both develop Oman and defeat the insurgency. This made him a suitable potential replacement for his reactionary and,

POLITICS AND DIPLOMACY

in British eyes, somewhat troublesome father. The fruit of this long-term UK investment is illustrated by Marc DeVore's comment that 'the British artisans of the Omani coup d'état expected [the new] Sultan Qaboos to increase spending on the armed forces and development projects, while also implementing British-inspired political reforms'.[73] Alongside examples of key historical British influence in Oman such as the 1958 'Exchange of Letters', the UK state investment in the future Omani rulers therefore gave Britain a ready-made governance alternative if required; a point illustrated clearly in July 1970. The coup was a key turning point in the Dhofar War but was only possible due to the alternative ruler presented by a long-term British process of mentoring and grooming Crown Prince Qaboos for potential power. This can be considered a triumph of long-term UK political strategy to guarantee both Oman's stability and its own interests in 'a classic example of the long-practised diplomatic art of exercising indirect power; as in a game of chess, the pawns are carefully placed on the board with the long-term aim of achieving the desired result'.[74] It is therefore a key indication of the level of historical political and diplomatic influence held by Britain in Oman, its governance, and the path towards victory.

Assistance for Oman in both a historical and specific Dhofar War context would not have been achievable without domestic political UK support. Although FCO Political Residents, Consuls-General, and Ambassadors had much autonomy and key in situ relationships and influence, home-based UK political agreement and support for any substantial actions was required. In the context of the Dhofar War and despite the domestic economic issues facing the UK in the 1960s and 1970s, it is notable that there was consistent general support for British assistance to Oman in all its guises from across the political spectrum when individual parties were actually in government. The more cautious Labour government under Harold Wilson (October 1964–June 1970) can, however, be contrasted to the instigation of the 1970 coup, which occurred only a month after the Conservative Heath government (June 1970–March 1974) came to power. Certainly the relatively parsimonious and minimalist support attitude of the British government with regard to material support for the Sultan was cross-bench in nature, but the point remains that existing contingency plans were likely enacted and Sultan Said was both deposed, and UK SF troops were operating *en masse* in Oman, within six weeks of a Conservative government taking power in 1970.⁷⁵ Following the coup, tangible UK support for the new Sultan was increased substantially to the benefit of the incumbent CSAF, Brig. Graham, who stated: 'The result of the 1970 UK election turned out to be a boon for Oman and for us in her service. Had Labour remained in office the course of events in Oman would not have been so happy for both countries as they have.'⁷⁶ This support included loaned British army instructors and eventually, and most importantly, initially by a troop, but eventually up to two full SAS squadrons (as at the time of the Battle of Mirbat with squadron changeover).⁷⁷ Amongst other taskings, the SAS were utilized for various training, intelligence, and 'hearts and minds'-related activities, all of which significantly helped the campaign towards overall success.⁷⁸ By the time Wilson returned to power in 1974, the pattern of support was already entrenched and via a process of inertia was effectively continued until the end of the war. Therefore, through two Labour and one Conservative administration, Omani war assistance, although at times justifiably considered frugal (especially in the early war years), was agreed and supplied. This cross-ideological party policy consistency was key to providing the required assistance to fight and win the Dhofar War.

As with the host nations of other post-war British COIN campaigns, one of the key benefits of the Dhofar COIN campaign for Oman was continued stability and viability. The Sultanate's governing status quo had both survived and avoided the descent into a full-scale national insurgency and potential provincial or nationwide Communist domination. Oman had also emerged from the war territorially intact and the COIN win reinforced both Sultan Qaboos's own, and his country's legitimacy in the eyes of not just its population, but of the entire Middle Eastern region, and indeed the world via Arab League and UN membership from 1971. The Sultanate had developed 'from an isolated country under Sai'id [sic], to a small and respected participant in the global community under Qaboos'.⁷⁹ Oman, therefore emerged from accusations of merely being a British puppet state and onto the international scene with reinforced legitimacy, therefore transitioning from a situation of UK protectionism to one firmly lodged in the 'Westphalian order'.⁸⁰

In addition to general historical influence and political support, there were several specific instances of key British political and diplomatic influence on Oman with direct effect on the Dhofar War and general stability of the

POLITICS AND DIPLOMACY

Sultanate. These examples collectively highlight the importance of the UK influence on the war, and include the July 1970 coup, the Habrut Fort Incident and Operation AQOOBA retaliatory airstrikes, Omani diplomatic development and Arab League/UN Memberships, and regional alliance-building.

It has been suggested in the historical literature that it is unusual in an insurgency or COIN situation to be able to pinpoint the specific milestone or event that turns the tide of a particular conflict, but that in the case of Oman it was 23 July 1970, when Qaboos brought about 'his father's abdication and removal to a comfortable exile in Europe'.[81] Almost overnight the parsimonious attitude of his father towards spending on his armed forces was swept away, civil development was prioritized, and an amnesty put in place to encourage the flow of Surrendered Enemy Personnel (SEP) to the government side. These developments were all long-held desires of the British government and UK military figures serving in Oman.

The coup was a key moment in the campaign. This event put Oman on the path to eventual victory from a situation many thought was heading towards a defeat for the COIN forces due in large part to Sultan Said's influence.[82] From a perspective of gauging the level of UK influence over the Dhofar War, the importance of the coup cannot be overstated, and Britain is widely considered to have been behind the event.[83] Although to date the available archival materials have been 'sanitized' on most key coup-related material, the historical literature includes comments such as 'The British government in 1970 orchestrated a coup d'état [in Oman] that installed the former Sultan's Sandhurst-educated son as head of state', or that 'On 23 July 1970 the Sultan was forcibly deposed in an almost bloodless coup and the British installed his son, Qaboos bin Said, in his place', as he was 'thought a better figurehead for the reconquest of Dhofar and the safeguarding of British oil interests'.[84] In terms of the reasoning behind such a move, James Goode states: 'The British ... who had become increasingly frustrated with his [Sultan Said's] ineffectual rule, decided to support a coup.'[85] Rory Cormac adds perspective to the debate by stating the 1970 Omani coup should be viewed in the perspective of previous British form in backing such regime change which remained 'plausibly deniable', as had been the case in other Gulf protectorates in the 1960s.[86] Whilst not all are as unequivocal, in many sources the coup is described as British, UK-backed or supported, and involving at least 'some British

49

involvement in the coup's orchestration and clear tacit British approval'.[87] This even includes a reference in former CSAF Maj-Gen. Ken Perkins's 1991 novel *Khalida*. This book was penned in retirement by Perkins and contains many details of real (and then largely unknown, and technically 'secret') events woven into a work of fiction, presumably to circumvent Official Secrets Act constraints, and refers to the 1970 coup being 'Assisted by unseen British hands'.[88]

Available archival documents at the time of writing back up such assertions and point to the view within British governing and military circles that a change in Sultan was vital to reversing a failing Dhofar campaign, and for the war to eventually be won.[89] The very limited available documentation pertaining to the subject (from UK authorities) indicates that detailed planning for different scenario outcomes of the potential coup was clearly undertaken. This was especially the case for how to deal with Qaboos (and whether he should be handed over to his father or not) if the coup failed, and the potential role of seconded personnel in this regard.[90] It also went further to detailed planning for the composition and tasks of what was suggested to be called an 'emergency committee' to be able to 'plan and take executive action' and to 'consolidate his [Qaboos's] rule'.[91] This was effectively the plan for the Interim Advisory Council (IAC) which was implemented after the coup. Such records also show that a systematic trail of misinformation and official denial was planned by British officials. It is recorded in archival materials, for instance, that 'PRPG states ... that, "We would of course maintain the public position that we had no foreknowledge [of the coup]".'[92]

Without potentially missing or unavailable archival information, however, it is difficult to state with absolute certainty that the coup was devised and implemented by Britain. British nationals, including members of the civil service and military (the latter on seconded duties with the SAF), were, however, highly likely to have been intimately involved in both the planning process and subsequent execution of the coup and evidence is increasingly now coming forward to support this view.[93] At the lower end of the scale, the British influence on the coup can be seen as simply not getting in the way of something that had already been decided by Qaboos. This is illustrated by the visit of Capt. Tim Landon and Lt. Col. Teddy Turnhill (CO of DR) to the CSAF not long after his arrival in-country to take up the post. Here, they collectively asked him in cryptic terms what he thought of the incumbent

POLITICS AND DIPLOMACY

Sultan and about the war status in general.[94] This element is further enhanced by the conversation (out of earshot of other bathers whilst swimming in the sea) between Col. Oldman and Brig. Graham where the former mentioned the possibility of a coup and the Qaboos plan in passing, just to see what the SAF commander thought and how the armed forces might react to such an event.[95] Graham was allegedly to answer that there would be a generally favourable response, but because of the potentially more deep-seated loyalties of long-term contract officers, only seconded officers should be involved.[96] This is backed up by the 'appallingly difficult dilemma' later described of the Muscat Regiment CO, Lt. Col. Peter Thwaites, who was asked if he would provide military assistance for the coup, which ran opposite to his personal deep-seated loyalty to, and personal affection for, Sultan Said.[97] Resultingly, it has been stated that 'the coup was arranged by John Graham, commander of the sultan's armed forces', and at a time deliberately coinciding with a military holiday in Oman so loyal British officers were on leave, and when the CO of the SAS and three of his officers were also somewhat conveniently arranged to be in Oman from 23 to 25 July.[98]

The subject of British complicity in the 1970 coup, however, remains contentious. Culpability cannot be wholly proven without original archival governmental papers clearly stating as such, as many of the relevant files remain, at the time of writing, closed to public scrutiny, but future archival releases are likely to back up this assertion.[99] If and when this occurs, the 1970 coup will likely be revealed as a highly choreographed and precision staged-managed event by the UK authorities and the unequivocal 'outcome of British design'.[100] Indeed, in a BBC radio interview, the then long-retired Gen. John Graham stated he was ordered to assist the coup and to not only make sure the SAF switched allegiance from Said to his son after the event, but to actually stop it from failing if necessary.[101]

The coup and its likely clandestine and covert planning and facilitation by UK authorities had a profound effect on the Dhofar COIN campaign. Almost immediately, the old policies of Sultan Said were swept away and Qaboos implemented many of the suggestions made for a long time by British authorities or the CSAF; the character of the Dhofar COIN campaign was to change both 'decisively' and positively.[102] In addition to a swift expansion of the SAF and an increase in funding for the military as well as civil development projects,

British support was also elevated to a much higher level. The secret deployment of the SAS was initiated to provide security, training, and to implement a 'hearts and minds' campaign as part of the wider COIN approach, which developed into the large-scale Operation STORM. This was implemented to prise the initiative away from the insurgents in the war and back to the government side. The coup ushered in a new phase of the Dhofar COIN campaign. Its outcome was cause for much positivity compared to the years of stagnation under the previous Sultan and path towards potential defeat and contributed significantly to setting the stage for the eventual campaign victory.

One of the key stability-related issues for Britain to manage in Oman was the threat of the expansion of cross-border tensions and minor incidents into full-blown inter-state war with the PDRY. This could have been potentially disastrous militarily for the SAF, and diplomatically and politically damaging for the UK itself. In this respect, British diplomacy managed to temper the Sultan's more impulsive desires towards retaliation and therefore the concomitant SAF response. Ultimately, this had the effect of outmanoeuvring the PDRY government in diplomatic terms whilst still enabling a strong SAF response. When PDRY forces attacked the Sultanate Fort at Habrut in close proximity to the PDY border in May 1972, an indignant Sultan Qaboos demanded reprisal airstrikes. This was to both deter further PDRY artillery bombardments and cross-border regular troop insertions, and to hit back militarily to maintain honour. UK officials and several of the Sultan's British advisors questioned the wisdom of such a move due to the potential not just for Oman but the UK also to be drawn into an inter-state stand-off or even conflict with the PDRY. The harmful implications of this potential scenario for the war could have included international arbitration efforts or monitored ceasefires which would have impacted operations and diverted diplomatic and military assets away from the main military effort.

Ultimately, against the direct advice of many of his key advisors and British officials, Sultan Qaboos largely got his way and with the overall support of Brig. Graham, retaliatory airstrikes were launched in May 1972 against the opposing PDRY fort as well as the PFLOAG's Hauf stronghold in the PDRY. The UK government, via its resident Ambassador and the influence of the CSAF, could only insist on a compromise to avert the worst potential political repercussions that no seconded (serving) British officers were to take part in the action. In an unorthodox workaround, after consultation with the British Ambassador in Oman, blank pages of paper were signed by DCSAF (Col. Colin Maxwell), SAF's senior contract officer, and later retrospectively completed with specific orders for Operation AQOOBA as dictated by Brig. Graham himself.[103] In addition, Graham penned the official incident statement that was delivered by Oman's mission to the UN, where he stated: 'The Sultanate Government therefore affirms its legal right to defend its Sovereign territory against the crimes perpetrated by the PFLOAG—PDRY partnership: and in so doing to defend the security of all the Sultanate's friendly neighbours who are threatened by this hostile partnership.'[104] So skilfully was the episode handled in terms of both the airstrikes themselves, but also with the British CSAF-penned diplomatic statement of justification, that Omani actions encountered much sympathy within the UN. This, in turn, helped to mute insurgent propaganda not just pertaining to the incident itself, but provided much international diplomatic goodwill for Oman in the remaining years of the war.[105] The whole episode's solution provided a level of deniability to the British government, allowed the Sultan to maintain 'face', and in both military and political terms achieved nothing short of the CASF's understated verdict of: 'good results'.[106] This British-managed episode was also a morale-boost for the SAF, who witnessed the determination of their Sultan to take the fight to the insurgents and their backers, and as such was a triumph on several fronts in political and diplomatic terms.

In part to solidify credibility for the new Sultan before the anticipated end of the post-accession goodwill honeymoon period and to limit the potential liability for future war expense to the UK, Britain proactively also helped to boost Oman's diplomatic credentials. It did this by assisting the Omani administration and the new Sultan to navigate the necessary diplomatic hurdles to gain recognition and 'international legitimacy' on the world stage.[107] Previously, Sultan Said had effectively left Britain to manage his foreign affairs and the UK had represented Oman's interests in the UN for decades.[108]

Apart from a small-scale Indian presence in the form of a consul, the only foreign diplomatic representation resident in the Sultanate's capital, Muscat, was the British mission represented by the UK Consul-General.[109] The Consul-General reported to the PRPG within the overall chain of authority of the UK Foreign Office, thus Oman's external affairs were managed through this archaic administrative arrangement, which was inherited from the colonial Indian Political Service.[110] After returning from his 1964 visit to London, Sultan Said never left Oman again until his exile in 1970. In addition, he had been absent from Muscat since 1958, when he relocated permanently to Salalah. These points both indicate the primacy of Britain in effectively running Oman's foreign relations, and from the beginning of the Dhofar insurgency and resultant COIN campaign in 1965 right up until late 1971. After the accession of Qaboos as Sultan, however, this situation evolved. Realizing the war was at a critical juncture and a change of leadership was vital to reverse the tide of stalemate or from potential defeat, the British seemingly reappraised their outwardly visibly dominant role in the relationship with Oman after instigating the 1970 coup.[111] Then, as a result of UK guidance, the new Sultan, via his Prime Minister and uncle, Tariq, took the initial steps to end Oman's regional and worldwide diplomatic isolation as well as proactively acquiring representation in the World Health Organization (WHO) in May 1971, then more importantly the Arab League, and subsequently the UN (in September and October 1971 respectively).[112] Britain's diplomatic experience and influence were invaluable in working behind the scenes to advise on the best timescale and process of applications as well as to facilitate the removal of objections (e.g. from Saudi Arabia)—and smooth raised eyebrows from Tariq's often ham-fisted initial application in breach of normal protocols—to Oman being recognized in both of these institutions by October 1971.[113] Whilst the successful coup enabled the faltering Dhofar campaign to be revitalized and the stalemate broken, Britain was not in a position politically, diplomatically, or militarily to supply the forces required to win quickly on the battlefield. The UK's strategy therefore changed to one of assisting Oman to help itself, by utilizing its established diplomatic leverage and influence.

The efforts expended to bring Oman into the diplomatic fold were partly a result of the UK's desire to have the stigma of the 'Question of Oman' removed. More practically the enhanced visibility of the Sultanate on the international stage and the increased legitimacy this brought was calculated by Britain to assist the Dhofar COIN campaign in a practical manner, and at limited—especially reputational—cost.[114] British-facilitated UN representation was notable as the key to diplomatic success in outmanoeuvring the PDRY over objections to the Omani retaliation at Hauf (Operation AQOOBA) in May 1972. Such diplomacy had the effect of generating widespread support for both Oman, and Sultan Qaboos personally, and even from a previously hostile Saudi Arabia and Egypt, for its conduct relating to the Dhofar campaign in general.[115]

In order to continue to be able to prosecute the Dhofar War COIN and continue to limit both liability and cost to themselves, the UK authorities also undertook concerted efforts to widen the scope of Omani alliances.[116] Economic problems in Britain in 1967 contributed largely to the future policy decision to downsize military commitments and withdraw East of Suez.[117] The untidy 1967 departure from Aden also further weakened the British ability to influence events in Oman and Dhofar from a military perspective.[118] With a still formidable range of military commitments around the world, there was a concerted effort to proactively internationalize the conflict by Britain and supplement its own, necessarily limited, assistance. British officials took to the diplomatic offensive to both help Oman to win the Dhofar War but also to limit its own liability or weight of expectancy of assistance. This was a situation which was pursued with even more urgency with the incoming British Labour administration in 1974.[119] Alongside the efforts of Qaboos himself, UK officials, especially via the Foreign Office, pushed for and helped broker talks and agreements with Saudi Arabia, India, and Pakistan for the provision of additional aid and assistance to Oman. Abu Dhabi Emirate was also lobbied to potentially provide assistance in the shape of troops, helicopters, and armoured cars.[120] The greatest and most successful efforts made were directed towards Jordan, and especially to Iran. This British-backed assistance was a key factor in the latter stages of the war to increase military campaign momentum and subsequently secure overall victory.

While Sultan Qaboos had an important personal diplomacy-related role to play in forging external links, the overall strategic planning required was primarily carried out by the British, via its regional diplomatic representatives including Brig. Graham, and later his successor, Maj. Gen. Creasey. Graham's personal relationship and liaison with both the Jordanian and Iranian ambassadors in Muscat was also a key factor. Although initiated by a request from Sultan Qaboos, only after Graham chaired an Omani–Iranian conference in Salalah in August 1972 did sixty C130 planeloads of supplies from Iran arrive as a gift to the Sultan from the Shah as one of the first large-scale, tangible non-British foreign contributions to the campaign, and coined by Graham as 'Operation CAVIAR'.[121] From this point, both Jordanian and Iranian aid and eventually military units were deployed to Oman to help bolster the SAF and its new overall and Dhofar Brigade Commanders (Maj. Gen. Tim Creasey and Brig. Jack Fletcher respectively) and tip the balance in the Dhofar COIN campaign. British personnel such as the Secretary of State for Defence, Lord Carrington, and the subsequent CSAF, Maj. Gen. Creasey, also undertook a sensitive (and direct) diplomatic mediation role directly with the Shah, independent of the Sultan's interactions.[122] This was due to a proactive British policy deemed necessary to discreetly educate the Shah as to the complicated politico-military situation in Dhofar and the need to avoid actions which could raise sympathy for the insurgents or foster direct military confrontation with PDRY forces.[123] Britain was effectively brokering the aid and support provision to be used in the campaign, as well as ensuring also that the Sultanate, as the end user, utilized these to best effect.

To both assist Oman to help itself in the Dhofar War and relieve reliance on Britain, the UK authorities focused on efforts to build up Omani state capacity and facilitate internal development via proactive state-building measures from political, institutional, and social and economic perspectives.[124] Without such widespread British assistance, Oman would not have been able to develop at a quick enough pace—or indeed at all—to be able to develop institutional robustness and gain the support of the people to positively impact the war effort. From this political and diplomatic perspective, Britain was key to securing the Dhofar win.

An important aspect of Britain's influence in Oman in relation to the Dhofar War was the issue of political tutelage, aimed at assisting Omani governance. During the reign of Sultan Said, the combined efforts of British officials to guide, but not to overrule, his administration was evident during the war years. The influence of the Bahrain-based PRPG and the Muscat-located Consul-General provided considered and valuable advice for the ruler, especially on the prevailing attitudes in London's corridors of power. As he was by the time of the Dhofar War start an experienced ruler, Sultan Said was not always amenable to this advice. On occasions he ignored diplomatic and military advice given on a range of issues including granting an amnesty to insurgents, investing in extra troops and new military equipment such as helicopters, changing widely unpopular policies, or even being seen more in public and out of his palace in Salalah.[125] The political tutelage aspect was even more applicable to the reign of Sultan Qaboos once he came to power in 1970. With an inexperienced ruler in place who had never even visited Muscat and had been isolated with vetted visitors only allowed by his father in Salalah, Qaboos relied extensively on British-derived advice. From those in the existing Omani government establishment such as Col. Hugh Oldman, seconded officials such as Brig. John Graham, and other influential advisors such as the then seconded intelligence officer Capt. Tim Landon (who retired to join the SAF on contract), British advice was always on hand. This British advice and political tutelage or grooming of Sultan Qaboos continued throughout the Dhofar War, and ranged from social development, to political, economic, and direct military guidance. Although Qaboos gained a greater sense of self-reliance over time and diversified his inner circle of advisors, often to Britain's ultimate political and diplomatic detriment, it helped the new Sultan to establish himself, further the development of his country, and prosecute the war.[126] An example of how far Qaboos had come in his role and confidence from the shy twenty-nine-year-old who was launched to power in 1970 was his somewhat impertinent question to the British Prime Minister on a visit to 10 Downing Street in September 1973 when 'he asked whether the RAF could drop some bombs instead of [just] taking photographs'![127] UK political tutelage therefore had a significant effect on preparing and progressing Qaboos in his leadership role in Oman and to be both the accepted Dhofar War and national figurehead.

When he assumed power in 1970, the new Sultan Qaboos had no formal governing experience, and had been given no official Omani government role or provided with any tutelage by his father other than as a result of his UK sojourn. Under such circumstances, British personnel unilaterally set up the IAC to temporarily run the country. In doing so, UK officials and personnel effectively administered the state of Oman from 23 July through to the latter half of August 1970, until the return of Qaboos's uncle Tariq as Oman's Prime Minister and the full establishment of his cabinet.[128] The new Sultan had been sequestered by his father in Salalah most of his life. In addition to having no governing experience, Qaboos had also never been to Muscat, the capital and hub of power in his own country, and therefore never been seen by the general populous.

Amid the general euphoria following the ousting of his father, the country still had to be governed and a war conducted in Dhofar, and Salalah was surrounded by the enemy. As such, there was an urgent need to create a governing continuity and bolster a potentially crippling power vacuum. To this end, senior, influential, and well-connected British military, political, and business leaders formed the IAC to take control of the Omani government under the chairmanship of Briton Hugh Oldman. This included several Omanis but consisted primarily of key UK state officials such as Brig. Graham, and private British actors such as PD(O) manager Francis Hughes, and British Bank of the Middle East (BBME) head, Peter Mason.[129] For approximately one month, the British-dominated IAC therefore effectively ran the entire governmental apparatus of Oman and enabled military, financial, and other decisions to be made.

In terms of aiding Omani governance, the IAC, in consultation with the British government, invited Qaboos's uncle Tariq to join the new Omani government as Prime Minister. This was likely done without prior consultation with the new Sultan and was a wholly British initiative.[130] Previously, Tariq had publicly called for the overthrow of his brother (Said) as Sultan, and he held significant support from many followers both in Oman and abroad. British officials, who were keen to present a more inclusive Omani administration to the public and wider world, negotiated Tariq's return primarily because he had a considerable following in Oman for his anti-Said stance. It was hoped that Tariq's return would facilitate the formation of a broad consensus of different Omani interest groups to aid the survival of the new Qaboos administration. This action was important and again helped maintain and reinforce the image of Omani legitimacy and of a Sultanate ruled and administered by Omanis which the British government and advisors in Oman knew was essential. The urgent creation of the IAC was also important to enable the new administration to initially survive politically and economically as well as militarily, so as to continue the high-tempo Dhofar COIN efforts. The mix of (formally or informally) well-connected state and private UK actors involved shows the ubiquitous British role in this key act to maintain Omani stability and prevent a de-railing of the war effort. The council was dissolved soon after Tariq's arrival to further promote the perception of Omani governance of Oman, and the British then reverted to a low-key advisory role so as not to undermine this fostered image.

Post-IAC, British advice remained central to helping the new Sultan to govern, gain legitimacy and, in effect, stay in power. It also kept the momentum going in the Dhofar War, which was at a critical juncture, as the insurgents firmly held the initiative. In the coming years, Qaboos cemented his authority within his administration and government. He built up his own circle of alternative (non-British) advisors which resembled a mafia-like cabal, effectively providing a 'shadowy cabinet' in an attempt to counterbalance UK influence which, as per the 'sliding scale of influence' framework, caused Britain to become increasingly sidelined, especially from governmental and economic affairs.[131] Initially, however, British advice remained the key voice of guidance in the spheres of military strategy and procurement, economic management, social and economic development. This was effectively the establishment and nurturing of a new governing administration, described by Amb. Hawley in its early days as: 'a tender plant'.[132] This support was continuous by necessity due largely to the young Sultan's inexperience, and the fact even in 1974 that 'Qaboos lacks the remarkable grasp of detail which his father held over every aspect of government'.[133] Indirect diplomatic guidance and support was also provided to Sultan Qaboos's advisors such as Timothy Landon, to bolster the Omani cause and the new administration. It was reported by Donald Hawley, the UK's ambassador to Oman, that 'He [Landon] can be naive and on several occasions has been prevented from making serious "gaffes" by our advice', including a draft letter to the Iranian ruler which was 'terse, alarmist and in no suitable form for delivering to any Head of State, let alone the Shah'.[134] Expansive, proactive, and timely British assistance therefore enabled the fledgling administration to firstly survive, then to help it both develop and flourish. This, in turn, enabled the campaign in Dhofar to continue to prevent an all-out defeat. Momentum was then able to be established, and new developments of British origin were subsequently able to be adopted within the COIN campaign.

The UK's state-building efforts in Oman also helped transform the country from a virtual medieval backwater into one firmly on the road to civil and economic development.[135] Such concerted efforts also helped to forge a new national identify in a country racked by internal divisions. The true extent of UK state-building efforts is largely glossed over in historical literature, with James Worral a stand-out example of an author affording them the recognition they deserve.[136] Unlike in previous UK campaigns, in Oman there was very little government apparatus to work with to aid COIN efforts. The British-officered SAF was the only effective and fully functioning state organization in the country, and essentially held it together.

From an administration where decisions were made almost solely by Sultan Said from his Salalah palace and transmitted (in the case of military decisions or orders) by radio telephone to advisors in Muscat, the large-scale task of introducing or developing the various institutions of state began in a process guided by British advisors.[137] In terms of internal governance, although Oman remained an absolute monarchy, post-coup there were concerted efforts to develop and put in place the wider organization of governmental bureaucracy essential for the functioning of a modern state. When Tariq bin Taimur returned to Oman as Prime Minister in August 1970, he was tasked to develop the governmental infrastructure, and oversee the formation of a new government.[138] Under his authority, but largely through UK guidance, new government departments were established, largely led by Omani nationals. This was done to showcase to the outside world both the perception and reality of 'native control over governance', necessary for both increased internal and external legitimacy.[139]

One of Britain's key priorities in terms of state-building was to extend the capability of the SAF to both facilitate internal cohesion and prosecute the war effort. With Sultan Qaboos's agreement, the main recommendations of British advisors Hugh Oldman and Brig. Graham were approved. A key development was the confirmation of the formation of the new Jebel Regiment (JR), the formation of an armoured car squadron, ships purchased for the SON, and the expansion of the SOAF to four squadrons.[140] In all, the SAF increased in size from approximately 3,000 men prior to the 1970 coup to over 10,000 less than twenty-four months later.[141] To further boost SAF capability, for the first time in the war, the British government provided large-scale regular UK armed forces support. Specialist British units such as a Field Surgical Team (FST), the RE, and an RA 'cracker battery', as well as training teams and extra equipment were deployed to Oman from 1970.[142] Such efforts also included the raising of the Firqa units, made up of a large percentage of SEPs with a view to taking the fight to their ex-comrades in the PFLOAG. Initially SAS-trained and led, despite a number of teething problems and the

POLITICS AND DIPLOMACY

view that they were 'fickly, quarrelsome and greedy', the Firqa were to prove key to turning the tide of the war.[143] All such developments helped towards developing a more effective SAF which was more capable of taking on the expanded, well-trained, and equipped PFLOAG forces in Dhofar as well as carrying out security duties concurrently across the whole of Omani territory. The realization of British-developed SAF expansion plans helped to stabilize the dire situation the government forces faced after five years of Sultan Said's ultimate control over the campaign. This enabled the profile of SAF to be raised, and ultimately the war to be won.

In terms of much-needed social and infrastructure development, a fast-tracked nationwide scheme of building schools, hospitals, and other infrastructure projects such as roads and port facilities was instigated, which helped propel the country from almost medieval-level underdevelopment to become a modern nation state.[144] This was recognized by the British as essential to gain the backing of the Omani people for the hitherto unpopular and expensive Dhofar War in a country which had only three primary schools and one hospital up until 1970.[145] Such social development was extended to the even more deprived Dhofar region and the Jebel initially via the SAS-instigated and 'hearts and minds'-focused Civil Action Teams (CATs). Activities included the introduction of medical assistance for civilians and construction of wells for human and animal water supplies, and amenities such as schools, mosques, and shops via CATs on the Jebel as well in the government-controlled areas such as the coastal towns (including the Kuria Maria Islands) and the Negd plain area.[146] In Dhofar, this COIN campaign-led civil development activity eventually morphed into the formal establishment under ex-Gurkha and previously second-in-command of the Muscat Regiment, Lt. Col. Martin Robb of the Omani Civil Aid Department (CAD) in 1975.[147] The CAD followed military pacification efforts with the construction of government centres, schools, wells, road-building and even a flying doctor service.[148] Such efforts contributed significantly to the velvet glove (as opposed to the 'closed fist' of military action) or 'open hand of friendship' COIN element that aimed to win over the Jebalis as well as Dhofaris in general to the government side and were therefore essential to the war effort.[149]

As a national state-building issue, modern internal state policing was also developed in post-coup Oman under British guidance. Under Sultan Said's rule, law and order had been administered primarily through the twin pillars of the traditional sovereign-appointed Wali governor system, with policing up until 1970 delegated to the military's Oman Gendarmerie unit. Under Qaboos, a new national police force named the Royal Oman Police (ROP) was established, with full functions and responsibility subsumed by the new unit by 1972.[150] A similar story was apparent with the development of an internal state security and intelligence apparatus. This organization was first called the Oman Intelligence Service (OIS) and set up and directed initially by officers of Britain's Secret Intelligence Service (SIS) and developed into the Oman Research Department (ORD) by 1974.[151] This gave the Omani government an effective non-military intelligence capability for the first time. In tandem with reforming policing organization itself, legal changes were also instigated to contribute to state-building efforts. Via British guidance, the repressive laws imposed on his subjects by Sultan Said over decades of rule (especially in Dhofar) were either relaxed or removed, including the restrictions on movement or travel, and from the long-standing rules banning 'wicked Western imports' such as transistor radios or cameras.[152] Such developments initiated during the Dhofar War helped to reduce or even remove many of the fundamental reasons why the original nationalist-led insurgency first developed in the early 1960s. Reinforcing the primary impact of UK state-supported governmental and institutional development, as a secondary effect, private British efforts also helped to forge a level of national consciousness or unity which would rally the country around the flag to support the hitherto unpopular ongoing COIN campaign in Dhofar. In the last few months of Sultan Said's reign, the BBME managed the introduction of a new national currency. The BBME controlled the phasing out of the anachronistic Maria Theresa silver dollar, hitherto the official coinage in Oman, as well as other unofficial denominations such as the Indian Rupee and the implementation of the new Omani Saidi Rial. This new central currency as a nationally bonding exercise was joined in the first few months of Sultan Qaboos's reign by the country's name change from Muscat and Oman to the Sultanate of Oman, and a new Omani flag. The latter was designed by SOAF's then Administrative Officer, RAF officer Flt. Lt. Bill Goodfellow, and chosen as part of a nationwide competition, remaining the national flag to this day.[153]

Whilst many initial problems were encountered in setting up such infrastructure and state-building developments, it was nevertheless a positive, and

POLITICS AND DIPLOMACY

successful, process for Oman. What previously had been a country run by a reclusive Sultan, remote from the capital city in his palace in Salalah, changed radically. Such British-instituted, supported, or managed state- or nation-building efforts firstly cemented support for the new regime. This enabled the modified Al Said dynasty status quo to survive and the country itself to flourish and develop over a rapid timescale into a more modern country with all facets of a functioning state. As such, the national support for the war in Dhofar was maintained. In Dhofar, the 'hearts and minds' aspects of the COIN campaign were also given extra credibility in the eyes of the Jebali population when they could witness local development, including on the Jebel itself. As Ian Beckett states:

> In Oman, the reforms begun in 1970 have been extended to produce the infrastructure of a modern state with improved communications, industry, and medical and educational facilities. In Dhofar, modernisation has also proceeded apace, and the *jebalis* have a significant measure of autonomy, increasing their vested interest in the *status quo*.[154]

All such state capacity and internal development facilitated, undertaken, or carried out primarily by British government agents and secondarily by private UK actors was aimed to increase the resilience of Oman in terms of governance and development. This, in turn, supported the war effort and demonstrated to Omanis, and Jebalis in particular, that the government was of benefit to them and was likely to ultimately win the war. Overall, the British government achieved its key strategic aims whilst adhering to an essentially highly frugal attitude towards the cost or length of the support given to Oman, and therefore without committing overly large resources to the campaign.[155] Despite some negative factors, such as a greater overall expense than was necessary and general loss of influence in Oman, the UK achieved its strategic objectives at relatively modest commitment and cost. When the Dhofar campaign began in earnest in the mid-1960s, Britain was already involved in COIN operations in Brunei/Borneo and Aden. The UK needed to achieve its strategic aims including encouraging both Omani and regional Gulf stability, the general resistance to Communist infiltration, and access to vital strategic oil supplies, whilst at the same time avoiding a protracted large-scale commitment or genuinely feared potential 'mini-Vietnam' scenario.[156] In accordance with the 1958 'Exchange of Letters', Britain provided relatively limited financial assistance and seconded officers. This was especially the case when viewed in the context of other contemporary actions such as that in Aden or even the much larger-scale deployment of regular British military units involved in Palestine, Malaya, Cyprus, Kenya, Borneo, and Northern Ireland. Additionally, in terms of limiting costs, UK assistance to Oman was largely paid for in full by the Sultanate, which further limited Britain's financial liability.[157] This scenario meant that, at least up until 1970, Britain was able to prosecute the Dhofar War in a relatively inexpensive manner as compared to the full 'state power' approach taken in several previous larger COIN campaigns where the UK authorities had to shoulder the cost of a wider and more extensive commitment.

Due in part to this general highly cost-conscious policy, the relatively limited scale of cost to the UK was also prevalent in terms of campaign casualties. Although the Dhofar COIN campaign was conducted in relative public secrecy, high British soldier casualties would have been politically unacceptable. Britain suffered only thirty-five military personnel killed in the Dhofar War, including twelve deaths suffered by the SAS during the unit's covert deployment from 1970 to 1976.[158] This was a very low casualty rate compared to the 1,845 members of the British-run security forces killed in the Malayan Emergency or even the 590 killed in the Kenyan Mau Mau campaign.[159] Although, to a large extent, the low attrition rate was due to the length and tempo of the conflict, there were still nearly 1,000 security forces fatalities in Northern Ireland up to the late 1990s, with 103 soldiers killed in 1972 alone, the year the Dhofar campaign was turning the corner to success.[160] With such casualty figures in Northern Ireland being sustained in a COIN campaign at the same time as Dhofar, the scale of the latter is put into perspective. By limiting the scale of and commitment to the Dhofar campaign, Britain was able to avoid the larger numbers of casualties as suffered during previous UK COIN ventures.

Additionally, in a concerted attempt to limit Dhofar War involvement and the attendant costs involved, British diplomats and military personnel embarked on a diplomatic charm offensive to attempt to widen regional involvement in Omani government COIN efforts. Whilst there are some exceptions to be found in the classical British COIN historical record, most campaigns featured only British, Commonwealth, or UK-raised and officered forces as the combatants. This was the situation prior to 1973 in the case of the Dhofar War, with

POLITICS AND DIPLOMACY

British-officered Omani and Baluchi troops conducting the military campaign. By 1970, it was clear the SAF were at that point unable to defeat the insurgents and at best a situation of stalemate had developed. At worst, it looked increasingly possible that the war in Dhofar might even be lost to the insurgents, so a more radical solution was required.[161] After the accession of Sultan Qaboos, determined efforts were put in place primarily by British state-level advisors to end the military stalemate, and one of the avenues both explored and subsequently fully exploited was the engagement of foreign allied forces to boost the SAF's capability and assist the campaign.

As a result of the growing links and relationship between the Sultan of Oman and the Shah of Iran, as cemented at the Iranian Persepolis celebrations in 1971, large-scale additional assistance was soon to result.[162] This steady build-up of links was continued via the new Iranian Ambassador in Muscat and through much behind-the-scenes diplomacy by military staff between the Omani, Iranian, and Jordanian administrations, to which Brig. Graham, and subsequently Maj. Gen. Creasey were key.[163] This British-instigated diplomatic activity in turn led to the deployment of Jordanian SF troops and combat engineer units, and eventually to an entire Iranian battle group by 1973. This included SF troops, vital heavy lift helicopter support, and some 3,000 men.[164] This situation triggered a significant change in the composition of the Dhofar COIN forces through a process of internationalization. By 1975, Iranian combat units actually spearheaded many of the key late-campaign offensives and Jordanian engineers and SF fortified and defended key locations.[165] Infantry from the UAE were also made available to assist with internal security duties in northern Oman to release two OG squadrons for Dhofar deployments.[166] By 1975, therefore, of the 14,000 plus troops serving in Dhofar, it was the case that up to 1,000 only were British regular forces, with these outnumbered almost four to one by foreign troops.[167] In addition to the large numbers of non-British troops brought into the COIN campaign, most additional regular troops supplied by the UK were withdrawn soon after the conflict ended in 1975. The ultimately political decision for RAF Salalah and RAF Masirah to remain fully manned was made but alongside the FST capability, the deployed RE squadron did not leave Oman until the completion of Operation TENABLE in late 1977, and a twelve-man SAS formation stayed until 1978, nearly three years after the war was won.[168]

65

THE DHOFAR WAR

The widening of the military assistance for Omani COIN efforts in Dhofar, especially the deployment of Iranian troops and other military assets, greatly boosted the capability of the SAF to engage the enemy and progress towards victory whilst enabling direct British assistance to remain limited. Alongside the political imperative of a swift return home for most of the deployed British forces once victory had been declared, this created a situation where the UK was able to pursue and attain its military—and therefore political and diplomatic—goals in Dhofar and beyond, whilst limiting both physical engagement and other potential associated costs.

Despite the British desire to maintain both political and economic influence in Oman, domestic political and economic realities meant that British politicians and diplomats worked to an agenda of providing only discreet, and largely covert, assistance to the Sultanate.[169] This policy was pursued in the full knowledge that UK influence would ultimately diminish. This was due firstly to the necessity to keep knowledge of the intervention to a minimum in the UK. British public opinion would be unlikely to take kindly to large deployments of troops and the potential for casualties, and even more so at a time of economic stagnation in the UK and stringent control of the public purse. The second reason was to not tarnish the carefully nurtured British policy of maximizing the international perception of Oman's sovereignty and legitimacy.[170] Prior to the 1970 coup, this policy enabled the UK to deflect neo-colonial allegations in the UN apropos its actions in Dhofar. It also helped to largely maintain international support for UK-backed Omani actions for the remainder of the war. Thirdly, at the beginning of the Dhofar War, Britain already had substantial forces operating in Borneo and involved in COIN operations in Aden, and the latter was suffering significant casualties.[171] Harold Wilson's Labour Party, which formed the UK government from 1964 to 1970, needed to balance national strategic interests with the predominantly anti-colonial stance of its party membership. Partly because of this, the Dhofar COIN campaign was largely covert and secretive in nature and virtually unknown outside of military and political circles in the UK, and debate in Parliament (then non-televised) on the subject was limited. After the establishment of the Conservative government in 1970, despite higher levels of press coverage following the coup, which did actually highlight the UK's assistance to Oman's new Sultan, information on the precise role of British

POLITICS AND DIPLOMACY

forces, the extent of wider UK military support, and especially the secretive role of UK SF units remained scarce.[172] The involvement of UK forces in Oman was also little publicized to the British people, and this was especially the case with the large-scale and politically sensitive role of the SAS.[173] This had the effect of giving UK politicians and military (seconded and contract) commanders greater leeway and flexibility in terms of theatre actions than elsewhere, as John Peterson states:

> Another advantage of both wars in Oman was their general obscurity. Vietnam is the most famous example of how the war effort was affected by adverse publicity and extensive television coverage but Britain also faced similar problems in Aden and Northern Ireland.[174]

This situation enabled decisions to be made at all levels which may have been potentially vetoed in other more 'public' campaigns such as in Palestine or Aden and helped to secure eventual military victory. This was because operations were mainly conducted in a 'generally benign media environment', where rules of engagement were often more flexible.[175] This in turn allowed firmer or more direct action against insurgents such as free-fire zones with less potential political risk. Primarily then, through the skill and actions of Britain's politicians and civil servants, the potentially complicating factor of UK domestic public opinion regarding Omani assistance was effectively sidestepped, and related complications therefore never became a major national or political problem for the incumbent governments. Thanks largely to the UK's highly experienced diplomatic corps, the impact of Marxist propaganda, UN General Assembly animosity, and world opinion in general never succeeded in destroying the shield of legitimacy over the Sultanate which was carefully crafted by Britain. Through a process where 'we should encourage, though unobtrusively, contacts between Oman and other Arab countries and Omani membership of international bodies', once discreet British efforts to smooth the path of Omani membership of both the Arab League and UN were successful, and the equally UK-encouraged development of Oman's own diplomatic corps and inbound foreign diplomatic representation, such strident anti-British, anti-colonial rhetoric was discredited.[176] This also paved the way for further regional alliances which also benefitted the Dhofar COIN campaign and contributed to the British-facilitated final victory.

It can be seen, therefore, that although it diminished over time as per the 'sliding scale of influence' framework, Britain's political and diplomatic influence remained strong and was one of the key facilitators of success. Britain also largely achieved its desired strategic outcomes and Oman and UK-centric goals as pertaining to the Dhofar War. After the highs of the UK-instigated 1970 coup, the largely British-comprised (both state and private actors) IAC and the implementation of plans for government, civil development, and especially military expansion, government policy evolved. Alongside the increasingly assertive and experienced Sultan Qaboos, a deliberate policy of discreet assistance was followed by successive UK governments so as not to damage the legitimacy of the new regime. As a result, Britain's influence on Oman and the Dhofar campaign diminished from a political and diplomatic perspective. British state (and private UK actor) commitment continued, however, in keeping with the UK's historically significant support to Oman. The emphasis centred on political tutelage, support for the fledgling Omani administration, and its UK-mentored ruler as well as unprecedented efforts in state-building in the modern age. All these factors were key to avoiding defeat in the Dhofar War. The UK's political and diplomatic commitment to Oman was subsequently central also to the later turnaround in the COIN campaign's fortunes and eventual achievement of victory, thereby allowing the governing status quo in Oman to endure and the attainment of Britain's key strategic, domestic, and Oman-centric aims.

4 Military Strategy

As an example of the utilization of the military instrument of state power to achieve policy goals, Britain set out and dictated military strategy from both a UK and Omani perspective, and tightly controlled its execution throughout the Dhofar War. Due to this input, the broad, overarching aims were largely achieved for the UK and Oman with the defeat of the Adoo and, in Dhofar Brigade Commander Brig. John Akehurst's words from 1974, 'To secure Dhofar for civil development.'[1] Unlike in other areas covered in this book, British control of military strategy was virtually total from the start of the Dhofar campaign in 1965 to its completion a decade later.[2] Whilst Britain's military strategy can be criticized in certain areas and especially earlier in the war, the UK's control of such at all key levels remained one of the vital factors in the eventual victory in 1975.[3] Some historical narratives alternatively suggest Britain was not actually in charge of strategy as this was the realm of the Sultan.[4] This was true to the extent that the ruler was Commander-in-Chief of the Omani Armed Forces and could, and did, interject as he saw fit, such as the general policy of support for repressive measures by both Sultan Said and Sultan Qaboos, including food denial and effective free-fire zones, and the latter's insistence on the Operation AQOOBA airstrikes on PDRY territory.[5] The situation, however, just meant that military strategy, as delegated to the British CSAF and SAF command, had to adapt to accommodate the whims, viewpoints, or wishes of the Sultan to achieve the overall aim, and he was not substantively involved in its formulation. With overall success achieved because of UK military strategic input in 1975, Britain's wider strategic aims on all levels were realized.

Military Strategic Goals

Concerning the Dhofar theatre, Britain's chief strategic military aims were to initially contain the insurgent threat, avoid defeat, and subsequently to stabilize the campaign, expand (and supplement where neccesary) SAF capability, then defeat the insurgency.[6] Although on the surface these can be considered as relatively standard military strategic aims, they did, however, follow the unique and case-specific historical pattern of the Dhofar insurgency. They also highlight the initial British mistakes which had to evolve to be subsequently addressed and rectified mainly post-1970.

The role of the UK political and diplomatic hierarchies was to support the military strategy formulated by the CSAF, who represented their seconded British army military expert on the ground. The CSAF had a high level of latitude on development and execution of military strategy, working within the limited constraints imposed by the UK government and the Sultan himself. The first CSAF, Col. David Smiley, described how, although he had a special clause in his terms of service to ensure his actions ultimately 'did not conflict with my allegiance to Her Majesty' and therefore British interests, he nevertheless directly served the Sultan and it was to him that he owed his allegiance.[7] This wide scope of freedom of action for the CSAFs to develop and implement military strategy is also illustrated through Brig. Corran Purdon's comment that 'I was in the happy position of being totally independent. I had no [direct] boss, other than the Sultan, who was Commander-in-Chief of his Armed Forces.'[8]

Whilst ably and loyally backed up by UK contract officer Col. Colin Maxwell as the DCSAF from 1958 all through the Dhofar War years, primary control of military strategy was in the hands of the incumbent CSAF. This meant that the two most senior wartime military SAF commanders were UK-trained nationals, with the ranking officer a serving Crown agent. The DCSAF and other contract officers were largely UK armed forces-trained, so their overall approach to warfare was resultantly similar. Although largely recruited via Airwork Ltd., as privately contracted individuals to the Sultan's administration, they still remained part of the 'old boy' British military network and hailed from the same strata of society. As such, they were considered loyal, yet largely deniable assets by the UK government; indeed CSAFs tended not even to

MILITARY STRATEGY

publicly differentiate between the contractual arrangements, seemingly considering them effectively a collective British officer corps.[9]

As previously alluded to, Britain's main latent influence over military strategy in the Dhofar War came in the guise of the seconded CSAF as this was his sphere of responsibility. In a scenario that may seem anachronistic today, the CSAFs seconded by the UK government were effectively given full charge of a sovereign foreign county's entire military resources and structure in order to fight a war in a province of that state. This scenario was in force from the official start of the war in 1965 to its declared end in December 1975, and beyond. It is relevant to the success of the overall campaign precisely because the eventual victory can be largely attributed to the military strategy developed and executed by these serving British army officers, supplied to Oman by the British government, and individually nominated by the respective branches of the UK armed forces. Oman was indeed fortunate that officers of high quality and experience were selected to lead the Sultanate's military. The momentum of improved organization and preparedness was initiated and built up by Col. David Smiley as the first CSAF and built upon by subsequent commanders. These individuals possessed a wealth of wartime and COIN experience as well as regional operational knowledge and familiarity and were able to utilize this to devise and implement workable theatre-level strategies.

The Dhofar War saw the high point of the British Army's historical COIN experience, actioned through UK leaders (including the CSAF), and helped achieve overall victory. The conflict represented the culmination of three decades of accumulated UK wartime combat and especially irregular warfare and COIN experience of its leaders.[10] All such UK COIN operations, including Dhofar, were to benefit from the unique and cumulative campaign experience gained from unconventional World War Two operations, then from Palestine onwards and especially during the series of overlapping COIN theatres and campaigns from the late 1940s through to the late 1960s in Palestine, Kenya, Cyprus, Oman (Djebel Akhdar campaign), Brunei/Borneo, Aden, and Northern Ireland.[11] From Palestine onwards, all British COIN campaigns benefitted from the wartime and/or accumulated anti-insurgent operational experience of both the senior officers commanding operations and even the more junior officers, NCOs, and troops executing them on the ground.[12] In Dhofar, a general implementation of hard-won COIN experience by UK military veterans

THE DHOFAR WAR

Table 4.1: COIN and warfare experience of CSAFs

CSAF NAME/TENURE	STANDARD AND IRREGULAR WARFARE/ COIN EXPERIENCE
Col. David Smiley (1958–1961)	WWII SAS and Special Operations Executive (SOE) experience. Irregular operations in Albania and Thailand, Omani Djebel Campaign Commander
Col. Hugh Oldman (1961–1964)	WWII Military Cross (MC) winner, Sudan Defence Force, Aden Protectorate Levies. Later Military Secretary of Oman (1970–1973)
Col. Tony Lewis (1964–1967)	WWII Commando operations, and Distinguished Service Order (DSO)/Croix de Guerre winner, Omani Djebel Campaign
Brig. Corran Purdon (1967–1970)	WWII Commando operations (MC won at St. Nazaire Raid), Palestine Emergency, Malayan Emergency, Cyprus Emergency
Brig. John Graham (1970–1972)	WWII, Palestine Emergency, Cyprus Emergency
Maj-Gen. Tim Creasey (1972–1975)	WWII, British Indian Army, Kenyan Mau Mau campaign, Aden Emergency
Maj-Gen. Ken Perkins (1975–1977)	Palestine Emergency, Korean War, Suez Crisis, Malayan Emergency (Distinguished Flying Cross (DFC) winner)

of earlier British campaigns is apparent and was a significant success factor. Nowhere is this seen more than in the CSAFs who served immediately prior to and during the Dhofar War. Such seasoned professionals were ultimately in charge of the development and execution of military strategy and brought their experience to bear in the Dhofar War.

There are numerous examples of this large, accumulated reserve of regular, unconventional military and especially COIN experience to draw from when considering the case of Dhofar. In terms of senior officers, Brig. Purdon won the MC at the famed St Nazaire Raid of World War Two. He later saw action in the Palestine, Malayan, and Cypriot COIN campaigns and commanded a regiment in the Borneo action prior to bringing this experience to the role of CSAF in 1967.[13] Brig. Graham saw action in both the Palestine and Cyprus COIN campaigns, Maj. Gen. Creasey in the Kenyan and Aden actions; latterly as a battalion commander with the Royal Anglian regiment. The final Dhofar wartime CSAF, Maj-Gen. Perkins, was decorated MBE and DFC for his

MILITARY STRATEGY

COIN-related actions in the Malayan Emergency, primarily as an army helicopter pilot.[14] All this accumulated experience was available to feed into the mindset, attitudes, and military strategies implemented in Dhofar, including the use of innovative cross-theatre blocking lines such as the Hornbeam Line.[15] It was not, however, just the CSAFs who had the relevant wartime and COIN experience to contribute to the strategic aspects of the Dhofar War. Most British staff and regimental fighting officers of the SAF, whether LSP or on private contract, as well as from the UK armed forces deployed to Dhofar, could boast often significant COIN experience. Of key importance was the COIN and regional-specific experience of the SAS soldiers and officers who planned the new 'hearts and minds'-focused COIN approach as implemented by the CSAFs from Brig. Graham onwards. Lt. Col. John Watts and later Lt. Col. Peter de la Billière had extensive COIN experience, both having served and commanded in Malaya and in the Omani Djebel campaign in the 1950s. The latter also commanded SAS units in the Radfan/Aden conflict and Borneo, including cross-border operations behind enemy lines, as well as having a role in the covert and deniable 1960s deployment of British mercenaries in North Yemen to support the ousted Royalist regime.[16] This level of experience from the SAS commanders afforded the CSAFs a coherent COIN plan or blueprint, utilizing tried and tested methods born from their widespread irregular and anti-insurgent operational backgrounds.

In terms of strategic development and implementation, there also exists the historical literature viewpoint that success in the war was influenced, decisively controlled, or even effectively won by the hand of the Sultan himself. Going further than the more reasonable explanation, which holds that Qaboos had a genuine and positive role in helping facilitate victory via helping to develop popular support against the insurgents, this view purports that the war was actually won because of his leadership and wise, strategic acumen and 'decisive, analytical skill'.[17] This minority viewpoint also holds that Qaboos was the driving force behind liberating his country from his father's oppressive authoritarian rule, which kept the country in a state of 'backwardness', and that his leadership was the real reason for the eventual war victory.[18] Such claims include that 'the crucial element [to winning] was Qaboos bin Said's [strategic] talent as a military leader. His military education enabled him to conduct a difficult campaign in accordance with modern requirements and to foresee the actions of the rebels'.[19] Both Sultans were influential in many aspects of the war, and even intervened at times at the tactical level, but in terms of overall military strategy, the CSAF was wholly responsible within the boundaries of circumstances, including Sultan-controlled funding. Beasant and Ling highlight further aspects of this Qaboos-centric viewpoint, including the fact that:

> The [Omani] official version, spelt out in a succession of nicely produced booklets aimed at journalists and other opinion-formers for 'guidance', is that Qaboos sprang fully loaded, so to speak, onto the stage, waved a wand ... and transformed his country [and won the war] overnight.[20]

Such writers go further to suggest that this general viewpoint was 'simply spin and nonsense' and that such excesses throughout Qaboos's reign were effectively propaganda narratives designed by the Omani Ministry of Information, and under the watchful eye of the notorious 'advisor' to the Minister for Information and one-time British spy, Anthony Ashworth.[21] This tendency for revisionism and whitewashed official narratives with reference to the 'rebirth' of the nation or descriptions such as 'the butterfly emerged from the chrysalis and made its first ecstatic flight' after Qaboos's accession acts, however, to rather unfairly devalue his valuable tangible, and very real, achievements in many areas.[22] These important contributions included vital support for, and the provision of, military expansion as initially requested by the CSAF and Col. Hugh Oldman, his Military Secretary, and of much-needed social development programmes, all of which helped towards both bringing the Dhofari population psychologically into the government camp and helped facilitate the military defeat of the insurgents. Despite this, although the Sultan was Commander-in-Chief of his own armed forces, military strategy was very much the preserve of the UK's seconded CSAFs throughout the Dhofar War and was probably Britain's greatest tangible contribution to the war effort.

Containing the Threat

British control and implementation of military strategy was paramount from the very start of the Dhofar War. This factor contributed largely to the containment, within the bounds of SAF capability, of the Adoo threat and the

MILITARY STRATEGY

avoidance of defeat to an insurgent force growing both in size and offensive ability. The initial SAF deployments to Dhofar as ordered by the then CSAF, Col. Tony Lewis, took place in December 1964 and May 1965. They were faced with a challenging tasking involving overland travel of several hundred kilometres with all required equipment from northern Oman to Dhofar. After two relatively uneventful deployments, the tempo of the insurgent campaign increased, leading to the official start (according to the DLF) of the war on 9 June 1965 when the DLF attacked an oil company lorry and killed the driver.[23]

At that time, the SAF consisted of small numbers of aircraft and a single naval boom, and its fighting ability rested primarily with the Muscat and the Northern Frontier Regiments. A new infantry unit was raised in 1965 as the Desert Regiment (DR) but was not fully operational until early 1968. In addition, the specialist Dhofar Force was administered separately from the SAF and CSAF authority under Pakistani contract officers who reported directly to the Sultan. In terms of personnel available, the SAF had to operate twenty-three separate military posts in its primary internal security role, and numbers to support large-scale additional deployments were scarce.[24] The initial NFR deployment in 1964 was only company-strength, with the subsequent MR force deployed in May 1965 doubling in size.[25] With the large size of the Dhofar operating area, the SAF simply did not have enough manpower to concurrently deal with the insurgency and its other roles. In addition, in the early years of the war from 1965 to 1970, the SAF only ever deployed (on rotation) one reinforced battalion of approximately 600 men to fight the insurgents in Dhofar, whilst 'In contrast, from their sanctuary in the PDRY, the PFLOAG could deploy up to 1,800 personnel(both fulltime fighters and militia) '.[26] This meant that although well-led by its British officers, for the first half of the war the SAF deployed fewer than 1,000 soldiers to Dhofar to counter an insurgency in a theatre as large as Wales, and such numbers were so removed from the minimum ten to one COIN force to insurgent ratio traditionally used as an indicator for campaign success that a positive result under such circumstances was unlikely.[27]

Similarly, in terms of equipment, the SAF suffered in the early years of the conflict with obsolete equipment, including World War Two bolt-action rifles, no helicopter casualty evacuation capability and limited in-country military medical provision. There was even a lack of basic uniforms, including suitable footwear, for the Jebel conditions. In Dhofar the (primarily) infantry operation was backed up by artillery when possible and slowly increasing levels of air support. Although the SOAF could field several small-scale transport aircraft, there were no helicopters or strike aircraft available to support Dhofar operations until 1969, when BAC 167 Strikemaster aircraft entered service and six Augusta Bell 205 helicopters were ordered. This provided a challenging operational and therefore strategic environment, and despite the severe financial limitations affecting the SAF, Col. Lewis and his successor Brig. Purdon forged effective fighting forces. These forces conducted several successful operations including supply interdiction actions on the Yemeni border in early 1967, but following a deteriorating security situation in the lead up to, and post-exit from Aden and the establishment of the PDRY, a deterioration in the strategic environment ensued where it was considered that nationalists in Muscat and Oman would be encouraged in their own struggle as a result.[28]

Firstly, support for the DLF and subsequently for the PFLOAG (from 1968) from Communist sponsors increased steadily. It grew to the extent that the insurgents were operating with better equipment and benefitted from many of their number attending military courses in China or the USSR. From indoctrination at schools in Hauf in the PDRY, to training courses in Peking and the benefit of foreign Communist advisor training in PDRY territory, the Adoo forces were committed and tactically astute. Combined with intimate knowledge of the Jebel terrain and the seasonal conditions, this made the Adoo a formidable enemy. Many British officers, including high-ranking commanders, learned to respect the abilities of their enemy and often held them in high regard.[29] Secondly, the Adoo forces were generously equipped by their Communist sponsors with the latest Soviet bloc weaponry in sufficient quantity, which resulted in a situation where the insurgents were often considered operationally at least the equal of the SAF.[30] As the final wartime Dhofar Brigade Commander Brig. Akehurst recalled: 'with anything like fair odds [the Adoo] would usually come off best in contact with [the] SAF'.[31] New equipment for the SAF was also not ordered early enough to make a theatre-wide strategic difference, due to the thrift-conscious approach of Sultan Said. Despite the small-scale and relatively primitive insurgent organization of the mid-1960s, the insurgency was not dealt with early and was eventually to last ten years.

MILITARY STRATEGY

Notwithstanding the introduction of Strikemaster jets in 1969, Brig. Purdon stated that if the required Iroquois and Jetranger helicopters and field artillery had been received 'A year earlier and we might have militarily won the War [*sic*] ... Final victory was not to come until 1974'.[32] Although faced with these almost insurmountable challenges, the SAF was not defeated. This was largely the result of both the development and the effective implementation of military strategy by the British CSAFs, staff, and regimental officers of the SAF.

Despite the best efforts of the SAF under Col. Lewis, the strategic military aim to defeat the insurgency early through halting the disrupting activities of the DLF under its instigator, Mussalam bin Nufl, was not achieved. This task was, however, no straightforward undertaking, especially with the constraints imposed on the CSAF, primarily in terms of funding and SAF manpower. With the withdrawal of Britain from Aden in 1967, the formation of the PDRY in 1968 and both the increase in resulting support for the insurgents and their growth and development into the more ideologically radical PFLOAG in the same year, this military failure was to prove costly in strategic terms. From 1967 and under the new CSAF, Brig. Purdon, the circumstances became even more challenging. Despite being by now well-trained, motivated, and led by British officers, the SAF remained undermanned and underfunded, and the momentum of the insurgency was firmly with the insurgents. By 1970, the SAF held no centres of population and no permanent presence in Dhofar except for the Salalah plain.[33] The strategic military priority towards the end of Brig. Purdon's tenure and for the first few months of his successor, Brig. John Graham, therefore evolved from an aspiration of defeating the insurgents quickly to merely preventing them from overrunning Salalah and therefore focused on 'holding the line'. This was achieved by withdrawing all SAF forces to the Salalah plain and fortifying this area against any insurgent advances, and the withdrawal was completed by Brig. Graham. He ordered the withdrawal of SAF troops guarding the Midway Road in one of his first actions after becoming CSAF in March 1970, as they were deemed to be too exposed and not defendable due to the dominance of the insurgent forces. This act effectively handed the insurgents complete control of the Jebel. They also controlled the remainder of the province bar Salalah and the surrounding plain area, covering a coastline area of approximately seven miles inland, and as far east as Taqa and Mirbat only.

THE DHOFAR WAR

The key aims of bolstering Salalah's defences and holding the line were subsequently achieved, and therefore defeat was avoided. As such, a stalemate ensued in the Dhofar conflict, with the SAF holding the Salalah plain, and the PFLOAG the remainder of Dhofar province. Salalah town and the airfield's defences were fortified and protected from any further insurgent encroachment. More importantly, a military defeat was avoided, an outcome considered eminently possible by many UK officers and officials in late 1969 and early 1970 in that the war could have actually been lost by 1971.[34] This success in holding the line and avoidance of defeat was the result of a switch in military strategy and the SAF withdrawal to the Salalah plain instigated by the British CSAFs. The pre-coup period therefore resulted in both strategic military failure and later, more modest relative success. Although an early military win was not achieved, the withdrawal to the relative security of the Salalah plain was necessary and therefore the requirement to avoid defeat and hold Dhofar province was achieved. This was, however, the necessary first stage towards the eventual victory and was achieved primarily because of the flexible military strategy developed and imposed by the CSAFs, and especially the heavily disadvantaged and effectively 'hamstrung' Brig. Purdon. Brig. Graham then consolidated his forces on the Salalah plain and, following the July 1970 coup, was in a position to expand and prepare for returning to the offensive.

Stabilize, Expand, and Defeat

Once the threat of being overrun by the insurgents had passed, British-devised military strategy was likewise the most important factor for the post-coup reversal of fortunes for the SAF. This was the result of the key input of the recently arrived CSAF, Brig. John Graham. The control of military strategy and its implementation in the post-coup period, allied to the SAF funding increases agreed to by the new Sultan, were to help reverse the then vulnerable strategic situation faced in mid-1970. The military strategy devised was to stabilize the campaign, expand SAF capability, and finally to go on the offensive. This was achieved whilst managing the key issue of the border situation with the neighbouring PDRY and preventing it from becoming a flashpoint factor in the conflict, both for Oman and the British position in the region.

MILITARY STRATEGY

In turn, this enabled the fight to be taken to the insurgents and their defeat to eventually be realized. In Benest's words:

> In conclusion, the insurgency was in the process of being lost up until 1970, was 'turned' by Graham and then won by Creasey/Fletcher and after them, Ken Perkins ... John Graham set the scene for what remains the most successful counterinsurgency in modern history.[35]

To convert withdrawal and a purely defensive posture into a win required a significant expansion of SAF capability. As a result of the coup and Sultan Qaboos's accession, the situation of his father's parsimony and unwillingness to spend the necessary funds on the SAF to enable them to challenge the growing dominance of the PFLOAG was reversed. The situation is summed up by Brig. Graham, who stated: 'One of Qaboos' first actions was to approve the recommendations which Hugh Oldman and I put to him for the substantial expansion of his Armed Forces.'[36] The priority for Graham was an expansion of the combat forces and therefore SAF fighting ability. To this end, and with Sultan Qaboos's full backing, Graham's plan for the formation of several new units was authorized and implemented. The pre-coup (but not actioned) approval by Sultan Said to raise a fourth infantry battalion to be called the Jebel Regiment (JR) was re-confirmed, the purchase of ships for the small Omani navy was approved, as was the enlargement of the number of air force squadrons.[37] The SOAF expansion was necessary to operationalize the long-insisted requirement for force helicopters and further transport aircraft (including De Havilland DHC-4 Caribous) which were finally delivered in September 1970. In addition to these much-needed developments, an armoured car squadron was also raised to bolster SAF capability.[38] From a pre-coup total SAF manpower count of only 3,000, with the raising of new units such as the renamed Dhofar Force (to Dhofar Gendarmerie; and newly under SAF command), and the Baluch Guard (which was later renamed the Frontier Force), in less than two years under Brig. Graham's tenure the SAF was increased to over 10,000 personnel with increased numbers of British LSP and contract officers (and NCOs) for command-related appointments.[39] The military strategy was designed to prepare the force for offensive actions, and therefore resulted in (over) a tripling of its size, with the attendant increase in potential and actual military capability.

In terms of SAF capability, it was not just Omani forces which contributed. Post-coup direct UK military assistance was provided as brokered via Brig. Graham and Col. Oldman, which significantly raised both the SAF's defensive and offensive capability. Although this was mooted pre-coup, it was either blocked by Sultan Said, as in the case of the SAS, or rejected by the British government. The expansion of Omani COIN forces was further boosted by Graham's request, and the UK government's agreement, to deploy limited personnel from regular British military units to assist in Dhofar. By early 1971, a both covert and substantial SF contingent was also in situ in Oman, through the incremental arrival of elements of the SAS Regiment (beginning in August 1970). This was key to the future COIN campaign success through their training and leadership role with the Firqa, 'hearts and minds' activities such as public medical provision, and latterly direct combat support. UK assistance also included Royal Corps of Transport (RCT) personnel, RAF Regiment mortar detachments, RA 'Cracker Battery', RE, and FSTs from the RAF and British Army.[40] These units carried out key support tasks such as the defence of Salalah airfield, Hornbeam Line development, and 'hearts and minds'-related construction tasks (including road-building and well-digging) and developing port facilities in the province, as well as combat support.

Eventually there were some 1,000 UK military personnel serving in Oman, with the majority deployed in Dhofar, which contributed greatly to the military campaign turnaround and eventual insurgent defeat.[41] Ultimately, this expansion of SAF size and capability was made possible by Brig. Graham's overall strategic planning and resultant negotiation with UK MOD and government officials who, post-coup, under the new Conservative Heath government, were more amenable than the previous administration to providing direct military assistance to the Sultanate.[42]

With a swift build-up of SAF manpower and equipment and direct British military assistance, which included the arrival of the SAS and the formation of the first Firqa units, by late 1971 the time had come to enact the next stage of Brig. Graham's military strategy. This entailed breaking out from the defensive line-holding posture and launching offensive operations against the insurgents across the Dhofar theatre. This was of key importance, as this element of the CSAF's military strategy was the first tangible step towards

MILITARY STRATEGY

the eventual 1975 win. The main thrust of the 1971 offensive strategy was to establish the SAF's first permanent base on the Jebel. This would challenge the physical dominance of the PFLOAG off the Salalah plain and demonstrate to the Jebalis that the government forces, and therefore central government, were strong enough to protect them and offer a viable alternative to the insurgents. Such an action would show that the SAF were taking the fight to the insurgents instead of retreating and hiding behind the Salalah plain fortifications. Although not as successful and decisive as hoped for at the operational level, with Graham reflecting that '[w]e have not however made the progress I had hoped for', the 1971 Operation JAGUAR and LEOPARD offensives were important in terms of theatre strategy and therefore progress towards achieving the insurgent defeat.[43]

The October 1971 offensives were the starting point on a long road to victory. They were important as positive actions that proved to the insurgents, Jebali population, the wider Omani populace, and importantly itself as an organization that the SAF could fight effectively on the offensive as opposed to undertaking defensive-only duties. It was the first stage of the new theatre-wide military strategy and allowed the initial theoretical aspects of the 'hearts and minds' approach to be turned into reality, as had been done successfully in previous post-war British COIN interventions. Following the autumn 1971 offensives, the 'strategically compelling' Operation SIMBA was launched to gain a foothold on the Jebel near the PDRY border at Sarfait in April 1972.[44] Through a bold helicopter-borne assault to secure the landing zone, the main features of the target area named 'Yardarm' and 'Mainbrace' were subsequently secured. Although a challenge to keep resupplied and bearing the brunt of concerted enemy mortars, artillery, and small arms fire, it was a masterstroke of strategic planning. In a single bold move, the SAF had moved its forward position deep behind enemy lines and both symbolically and practically demonstrated to all concerned a clear statement of intent, capability, and the will to take the fight to the insurgents and ultimately defeat them. The October 1971 offensives resulted in the first permanent SAF position on the Jebel in the Dhofar conflict and succeeded in changing the strategic balance of the war, despite drawbacks encountered such as problems involving the discipline of the new Firqa units. This position was named 'White City' and was an important step in the war and the first significant achievement towards a COIN

THE DHOFAR WAR

force win. Operation SIMBA showed SAF intent and capability and proved that government forces were very much on the offensive.

One of the key strategic-level UK aims was to contain the hostilities and avoid them becoming an overt inter-state war with the PDRY. A full-scale international war plus a domestic insurgency was neither desirable nor manageable and was a key concern for the CSAF and other senior British SAF staff officers, but especially for the for the UK Foreign Office and wider government.[45] The CSAF's military strategy had to maintain an approach to pressure the insurgents, and later regular PDRY forces, via cross-border raids by SAS-trained Mahra tribesmen, to reduce insurgent supply line capability from their PDRY-located Hauf base. It also had to deter or distract aggression by PDRY forces towards the SAF. Brig. Graham also had a responsibility towards regular UK forces such as those stationed at RAF Salalah. Thus, the balance had to be struck between achieving military aims, helping the Sultan avoid losing public 'face', and placating the key UK government concerns over the likely domestic political fallout which would result from potential British LSP casualties.

Ultimately, through British actions, the key military strategy objectives were achieved whilst avoiding a potential inter-state war with the PDRY. Britain's counsel (or compromise) in the guise of advisors such as the CSAF and regional or in-country British diplomats (including Amb. Hawley) prevailed over an incensed Sultan Qaboos on the extent of cross-border military actions. These included the 1972 SOAF attacks on Hauf and those of the Mahra tribesmen, both of which infringed sovereign PDRY territory.[46] The Operation AQOOBA Hauf raids were eventually of limited—yet effective—scale and were blended with appropriate diplomatic activities, with the scope of Mahra activity also being curtailed.[47] Through its influence, Britain thus balanced the delicate situation of needing to achieve its overall strategic war objectives alongside more subtle diplomatic necessities and a full-scale inter-state war was avoided. The UK had to ensure the war was conducted in a diplomatically appropriate manner and avoid unacceptable consequences to its regional and global interests. This was an outcome not always so successfully achieved in previous British COIN actions, most recently experienced in Aden up until 1967.

Whilst the new COIN campaign was the primary method for achieving its required outcomes, the overall theatre strategic approach, devised by Brig. John Graham and continued by Maj. Gen. Tim Creasey, was one of

MILITARY STRATEGY

'block and clear'. This was not a new strategy in the history of warfare (with effective use for instance by French forces in Algeria), but one newly implemented in Dhofar, and one that contributed decisively towards victory.[48] This strategy saw Dhofar, and especially the Jebel, divided up by fortified lines. This served to interdict enemy supply routes and disrupt the activities of the various insurgent units operating in the different province sectors. Once achieved, the SAF would switch to offensive operations and clear areas of insurgents, initially primarily in the east, and then progressively farther to the west. With the establishment of the original Leopard Line in the western Dhofar sector in 1971 and its development into the enlarged, extended, and considerably more effective Hornbeam Line, the overall 'block and clear' military strategy was instituted. The precursor to building the line itself, Operation HORNBEAM was begun in September 1972 under the auspices of the energetic newly arrived Dhofar Brigade Commander, Brig. Jack Fletcher, and by November he had Iranian SF troops patrolling the newly under-construction and mined barbed wire blocking feature initially consisting of linked picquet positions.[49] Although a drain on scarce SAF manpower, the Hornbeam Line, which was largely completed and operational in 1974, had a significant impact on the ability of the insurgents to resupply their eastern-based units from the major western supply hubs. Tangible success was evident from late 1972, when the still under-construction Hornbeam Line was developed enough under Brig. Fletcher's watch to be able to successfully disrupt Adoo actions. It achieved this by denying passage and logistical support across the Jebel from the PDRY-located Hauf base and Sherishitti Caves complex in western Dhofar to fellow insurgent units in the east and enabling the effective addition of a SOAF free-fire zone to be created west of the line.[50]

The Hornbeam Line was followed by further blocking lines during the war designed to pressure the insurgent supply lines. This was an approach reinforced under Graham's successor CSAFs with the Hammer and Damavand Lines in 1974. The Hammer Line was a series of linked 'patrol bases' established by Dhofar Commander, Brig. John Akehurst, as part of post-monsoon operations in the central and western sectors in between the Hornbeam Line itself and the vital Midway Road.[51] The arguably even more important Damavand Line was constructed wholly by Artesh forces and constructed entirely with Iranian-supplied materials. It was also completed a year faster than the Hornbeam

THE DHOFAR WAR

Figure 4.1: Cross-section of barbed-wire construction of the Hornbeam Line (soldiers of the SAF's Northern Frontier Regiment can be observed providing guard duties in the foreground). © Sid Pass 1974

Line and to a higher general standard.[52] Despite the oft-raised verdict of the poor training, and deficient tactical and operational performance of the Iranian forces in Dhofar, the Damavand Line was, however, testament to their importance and contribution to the CSAF's overall military strategy.[53] The original Brig. Graham-instigated block and clear approach for the Dhofar campaign was an eventual war-winning strategy. Graham had observed the efficacy of the French blocking lines in the Algerian War of Independence and COIN campaign whilst working in a NATO headquarters in France in the early 1960s and translated this concept into one suitable for the Dhofar theatre.[54] Whilst far from perfect, these elements of overall military strategy were both embraced and continued by Maj. Gen. Creasey as CSAF and his Dhofar Commander, Brig. Jack Fletcher, and eventually yielded the required results. After the Darra Ridge and Sherishitti Caves clearance by SAF forces in December 1975 and the dispersion of remaining insurgent forces, this British-conceived and implemented strategic approach achieved its ultimate aim of defeating the insurgents and was wholly vindicated.

MILITARY STRATEGY

Attempting the direct defeat of the enemy in Dhofar was not viable until 1973, some eight years after the start of the war. The realistic theatre strategic approach to achieve this objective was only possible after the British-inspired 'bloody nose' and comprehensive defeat of the insurgents at the Battle of Mirbat in July 1972, and the subsequent addition of Iranian forces in 1973.[55] Only at this juncture did the SAF and allied COIN forces have both the manpower and operational momentum to enter the 'defeat of the enemy' phase to fulfil Brig. Graham's ultimate goal.

Whilst the British-designed, and implemented, and largely covert SAS-led COIN intervention from 1970 was key to the incremental turning of the momentum of the conflict towards Omani forces, the final defeat of the insurgents was achieved via the use of CSAF-designed and implemented both large-scale and conventional military actions.[56] Complementary large-scale conventional manoeuvres had also occurred as part of the overall military strategy of previous British COIN undertakings in Malaya and in Kenya, for example, so had clear precedent. Amalgamating conventional and more 'hearts and minds'-oriented actions was another aspect of the traditionally flexible British COIN approach, and subsequently of the overall Dhofar military strategy. The large-scale push by Iranian forces southwards towards Rakhyut in December 1974, as ordered by Maj. Gen Creasey, was the initial element of the final act of defeating the insurgents. Utilizing a whole brigade, the Iranians, despite suffering ten men killed and numerous additional casualties in the initial thrust, eventually captured the town in early January 1975.[57] The simultaneous SAF push on the Sherishitti Caves, approximately 5 kilometres farther west, was also a conventional operation involving hundreds of soldiers as well as armour and supporting artillery. Due to stiff resistance, the Sherishitti operation was, however, a failure and the SAF suffered over thirty killed and wounded.[58] Despite this, these larger manoeuvres had the effect of wearing down the insurgents as an effective fighting force and causing substantial Adoo casualties. As a result, by early January 1975 Rakhyut was in Omani government forces' hands for the first time since 1969 and was visited soon after by the Wali of Dhofar in recognition of the achievement.[59] The stage was, therefore, set for the final act of the CSAF's military strategy.

The closing Dhofar War actions came in the form of the final assault on the Sherishitti Caves complex and the clearing of the Darra Ridge in late

1975 under the final wartime CSAF, Maj-Gen. Ken Perkins. This was the culminating act of the military strategy developed to defeat the insurgents in western Dhofar. Diversionary attacks took place in October 1975 by the Iranians, primarily from Rakhyut towards Sherishitti. SAF units based at Sarfait also struck out from their base area in a diversionary move, but in a last-minute change of plans advanced the same garrison further south than originally planned towards the coastal town of Dhalqut, cutting the insurgents' main supply line from Hauf en route and considerably weakening them.[60] By the last week of November, the Sherishitti Caves locality, the site of the abortive and fiercely contested action in January of the same year, was captured with virtually no resistance. After Dhalqut was formally liberated on 2 January, he final 'mopping-up' stage was undertaken, including on the Darra Ridge, in a much less intense atmosphere against limited opposition.[61]

The CSAF and his British staff officers devised the overall Dhofar War military strategy, and the enemy defeat phase was implemented only when possible after the preliminary elements of the overall theatre military were achieved. The final neutralization of insurgent capability was achieved with a switch to largely conventional military operations over the earlier post-coup emphasis on traditional British 'hearts and minds'-related COIN methods. This war-winning realignment of strategic military priorities and its implementation was almost solely the result of British knowhow and flexible, devolved leadership.

One of the most important strategic elements of winning the Dhofar War was the implementation of a new theatre-wide COIN approach post-coup, along traditional British lines. Brig. Graham realized the implementation was required of a more traditional British-style COIN approach for the Dhofar War, with 'hearts and minds' activities prioritized to help win over the population, allied to the use of indigenous forces in intelligence-gathering and combat roles. The subsequent new COIN approach, vital to turning losing into winning ways for the SAF and the Omani regime, was also designed and implemented by British officers, highlighting the key UK role in the overall insurgent defeat.

Even though ably led by British officers, because of Sultan Said's extreme frugality and the resultant impact on SAF capability, overall, the COIN approach adopted was failing up until 1970 as the PFLOAG was able to grow its logistical, numerical, and training capacity to support ever larger-scale

MILITARY STRATEGY

insurgency operations. Through the inability of the SAF to maintain and hold a permanent presence on the Jebel, it had effectively lost the moral and practical right to any support from the Jebali population who, for the most part, had no realistic choice, either through persuasion or oppression, to support the insurgents who dominated the mountain areas. There was a growing sense of unease among British officers serving in Oman, as well as in Middle Eastern Command based in Bahrain (to 1971) and key officials in the Foreign Office, that the war was not going well, and the approach insisted upon by Sultan Said needed to change. To assist, the MOD sent Lt. Col. John Watts, CO of 22 SAS and Jebel Akhdar campaign veteran, to Dhofar in early 1970 to undertake a situational study. He was ordered to report back on what could be done to improve the current approach, and to clarify the potential British SF role.[62] This was a significant move by the UK government and a clear sign of more interest in and commitment to the war effort.

The result of the study was Watts's 'Five-Point Plan', which ultimately developed into Operation STORM. The plan highlighted the need for the implementation of a classical British-style COIN campaign incorporating key elements of previous successful COIN undertakings such as in Malaya, Kenya, and the earlier stages of the Borneo campaign, including a substantial 'hearts and minds' component.[63] The Watts Plan included several important recommendations on how to improve the COIN situation in Dhofar and these were incorporated into British bureaucratic decision-making to establish final mission parameters. Paramount amongst these roles was the deployment of SAS forces to Oman and Dhofar specifically to undertake several key roles. Apart from important but relatively small-scale training roles (such as the raising and training of a new bodyguard unit for Sultan Qaboos and a weapons training programme to improve the skills of SAF infantry for Dhofar combat duties), one of the SAS's main tasks was in the field of intelligence and developing an intelligence-gathering capability in Salalah, providing training for the SAF in this field, and developing an accurate PFLOAG order of battle (ORBAT) to ascertain the enemy's dispositions, strengths, and locations as a basis for planning future SAF COIN-related actions.[64] The key recommendations of the Watts Plan were: firstly, the requirement to develop and implement an effective intelligence system; secondly, to encourage defections from the insurgent ranks; thirdly, to implement a veterinary assistance and water-provision programme; fourthly, to provide medical assistance to the Dhofari population; and, fifthly, to instigate a psyops or propaganda programme in the province.[65] All these elements can be viewed as constituent parts of a classic 'hearts and minds' approach to improve the perception of the Sultan's government and the SAF and to eventually win over the loyalty or support of the Jebali population. The idea was that if this could be achieved, it would enable insurgent support denial, and both deplete their fighting ranks and operational capability to facilitate their defeat. Despite further plan refinements made after the post-coup visit to Oman of the overall SAS Director, Brig. Fergie Semple, the essence of the original plan devised by Watts was not substantially altered during the remainder of the war.[66] In essence, the plan would enable the population to be won over, thereby contributing, by design, to Brig. Graham's overall military strategy of initially holding the military line, and then enabling the SAF to go on the offensive and eventually neutralize the insurgent threat. This would be subsequently achieved by bisecting the Jebel, utilizing fortified blocking lines, and use of the unique attributes of the Firqa to both sap Adoo morale, and provide intelligence on the enemy organization, capabilities, and dispersions to promote their overall collapse.

The covert SAS deployment was a key element of the CSAF's strategic military approach, and likewise the UK government's wider aim to discreetly revitalize the war effort. Prevented from operating in Oman by Sultan Said as he refused to accept their help, once Qaboos took the reins of power, the British were invited to provide further assistance and the SAS were officially despatched to operate in the Sultanate for the first time since the Jebel Akhdar campaign a decade earlier.[67] Alongside the increase in funding and expansion of the SAF, Watts's 'Five-Point Plan' became the blueprint for incrementally bringing the Jebali population over to the government's side and strongly resembled aspects of previous UK COIN actions such as the implementation of the 'New Villages' resettlement scheme during the Malayan Emergency.[68] The plan espoused a developmental 'sticks and carrots' approach and something familiar to the significant number of the senior officers in Oman who had served in Malaya including Watts himself and his successor, Lt. Col. Peter de la Billière.[69] This was an effective wartime approach that had hitherto been lacking.

Part of the British-devised and implemented 'hearts and minds' approach which eventually brought victory was the use of strategic messaging in order to undermine the insurgents. This was achieved by driving a psychological 'wedge' between the Marxist-indoctrinated commissars, who were by 1970 the key driving force within the PFLOAG, and nationalists and the natural affinity of the Dhofaris with the religion of Islam by spreading the key message or slogan that 'Islam is Our Way, Freedom is Our Aim'.[70] Numerous delivery methods were employed by the detached SAS-run psyops team. These included UK-produced pamphlets dropped from SAF aircraft and radio broadcasts from the newly established Salalah-based Radio Dhofar (allied to small transistor radios distributed on the Jebel), as managed by an SAS NCO psyops specialist.[71] All such methods were part of the strategic messaging approach launched to bring the Omani government's version of events and opinion to the Jebel. This was later enhanced by the employment of a specialist public relations firm by the Omani Embassy in London to counter Adoo propaganda in UK media and governmental circles.[72] Such efforts were also able to counter the stridently anti-Omani Sultan Radio Aden, which was then the sole radio service available, and which set the skewed strategic war narrative. Such messaging operations helped weaken Adoo morale and led to a significant increase in SEP numbers. The initial trickle of defectors to the government side later became a veritable flood through reinforcing the population's disillusionment and growing alienation from the increasingly militant and abusive Marxist-controlled insurgents. Only one SEP was recorded in September 1970, but by March 1971 this had risen to over 100, including, somewhat ironically, the ousted former leader of the DLF, Musallam bin Nufl.[73] Ultimately, such activities were deemed 'very effective', with 'Excellent work also being done in the ... psyops spheres ... [the] SAS's contribution in general has been vital and invaluable.'[74]

As part of the switch to the new Watts-designed COIN approach in Dhofar, and alongside the targeted information campaign, was the key element of the development of the SAS-raised Firqa units. The establishment of such units reflected a historically tried and tested British COIN approach of raising, training, and deploying unconventional, special, or paramilitary indigenous units using local tribes or SEPs. One of the key examples of this was the formation of the 'pseud' or 'counter gangs' incorporating former 'terrorists' utilized by the British military for deep forest penetration patrols in Kenya during the Mau Mau COIN campaign.[75] In a development inspired by the

To all people on the jebel.

Now is your time to claim your freedom. Throw off the yoke of the communist oppressors.

We, who are your brothers in freedom and in Islam, we who are from the jebel, we understand your hardships, for the communists destroyed our flocks and murdered our families.

Now we have returned!
We return in strength to take our revenge. Our brothers from all the tribes upon the jebel, now is your chance for revenge. Join us in the Holy fight against the ungodly communists.

Come to us in friendship, carry your rifle openly in your hand, join us in the fight as a fellow warrior of Islam to defeat communism.

Figure 4.2: British-produced SAF propaganda leaflet. © The National Archives

then Capt. Frank Kitson when seconded to the Kenyan Police Intelligence department, small units were formed where British officers and troops led operations in disguise as insurgents alongside loyal Kikuyu or SEPs to seek and destroy enemy units.[76] The approach was so successful that it was also used by British forces as part of anti-insurgent actions in Cyprus via undercover 'Q' unit detachments and the use of disguised SAS troops in 'Keeni-Meeni' operations during the Aden COIN campaign.[77]

The Firqa were also utilized for their knowledge of the Dhofari terrain and tracking skills. This also had UK COIN precedence, with indigenous tracking

MILITARY STRATEGY

units being utilized in both Malaya and Borneo; often working alongside and assisting British SF to seek out or provide reconnaissance on, or engage enemy forces.[78] Dyak tribesmen from Borneo were even brought into Malaya during the Emergency from as early as 1948 for such purposes and their tracking skills were invaluable in locating insurgent trails and camps.[79] Vital for intelligence-gathering, in Borneo, British SF personnel lived in jungle areas alongside tribal members of the Ibans, Dyak, Murut, and Kalabit peoples, who helped to provide information that the British forces could not generate themselves, and: 'As in Malaya, we [the SAS] found that the natives themselves were [by] far the best source of intelligence … [and] we depended on them to be our eyes and ears.'[80]

In Dhofar, the raising and subsequent training and deployment of the Firqa units by, and with, UK SF personnel was a classic technique which reaped significant dividends.[81] Such a task was not straightforward, as the Firqa personnel displayed a historically 'hot-headed' persona as also evident with Dhofaris recruited as soldiers in the TOS in the 1950s and 1960s.[82] The SAS, however, with their experience in employing indigenous irregular forces in previous British COIN campaigns, were able to mould the irregular Firqa into effective or even 'splendid' combatants.[83] They were effectively utilized as scouts, trackers, and guides for SAF operations, but also as home guard units to police 'sanitized' tribal areas post-military operations.[84] By mid-1974, there were approximately 1,000 members of the Firqa units (up to 1,200 by the war's end), which illustrates the scale of the undertaking and the perceived importance of their role.[85] The contribution of the Firqa units to overall victory was key, and, importantly, the concept, planning, and execution was British, as the SAF did not have the expertise to create, train, or, at the time, lead such units.[86] Graham stated that the Firqa proposal: 'was quickly and courageously supported in Whitehall and Hereford. The creation of the resultant Firqa Force was to be a campaign-winning factor of cardinal importance.'[87]

In addition to Firqa forces, from 1969 British Intelligence services also covertly supplied arms and money to, and later SF trained, engaged, and directed exiled Mahra tribesman for use as an unconventional militia force, with then Prime Minister Harold Wilson a 'fan of [such] covert action', sanctioning such activities over two premierships and up to 1975 in the case of the Mahra.[88] Exiled Mahra were encouraged, via exploiting their strident anti-Marxist sentiment, to foment their own brand of cross-border insurgency. They had the benefit for British authorities of being a relatively cost-effective and deniable proxy force conducting successful destabilizing operations in South PDRY territory. The Mahra operation began in earnest in 1972 and was known as Operation DHIB.[89]

The newly adopted COIN approach implemented as part of the CSAF's overall military strategy included a concerted civil development programme which was also launched to back up 'hearts and minds' activities. This offered Jebalis basic necessities such as water, medical assistance, housing, places of worship, and, importantly, a tangible governmental and military presence. These elements were implemented to provide a sense of security and provision of material needs which the insurgents could not match to gain their support for the Omani status quo. Such activities worked alongside the strategic military requirement of the SAF returning to the Jebel via offensive actions and holding permanent base areas. With the first such action at White City in the Eastern Sector in 1971, this integrated civil-military approach was begun.

Britain's pre-coup assistance in the civil development field through Hugh Boustead as a seconded development advisor achieved only modest success due in part to Sultan Said's efforts to slow down or even block the programme.[90] Large-scale tangible results were only discernible once Sultan Qaboos came to power. On the advice of the British authorities, extra financial resources were prioritized towards civil development as well as towards military necessities, supported by an increase in the national budget (from 68.5 million Rials in 1973 to 325 million Rials in 1975), largely resulting from increased oil income.[91] 'Hearts and minds' campaign-implemented CATs administered such plans and, by 1973, such successful yet ad hoc activities were cemented through British support and advice to Qaboos to enable a standalone CAD to be established in January 1975 to further institutionalize such efforts.[92] The British-instigated civil aid programme created no fewer than fifty new wells, forty-seven government support centres, and thirty-eight schools during the war in Dhofar alone, alongside agricultural and road-building initiatives; the latter of which resulted in some 155 miles of 'motorable' tarmac road build on the Jebel by 1975, where previously there had been none.[93] A 'Flying Doctor' service was also established, operated by and under the control of the CAD, to access areas not easily serviced by medical facilities set up in the

MILITARY STRATEGY

larger government centres, and serviced some thirty-five rural centres within Dhofar province.[94] The civil aid programme via the CATs, the SAS, the senior British SAF leadership, and latterly by the CAD, was to help ensure the survival of the ruling status quo, the support of the people, and their subsequent disengagement from the insurgent cause. This was primarily due to many of the underlying grievances against the regime, which stimulated the growth and development of the insurgency, being finally addressed.

In addition, a tried and tested UK COIN-style insurgent amnesty programme also commenced. This overturned a long-held policy against offering any leniency towards the insurgents by Sultan Said which, as utilized in previous post-war UK COIN campaigns, resulted in bringing increasing numbers of Adoo combatants over to the government side.[95] Alongside the Firqa units, there were less vital, but nonetheless important factors implemented such as agricultural or veterinary assistance to help Jebalis grow agricultural produce, as well as to maintain better cattle stock on which they depended for their livelihoods. The Watts Plan also provided a comprehensive COIN package and became the effective blueprint of the Dhofar COIN approach and one of the key reasons for the eventual insurgent defeat. The plan utilized tried and tested UK COIN methods and generally translated these successfully into specific Dhofar theatre circumstances. Chief amongst these was the build-up of intelligence capability as well as the raising of irregular indigenous COIN forces. These were utilized to weaken morale, absorb SEPs, and bring the fight to the insurgents by those familiar with their methods, psychology, and skills.

One of the key recommendations of the Watts Plan was to develop and implement an effective intelligence system. Experience had taught the British that an effective intelligence system was as important to a successful COIN enterprise as the lack of effective intelligence-gathering and utilization capability was a campaign-losing factor, as shown by the COIN losses in both Palestine and Aden.[96] The extent of intelligence utilization, especially early on in such undertakings, was a vital element in the winning or losing of all previous post-war British COIN campaigns. The eventual COIN success in Malaya was in part due to the effectiveness of the utility of intelligence material and the Special Branch (SB) infrastructure, whilst the failures in Cyprus and Aden were due in part to reductions in such capability due to widespread intimidation and targeted assassinations of SB officers (by EOKA 'Special Killer Groups' in Cyprus) conducted by insurgent forces and the intelligence establishment was resultingly 'severely tested'.[97] Sultan Said also hampered the vital asset of intelligence throughout his reign, including denying the SAF permission to bring specialist officers into Dhofar and, somewhat optimistically, stating that he would provide his CSAF with any intelligence that he needed.[98] Even though Col. Lewis subsequently covertly inserted Force Intelligence Officer (the then) Capt. Bob Brown into Dhofar, this attitude to intelligence was pervasive. The Sultan later insisted on Brown's sacking (as chief Dhofar Intelligence Officer), and Brig. Purdon describes how resultantly he was effectively blind after this point in terms of reliable intelligence at a vital stage in the war; stating as a result that; 'we never had worthwhile intelligence in Dhofar' for most of his tenure as CSAF.[99]

Despite their key contribution to his successful offensive against the Imamate rebels only a few years prior, Sultan Said also did not permit the SAS to operate inside Oman or Dhofar. The unit's specialized skill sets were not, therefore, formally utilized in Oman until after the 1970 coup, some six years after the insurgency's start, despite Brig. Purdon's extensive lobbying. As part of the new, post-coup theatre-wide COIN approach, the SAS provided a substantial intelligence capability uplift, including the enemy ORBAT utilizing the latest intelligence possibilities of the newly developed Firqa organization and the creation of a functional military intelligence cell.[100] This cell collected, collated, and disseminated all such sources as part of 'the classic intelligence cycle'.[101] For this purpose, members of the British Army's Intelligence Corps (IC) were deployed to Dhofar for the first time in 1970 alongside BATT, which included a specialist interrogation team euphemistically known as the BATT 'Radio Detachment'.[102]

These British-designed and implemented developments, in tandem with the intelligence-gathering and utilization capabilities of the SAS and IC personnel, significantly boosted the usability of the intelligence picture in the country and benefitted CSAFs in developing theatre strategy for the overall war execution. The situation which resulted was one of a virtuous cycle, where success reinforced success. Such developments also had the effect of enabling Operation JASON to be successfully undertaken in December 1972, wherein upwards of forty suspects and members of the PFLOAG's affiliate

MILITARY STRATEGY

organization, the National Democratic Front for the Liberation of the Occupied Arabian Gulf (NDFLOAG), were rounded up in northern Oman, including military officers and members of the Oman Gendarmerie.[103] In addition to the personnel arrested, large caches of weapons and ammunition were seized, which collectively were enough to start a small war. The inventory included over 150 rifles (largely SKS and AK47), over 60 mines, over 300 grenades, over 900 slabs of TNT explosive and approaching 50,000 rounds of ammunition.[104]

Operation JASON was a relatively close-run episode and could have been disastrous, not just for the Dhofar War, but Oman in general, had it not been discovered and thwarted. As such, Maj. Gen. Creasey stated: 'To date, Operation JASON has been successful. However I consider it would be dangerous for us to become complacent or over confident as a result of this success.'[105] The military ringleaders were subsequently executed in June 1973—including as many as six SAF officers—clearly demonstrating to all the price of treachery against the Sultan.[106] That the second front activities in northern Oman were detected, and the organization behind it disrupted if not largely dismantled, was a key output of the UK government's concerted efforts to improve the Sultanate's intelligence capability. These fortuitous outcomes further reinforced the key UK contributions to both Omani state capacity and eventual war success.

Unlike in other areas of influence, Britain's wartime role in terms of military strategy was virtually total and did not diminish during the conflict. The UK's development, and wider control of war strategy in all senses served as the master plan for countering the insurgent threat and ultimately for delivering the final victory in 1975. This, therefore, allowed the province to be secured 'for civil development' as per Brig. Akehurst's directive for Dhofar Brigade, and the UK's overarching and regional strategic aims to be realized.[107] The overall military strategy as developed and implemented by the British CSAFs and their subordinate officers did ultimately result in a victory for Britain, the Sultan, and his allies and was a rare occurrence against Marxist or Communist-backed insurrection, despite the drawbacks and failures encountered over ten years of fighting.[108] More impressive was the fact that this was achieved despite the limited resources available. As a result, it has been argued that the Dhofar War was Britain's most unambiguous counterinsurgency victory since Malaya and should be viewed favourably against both the British and general Cold War-era COIN record.[109] Defeat of the Dhofari insurgents was a timely boost to the West as well as the non-Communist or free world in general, with the Dhofar War being perhaps a more significant strategic-level victory than was even appreciated at the time.

5
Military Operations and Tactics

In small wars such as in Dhofar, there is significant crossover between the operational and tactical levels including a relatively small campaign, allied to relatively large battles at the 'fighting' level. As such, the dividing lines between the usually distinct levels of warfare are often blurred. For this reason, this chapter covers both levels to minimize overlap. Due largely to the expansion of non-UK assistance to Oman post-1973, in accordance with the 'sliding scale of influence' framework, it can be considered that British numerical influence on Dhofar War operations in terms of personnel reduced in the latter stages of the war. The campaign should still, however, be deemed very much British-controlled, primarily because operational direction was always in UK hands via the seconded CSAF and his staff. Whilst the relative physical contribution of Britain to operations therefore reduced throughout the war's duration, its influence or control *over* operations never wavered. At the same time, influence, and control at the tactical level via the quality of British junior officer leadership, and language capability of often COIN-experienced personnel, was virtually complete from the start of the war. This helped form cohesive, tactically effective units and ensured integration and cohesion in action at the 'fighting level'. The combined effect of influence and control at both the tactical and operational levels of warfare in the Dhofar COIN campaign can be considered as potentially the primary factor in achieving the insurgent defeat.

Operational-level actions in Dhofar were, as in other COIN campaigns, undertaken to directly support the strategic goals of the war. The required end-states were therefore similar, with operational success supporting the achievement of the required overall strategic military outcomes of containing the insurgent threat, avoiding defeat then stabilizing the campaign, expanding military capability then defeating the insurgency. Certain general aspects of British influence on operations endured throughout the Dhofar War, and cumulatively helped to achieve the overall (strategic) victory goal. Of these, the UK's main contribution to the Dhofar War win at the campaign level was the primacy of British officer control of operations. This was achieved primarily via the SAF chain of command and operational control over British and other military assets. Although officers of several countries such as India or Pakistan also served in the SAF, the majority were British, either seconded or employed via private contract.[1] The CSAF was always British throughout the war years, as was his Deputy. The CSAF was a seconded officer but served a foreign ruler, and although conducting the war for the Omani Sultan, he was still a serving member of the British armed forces who could receive orders from his superiors and therefore from their UK political masters. The DCSAF, Col. Maxwell, as a SAF contract officer was under no such direct control by London and worked solely for the Sultan. The majority of SAF staff officers and the CO, second-in-command, and all other subordinate officers in every SAF combat unit were also UK personnel. This situation was further reinforced with the establishment of the separate Dhofar Command in early 1971, with a British officer directly in charge of all military operations in the province.[2]

The main SAF staff headquarters was based at the Bait Al Falaj fort in Muscat and was almost exclusively British-manned from the start of the war. As an illustration of how dominant British influence was in the SAF, in his 1993 biography *Reminiscences of an Irish Soldier*, Brig. Corran Purdon vividly recalls arriving to take over from Col. Tony Lewis as CSAF in 1967. On arrival, he was welcomed at the airstrip at Bait Al Falaj fort by a group of serving or ex-British officers including the Omani Military Secretary, Brig. Pat Waterfield, his predecessor as CSAF, Col. Lewis, the DCSAF, Col. Colin Maxwell, and the SOAF Commander, Sqn. Ldr. Brian Entwistle. Purdon further highlights how the Assistant Military Secretary (Col. Louis Sanderson) and nearly all staff officers at Bait Al Falaj were either British seconded or contract officers.[3] This illustrates the control or influence of Britain and UK personnel exerted over the SAF in general, and specifically over the conduct of the Dhofar COIN campaign. As a result, it was an almost completely British-administered and managed war on the Omani government side.

MILITARY OPERATIONS AND TACTICS

Command of the SOAF was also in British hands, and virtually all pilots were UK citizens throughout the war. The modestly apportioned Sultan of Oman's Navy (SON) was also always commanded by a British naval officer. In addition, the commander of operational forces on the ground in Dhofar was also always a British officer and was initially the CO of the resident SAF battalion. This role then became a fixed staff officer position in January 1971, when Lt. Col. Turnhill of the DR handed over all command responsibilities to the new permanent senior officer, HQ Dhofar, Col. Mike Harvey.[4] Later, this position was upgraded to a one-star command and filled by Brig. Jack Fletcher from August 1972, and finally by Brig. John Akehurst in August 1974, illustrating the near-total dominance of Dhofar War operations by UK officers. Regimental officers in all combat units were also almost entirely British. The CO of each infantry regiment was usually an LSP British officer and the second-in-command a UK officer on private contract to balance the perception (and contractual status) of responsibility.[5] The British army-controlled chain of command all the way up to CSAF therefore remained intact. The SAF operational command structure was therefore effectively British to its core, from the CSAF to regimental officers. This had the effect of ensuring that from planning to execution, all stages of military operations were controlled either by serving British officers, or former UK military officers employed on contract.

Further reinforcing this dependence on British leadership, due to the fear of potentially being overthrown by his own native officers (as had occurred in other Middle Eastern countries as he considered them more 'coup-prone'), Sultan Said allowed only a small number of Omani Arab officers to be commissioned.[6] He refused to promote these officers past junior officer rank and prevented them from taking command postings.[7] SAF officer leadership was, therefore, effectively dependent on British seconded and contract officers under the rule of Sultan Said.[8]

Although relatively few in number, this dominance of British officers within SAF therefore gave significant indirect power to the UK authorities over the conduct of the war, as: 'While the UK never had more than a few hundred [officers and] troops in Oman during the Dhofar War, it had a disproportionate share of influence during the campaign because Britons occupied key decision-making positions within the Sultanate.'[9] McKeown adds that 'British officers

THE DHOFAR WAR

and NCOs led the military effort at every significant level throughout the war, and there is no doubt that this was decisive in maintaining the long struggle and [facilitating the] final victory.'[10] Resultantly, from an operational perspective, UK leadership and command were the key to both prosecuting, and later winning, the war in Dhofar. With key command positions largely in seconded officer hands, this also gave the British military and therefore UK government direct influence and even control of operations throughout the war.

With British operational command and control being one of the key factors for success in the Dhofar War, there were several key challenges identifiable that highlighted the quality of the leadership provided by the British SAF officers. In previous post-World War Two UK COIN campaigns, operations were largely undertaken in territory which was officially British-administered, usually by the UK Foreign or Colonial Offices. This was, however, not the case in Dhofar. In previous campaigns, this meant that all the arms of the state were in place and available to support the COIN forces. These included the local military forces, the police, and especially Special Branch, and the intelligence services. This integrated 'truimvirate of civil, military and police' was a situation exploited to the full and used so effectively in Malaya, for example, by Generals Briggs and Templer as 'Director of Operations' with virtual dictator powers.[11] Unlike in most other previous post-war British COIN campaigns, direct UK state support in all its guises in Dhofar, and especially up until 1970, was not available. This presented a situation where Britain effectively only managed the campaign and did not completely run or 'own' it as such as in previous undertakings. That operational success was achieved in Dhofar, and the eventual win secured is therefore noteworthy, and mainly due to the quality, experience, and impact of British military personnel.

Several previous British COIN campaigns also featured insurgent opponents who were not generally first-rate or professional-standard fighting units compared to those fielded by the UK, but in Dhofar the situation was, again, substantially different. With exceptions such as the variously described 'fanatical' or 'hard-core killers' of EOKA in Cyprus who carried out a ruthlessly effective campaign, British COIN forces were previously often pitted against poorly equipped and ill-disciplined insurgent adversaries.[12] Examples included the Mau Mau Land Freedom Army (LFA) fighters with almost nil military training, the semi-trained Communist and Indonesian-backed rebels and

MILITARY OPERATIONS AND TACTICS

insurgents in the Brunei/early Borneo campaign, '[mere] bandits' as the main insurgent force in Malaya, and the Egyptian-trained insurgents labelled as 'inept' and displaying levels of general incompetence' in Aden.[13] In terms of combat, such irregular and at best semi-trained insurgents were no real match for often multi-theatre COIN-experienced British units and personnel with thorough training and equipped with modern weapons and artillery and aircraft support. These insurgent groupings often countered such capability shortfalls by utilizing urban anonymity or difficult rural terrain as an effective form of protection. Defeating in battle was not necessarily the issue for full-time, professional, and well-trained UK COIN forces. It was more often a struggle against harsh terrain, lack of intelligence, and even finding the enemy to actually engage and potentially destroy them.[14] Although initially numerically few and poorly trained and equipped, the Dhofari insurgents were eventually to present a formidable enemy. This was especially the case after the withdrawal of British forces from Aden in 1967 and subsequent formation of the Marxist PDRY regime. Training of insurgent forces was consequently undertaken abroad as well as at Hauf, provided initially by Chinese and then Soviet benefactors. Allied to generous provision of modern weaponry, this soon translated into improved insurgent performance, which the SAF initially could not match. The Adoo developed into an effective small-scale, well-trained, and organized enemy. It operated utilizing the natural Dhofari soldiers' traits of both energy and enthusiasm to compound the difficulties for British-run SAF COIN forces.[15] Combined with intimate knowledge of the terrain and the seasonal climatic conditions, this made the Adoo a formidable adversary, and resulted in a situation where the insurgents were often considered the equal of the SAF in terms of ability.[16] Many British officers, including senior commanders, learned to respect the abilities of their enemy and often held them in high regard. Brig. Akehurst quotes Capt. Ian Gardner of SAF as stating: 'As men the *adoo* were truly remarkable. It would be an honour to command such a group.'[17] Akehurst adds that all things considered, the Adoo would usually prevail in any military contact with the SAF.[18] That British officers were able to counter such a situation through command and control and leadership, and to turn around a bleak operational picture in the late 1960s and early 1970s, makes the overall victory even more notable.

THE DHOFAR WAR

As highlighted previously, the Dhofar conflict was generally low-tech in its COIN conduct, and this was the case from the start of the war in 1965 and all throughout the reign of Sultan Said. This situation effectively endured right up until the final two years of the conflict when it was significantly reversed through large-scale Iranian troop deployments and military hardware and technology introduced to the campaign. This situation makes the British-planned and largely executed campaign successes particularly noteworthy. The SAF suffered in the early years of the conflict with obsolete military equipment, which contrasted with the modern weapons being supplied to the insurgents by their Communist sponsors. This included SAF soldiers being issued with World War Two British Lee Enfield bolt-action rifles, whilst the insurgents had access to mortars, automatic rifles, Spagin recoilless rifles, and Katyusha rockets.[19] Partly as a result of such disparity in weaponry capability in the early years of the war, the SAF was often out-gunned by the insurgents.[20] Towards the end of the war, the insurgents even had access to sophisticated surface-to-air missiles (SAM), with which they managed to down several COIN coalition aircraft.[21] Early in the war, the lack of basic equipment led the CSAF at that time, Col. Lewis, to state with regard to general funding that 'we didn't have Bucks Fizz for breakfast', and priority was given to essentials such as ammunition over less vital supplies.[22]

Working in an expansive area of operations, in the early years of the war, the SAF also had no helicopter casualty evacuation capability and extremely limited in-country military medical provision. In Dhofar, the primarily infantry operation was backed up by artillery when possible and slowly increasing levels of air support. Although the SOAF could field several small-scale transport aircraft, there were no helicopters or strike aircraft available to support operations in Dhofar until 1969. Ground attack BAC 167 Strikemaster aircraft then entered service and six Augusta Bell 205 helicopters were ordered and delivered in theatre a year later. These aircraft represented useful new capabilities but remained relatively outdated in terms of technology and were too few to make sufficient and timely inroads to a by then stagnating campaign. Thus, for the critical initial four years of the war, SAF forces operated at a significant disadvantage compared to previous UK COIN campaigns. With the arrival in Dhofar of the initial Iranian contingents in 1972–1973, numerous modern fast jets (including the McDonnell Douglas F-4 Phantom and Northrop F-5)

MILITARY OPERATIONS AND TACTICS

and heavy lift Chinook helicopters, for instance, were eventually made available to support the SAF for the first time. Prior to this and for the first eight years of the war, the luxury of such resources to support limited-scale infantry operations did not exist, which made for a challenging operational environment for the SAF's British commanders. These shortcomings were stark when compared to the even relatively limited availability of military technology or combat equipment available to support British forces in previous COIN campaigns. These include Malaya, Kenya, and Northern Ireland, for example, and ironically even previously in Oman during the Djebel War of the late 1950s. During the latter, troops were on hand and available from the Trucial States and (Muscat and) Oman as well as the UK, plus substantial RAF bomber and jet fighter support from bases such as RAF Khormaksar (Aden) and RAF Sharjah (Trucial States) to draw upon. Even British forces in Aden could, prior to withdrawal in 1967, call upon large-scale RAF forces and RN warship support as required.[23]

Although increasing levels of war-fighting technology were utilized in the Dhofar campaign after the 1970 coup, it remained a relatively low-tech affair. Although British units became available, while there was increased military expenditure with expansion and investment (boosted further from 1972 onwards via Iranian support), the COIN operation was in war-fighting technology terms effectively a poorly funded and equipped small-scale infantry-level fought campaign. The major counterweight to this was therefore primarily the experience and skill of the seconded or contract British officers leading such units coupled with the stoicism and determination of the Omani, and numerically larger contingent of Baluchi soldiers of the SAF. Similarly to earlier UK COIN operations elsewhere, the Dhofar War was for the most part a small-unit scale infantry operation where success or otherwise was in the hands of the skills and leadership of relatively junior British officers in the field.

Whilst British influence on operations, operational success, and the eventual victory in the Dhofar War was key, there were, however, other sources of significant influence. These include the Omani Sultans and the other foreign forces deployed towards the end of the campaign, including, notably, the Iranians. As highlighted previously, some modern historical narratives contend that victory in the war was majorly influenced, controlled, or even won directly by Sultan Qaboos. As part of an 'Oman-centric' viewpoint, this interpretation

103

promotes the view that the war success and ultimate win was down to the Sultan, whilst simultaneously downgrading the British contribution. Central to this view is that the Dhofar War victory was essentially due to Qaboos and his martial knowledge and talent as a military leader.[24] From an overall operational perspective, however, apart from during specific occurrences such as Operation AQOOBA, Sultan Qaboos did not personally have either a high, or indeed day-to-day campaign impact. Whilst Sultan Qaboos had an overall positive influence on the Dhofar War and contributed greatly from a non-operational perspective (for example repealing repressive laws and introducing policies such as the amnesty for insurgents), Sultan Said actually had a significantly negative impact on the conflict at the operational level. His influence was one of the main reasons for the poor operational situation of the Dhofar War from its beginning in 1965 up until 1970, the SAF retreat to the Salalah plain, and ensuing deteriorating stalemate situation. A misreading of the root cause of the insurgency and the Sultan's dogmatic refusal to accept British advice on issues such as amnesty for insurgents led to a situation where UK officials believed the Sultan, in Dhofar, 'may have written himself a prescription for ultimate defeat'.[25] Despite having a Dhofari wife, Sultan Said also displayed a dislike of his subjects from the province by dictating a stringent policy of repressive or 'collective punishment' measures including well-capping, burning dwellings, and destroying crops in food denial actions, which further alienated the Jebali population.[26] The Sultan refused to pardon SEPs against the strong advice of his British advisors, even when its central contribution to UK COIN success in Malaya had been explained personally in detail to him.[27] The Sultan was seemingly only interested in the implementation of harsh or oppressive measures against the insurgents with an attitude which, if different, 'could have brought the Dhofar trouble to an end there and then instead of ... [many] years later'.[28] Sultan Said also hampered operations by refusing to place the DF, his private Dhofar-based army, under SAF control (despite the SAF having never before operated in the province) and by refusing to commission many Omanis in the SAF with platoon commanders being staff sergeants only, which also placed more strain on the limited available British leadership resources.[29] The Sultan also regularly intervened in other operational-level military issues such as intelligence. This included initially refusing to let any British SAF intelligence officer (IO) into the province in

MILITARY OPERATIONS AND TACTICS

1964, and later insisting on the sacking of key Dhofar IO, Maj. Bob Brown. This act so hampered the conduct of contemporary operations that Brig Purdon stated: 'The lack of good intelligence was to be prevalent during my time and I often wonder if we could have seized an early victory had Bob remained; I believe we could have.'[30] Finally, Sultan Said was also overly controlling and often concerned with low-level campaign-related minutiae which distracted from operations. Wartime correspondence with a resident Dhofar SAF Battalion CO reveals a preoccupation by Sultan Said not even with operational-level issues, but on the movement of single weapons, for example, or small amounts of ammunition from the Salalah armoury, and for meddling in other junior-level decision-making, including the arrival dates in Oman of junior LSP officers and even the specific destination of building supplies distributed by resident SAF forces.[31]

It can therefore be seen that the Omani Sultans had largely either limited or even negative operational impact on the Dhofar campaign. Neither Sultan had direct operational command of combat forces and deferred on nearly all military matters to the LSP CSAF and his British staff officers, and this had the effect of reinforcing the latter's operational control.

From an operational perspective, it can be observed through the 'sliding scale of influence' framework that Britain's influence did reduce throughout the Dhofar War. During the first half of the war up to 1970, Britain was undoubtedly Oman's major military partner in prosecuting the conflict. UK forces, however, did not physically undertake a majority of the combat or operations in the Dhofar conflict. The SAF specifically fulfilled this role. Whilst Britain provided the leadership in terms of the key officers of SAF operational units, the organization's rank and file was almost exclusively Omani and (majority) Baluchi in composition, and it was the thousands of these men who carried out the fighting and to whom victory has sometimes been credited.[32] Unlike in terms of composition, the control of military operations was, however, always in the hands of British officers from the CSAF down through the SAF chain of command.

Even within the expanded and diversified nature of the Sultan's forces formed to fight the Dhofar War, Britain was never to have large forces involved in such operations. In the later stages of the war, several nationalities other than the UK were represented in the leadership and command structure of the Omani COIN forces and this situation of the influence of other nations was to accelerate, especially from 1973 onwards.[33] British direct military assistance was to be dwarfed from 1973 onwards by further outside or non-UK troop contributions. Jordan's King Hussein supplied a battalion of SF troops, combat engineers, intelligence officers, and later (in late 1975) some thirty Hawker Hunter jet aircraft as a gift to Oman.[34] The most significant military force addition to the COIN campaign came not from an Arab ally or the UK, but from the Shah's Iran.[35] The end of 1972 saw the arrival of the first Iranian SF troops in Oman. Iranian units were well supplied and essentially self-sufficient and at its peak the Artesh contingent in Oman exceeded 3,000 men, with over 15,000 serving in total through a system of regular unit rotation.[36] By 1974, this deployment included a full brigade supported by artillery, SF, fighter jets, and helicopters, which was known as the Imperial Iranian Battle Group (IIBG). Such increased military capability had a positive impact and undoubtedly contributed to the 1975 campaign win.

By 1975, campaign personnel numbers had expanded further to include upwards of 10,000 combined Omani and Baluchi soldiers of the SAF, and approximately 3,000 Iranian troops, well over 1,000 Firqa militiamen, upwards of 1,000 British regular service personnel, and some 800 Jordanians.[37] The British contingent was eventually therefore substantial, but the overall non-SAF forces on the side of the Omani government consisted mainly of the troops of other outside regional powers; principally from Iran. It is revealing that, at the time of victory in 1975, there were nearly four times the numbers of Iranian and Jordanian military personnel fighting on the Sultan's side than those of Britain, with many of the latter being solely employed to protect the RAF personnel required to serve at and operate the facilities at RAF Salalah and not even, therefore, combatant forces.[38] As such, Britain did not provide anywhere near the largest contingent of military personnel to the Sultan's ultimately victorious coalition.

Likewise, in terms of impact at the operational level, the intervention by Jordanian and especially Iranian forces was also of central importance. Not only were there more troops made available to fight or man the numerous and labour-intensive static positions, such as the Hornbeam Line, but there was also the welcome provision of ample heavy lift helicopter transportation. This was available on a large scale to the SAF for the first time so supplies

MILITARY OPERATIONS AND TACTICS

or troop units (including casualties) could be quickly moved around theatre in a way that would have been impossible, or at least taken much longer, in the early days of the campaign. The latter was undertaken via 'stretchers being man-handled down perpendicular slopes', or mule train, with eventual evacuation to medical facilities.[39] Such support also included Iranian naval assets and the provision of ship-borne supply and, importantly, naval gunfire support. Such large-scale tangible military support had hitherto been virtually unavailable to the SAF, especially so since the UK's withdrawal from Aden in 1967. In terms of quality of contribution to operations, Iranian forces are often criticized in traditional accounts of the war. Key criticisms include the 'Trigger-happy' nature of Iranian troops, below par fieldcraft, and often poor performance which resulted in large-scale self-inflicted casualties for their own units.[40] One particular example highlighted was the incompetence of an Iranian mortar team, which managed to injure three of their number by incorrectly loading their own mortar, or an Artesh officer who accidently shot and killed one of his own soldiers whilst cleaning his weapon.[41] Others include poor Iranian logistics and planning, limited intelligence capability, poor liaison and reporting (including failure to include required details in operational sitreps), a generally inflexible approach, poor command and staff procedures, lack of initiative and being 'fearful of doing anything without orders', and essentially needing hand-holding by British personnel to be effective.[42] One particular issue raised in a British military officer's memoir in terms of operating with them was the general outlook or attitude of the Iranian troops. A former British officer stated that they 'need not have been incompetent, but unlike the Omanis, you couldn't teach the Iranians anything; they knew it all. The sublime combination of arrogance and ignorance was a marvel to behold.'[43] Of more importance to the overall campaign than such generalized issues of quality, training, or mindset was the general stance or approach of the Iranian military leadership. The Chief Supreme Commander's Staff of the Imperial Iranian Armed Forces, Gen. Azhari, and his senior officers were initially strongly opposed to taking on any role in western Dhofar which would potentially involve large-scale operations and enemy contact for several military-related reasons, including that there were so few enemy that the men would become 'idle', lack of Arabic-speaking intelligence personnel, and concern that action in the west may cause antipathy towards the Sultan.[44] This was believed by most on the

THE DHOFAR WAR

British side to be more to do with 'cold feet probably stemming from the realization that the [military] problem is more than they can cope with', and was further illustrated by their manoeuvring in negotiations with the CSAF in terms of command arrangements (including offering to provide a battalion for the west under the SAF Brigade Commander) so Artesh commanders could blame others if required if they failed to achieve their objectives.[45] In short, it was stated of the Iranian commanders, 'They are frightened of failure.'[46]

Despite these drawbacks, the contribution of the Jordanian and especially the Iranian troops was significant as well as being important for the campaign and for facilitating the final COIN win. In addition, it has been stated that many earlier British accounts of the Dhofar War either 'downplay ... or even sometime[s] denigrate' the crucial Iranian contribution to the campaign.[47] The Jordanians and especially Iranians should be fully credited for their contribution to the Dhofar campaign and towards the overall win. In this regard, the CSAF who delivered the final victory for the Sultan, Maj-Gen. Ken Perkins, commented that 'Iranian support undoubtedly tipped the scales; without it the war would have dragged into a stalemate as [the] SAF alone had insufficient troops to achieve a clear decision.'[48]

Though important, the main Iranian contribution was in terms of numbers and equipment, especially helicopter lift capability, which the SAF lacked. Whilst their contribution was welcome, the Iranians played only a minor part in the campaign command and control structure. For the duration of their participation, they remained, despite being allocated a designated brigade operating area centred on the suggestion of a 'subordinate headquarters in their own area' as an 'organic formation' under their own command, under the overall operational command of the CSAF.[49] In addition, due to perceived quality issues, Iranian forces were utilized by the British SAF command on less technical tasks such as clearing or patrolling the Midway Road, changing the objective from Sherishitti to Rakhyut in December 1974, and building the Damavand Line in 1975, as opposed to complicated and large-scale combat-related manoeuvres.[50] The CSAF and SAF chain of command controlled the operational picture in Dhofar, the allocation of asset units, and ordered the thousands of men of the IIBG into action as and where required.[51] The Iranian military leadership were even sent draft operational plans for the proposed western offensive including their own role for their 'consideration',

MILITARY OPERATIONS AND TACTICS

and the Iranian Brigade command was required to provide detailed military operation phase plans to the CSAF for his vetting and approval before being undertaken.[52] Aside from this requirement to closely control Iranian actions to try to minimize the impact of their systemic drawbacks, the campaign was also laced with an undercurrent of both traditional Arab distrust of their Arabian Gulf neighbour, but also from the British commanders regarding Iranian intentions. Amongst such suspicions, '[Maj. Gen.] Tim Creasey has just begun to wonder whether there might not be some ulterior purpose in the Iranian tenacity over the Midway Road' and therefore potentially being able to 'effectively control land communications between Northern Oman and Dhofar', where memories of Iranian seizure of island territory in the Gulf as the British withdrew East of Suez were still fresh in people's minds.[53]

From an operational perspective, it can be observed that the British role was essentially one of management. Even at its height, the UK only had up to 1,000 men deployed in Dhofar, as compared to 10,000 SAF personnel and up to 4,000 Iranians and Jordanians.[54] Although British troops such as the SAS were key to many aspects of the Dhofar War, the actual combat element was not generally undertaken by UK troops. Rather, in terms of operational control and management, the British role in the Dhofar theatre was, however, decisive and was arguably even more important than the combat contribution of non-UK troops. While it is not disputed that a multi-national COIN coalition was a key contribution in sealing 'an international victory' in Dhofar, UK operational control and leadership was the most significant factor.[55]

In addition to the role played by British seconded and contract officers in operations via command and control, deployed and (primarily from 1970) regular units of the UK armed forces also played an important operational role. They helped both to stabilize the campaign and contributed towards the overall victory. After being deployed in secret to Oman in 1970 as part of British efforts to bolster the flagging Dhofar campaign, the SAS brought an extra dimension to COIN operations by supplying training and war-fighting capability in support of the SAF in a key UK contribution. Under the leadership of Lt. Col. John Watts, then Lt. Col. Peter de la Billière, the SAS provided several key operational-level benefits to the COIN campaign. Planned as early as February 1970 (and although initially devised as a limited six-month-only operation for smaller regimental sub-units 'for strictly limited periods', this approach developed into a full squadron deployment by 1971) larger two-squadron—or over half of total regimental strength—was deployed at times, with the unit also not departing Oman until 1976 and therefore a year after victory was declared.[56] Initially envisaged as a training and support role, one of the first taskings for the euphemistically named SAS British Army Training Team (BATT) was to train the new Sultan's bodyguard and to train SAF rifle companies in northern Oman prior to Dhofar deployments.[57] The BATT also had an important intelligence-gathering role to play and SAS teams, in addition to British army IC personnel, were despatched to Oman to improve the dearth of intelligence-gathering capability especially covering the Salalah area, but also to provide hitherto lacking interrogation and psyops expertise.[58] Strongly influenced by experience gained in previous COIN campaigns, another fundamental role of the SAS in Oman was to devise and implement a concerted 'hearts and minds' COIN package, which helped to turn the hitherto flagging COIN campaign around.[59] This included the introduction of medical assistance for civilians and the construction of wells and building of amenities such as schools through CATs in the government-controlled areas.[60]

The SAS assistance in this area also included veterinary services and help with implementing more effective agricultural practices with the introduction of demonstration farms to experiment with, and teach the best agricultural practices for the harsh Jebel environment.[61] Such 'hearts and minds' package-related assistance even went so far as sending soil samples to the UK for analysis to help improve crop yields, importing prime Hereford bulls to improve the Jebali bloodstock, and the large-scale movement of cattle from the Jebel to the Salalah market in Operation TAURUS.[62] The latter enabled the Jebalis to sell their livestock to the government to build much-needed trust and cooperation between them and the Sultan's authorities. Such 'hearts and minds' activities were not just ad hoc measures devised by individual SAS squadrons themselves, but part of an overall concerted plan devised by UK commanders.

A further key operational-level role of the SAS in Dhofar was the raising, training, and leading of the paramilitary Firqa units. It was not just in their formation and training where the SAS had the central role, in terms of operations they led them into battle too. This was beyond the remit initially envisioned by UK politicians but was vital to motivate the Firqa to operate in accordance with their training and as cohesive units. From the creation of

MILITARY OPERATIONS AND TACTICS

the first unit, that of the multi-tribal Firqat Saladin, by the summer of 1971 there were six Firqa units in existence, each formed of up to 100 indigenous fighters trained, organized, and led by SAS soldiers.[63] Despite initial issues with operational effectiveness and reliability, the SAS and the CSAF continued to place great faith in the larger strategic value of the programme, despite numerous teething problems with the initial units raised, and by the end of the war, the Firqa forces numbered well in excess of 1,000 men.[64] Keeping faith with the potential of the Firqa and leading as well as fighting alongside them in operations eventually bore the fruits of success. As Brig. Akehurst stated: 'I must reiterate how vitally important the Firqats were in the struggle. Their knowledge of the ground and their influence with the civilians were indispensable.'[65] The contribution of the Firqa to winning the Dhofar COIN campaign was key, and importantly the concept planning and execution was wholly British in nature, as the SAF did not at the time have the expertise to create, train, or effectively lead such irregular units.[66]

With the deployed SAS detachment doubled in size in 1971 to two squadrons and the addition of a psychological warfare detachment, the initially envisaged limited training and support role suffered mission 'creep', and became blurred with that of live combat operations, starting with Operation JAGUAR in October 1971 and even more clearly illustrated by the Battle of Mirbat in 1972.[67] Here, the small-scale deployed group of SAS soldiers and local resident Askars held off repeated attacks from a large Adoo force, inflicting dozens of enemy casualties, sapping morale, and facilitated the turning point in the campaign which helped to hasten the end of the war.[68] From the inability to win and subsequent withdrawal (to the Salalah plain) up until 1970, to underwhelming initial offensive operations from October 1971 onwards, the overall campaign was not proceeding well. With the bold SIMBA operation, followed by the retaliation against the PDRY over the Habrut incident in 1972, the overall outlook for the campaign subsequently improved. The Mirbat confrontation, however, provided the operational reversal required through insurgent battlefield defeat, which changed the whole Dhofar War trajectory.

Whilst there is much in the historical record highlighting the role of the SAS in the Dhofar campaign, it should be clearly emphasized that several other deployed regular British military units were represented and contributed significantly both to operations and to the overall victory. The Dhofar War win cannot be credited solely to the SAS. These units included the Royal Artillery (RA) which, although deployed primarily in a defensive capacity, was used to bolster the strategically important base of RAF Salalah. This was critical during the post-coup phase when consolidation, defence, and the avoidance of defeat on the Salalah plain were of paramount importance at the campaign level. The RA 'Cracker Battery' operated Green Archer ground radars, adding a new technological dimension to overall defensive operations with mortar-locating radar equipment, which enabled the launching point of projectiles to be determined and therefore pinpointed for SAF jets to accurately counterattack. The unit also included an RAF mortar detachment with experienced visual spotters who could effectively counter and reply to incoming projectiles using the data provided by the Green Archer equipment.[69] The RA personnel of the detached 'Cracker Battery' also provided additional fire controller capability for SAF artillery based in the vicinity, which helped to boost the capability of Omani government forces in general.[70]

A Royal Engineers (RE) detachment of approximately eighty-five men was deployed to Dhofar as part of Operational TENABLE, the first elements of which arrived in 1973.[71] The RE soldiers undertook many important tasks including civil development works and military construction projects. These included improving the 'Hedgehog' defensive positions around Salalah airfield and contributing to construction of the forward 'Diana' positions on the Jebel overlooking the Salalah plain, designed to deter missile attacks on the base. RE soldiers also created wire obstacles for various blocking lines (starting with the Hornbeam Line in December 1973), furnishing them with minefields, built airstrips and accommodation in base areas, as well as undertaking the training of newly raised SAF engineer units.[72]

The RE's civil development works supported the bold 'hearts and minds' initiative of the new post-coup COIN approach and included well-digging and building construction (including government offices) in new permanent SAF-backed settlements, such as White City, in support of the CATs. In addition, over an extended period, RE soldiers built much of the Hornbeam Line themselves. This constituted a construction project over 30 miles in length from the sea at Mughsayl over often extreme mountainous terrain. This construction involved building fencing over steep gradients but also laying mines either side of the barrier as well as the building of eight unit

MILITARY OPERATIONS AND TACTICS

observation positions.[73] The combined contribution of the RE detachment to operations, which did not depart Dhofar until the completion of Operation TENABLE in late 1977, was a boon for the Dhofar COIN campaign.[74] The civil development works undertaken by the RE, combined with the key enemy supply-blocking Hornbeam Line, contributed to the achievement of overall theatre military strategy and was, therefore, of a war-winning magnitude.

RAF (airfield and flight) and RAF Regiment personnel were also deployed to Dhofar. Although RAF Regiment personnel were deployed to protect Salalah airfield in 1969, this vital force protection role continued throughout this period, as the Salalah airfield was vulnerable to attack, especially up until 1972. RAF personnel also ran all aspects of the airfield from support services to day-to-day airport movements. This created a situation where all helicopter or fixed-wing flight movements not conducted from Muscat were launched from RAF Salalah and thus were under the control of RAF personnel. With the arrival of Strikemaster aircraft in 1969, extra transport aircraft in 1970 and later some thirty-one Hawker Hunter jet fighter aircraft to bolster the SOAF arsenal in 1975, this role was increasingly important.[75] A non-operational or poorly run RAF Salalah would have been disastrous for the COIN campaign, and RAF personnel provided this service up until the end of the war.

Members of the British Army's IC were also deployed in secret to Dhofar for the first time in 1970 alongside the SAS, which included the BATT 'Radio Detachment' interrogation team.[76] These specialist interrogators were used in standard intelligence-gathering roles such as the questioning of SEPs, but were notable particularly for their key role in gaining important leads from insurgent prisoners as a result of Operation JASON in December 1972, to help dismantle a potential existential twin front threat to the Omani status quo. The Adoo had arranged the smuggling of large quantities of weapons into northern Oman and had plans in place to launch attacks on military as well as soft commercial targets and to conduct Adeni National Liberation Front (NLF)-style assassinations of allied intelligence officers.[77] Over forty members of the PFLOAG's affiliate organization (NDFLOAG) were rounded up in northern Oman including SAF officers, officials of the OG, and even the driver of the OIS head, Brig. Dennison.[78] These prisoners were questioned by the British Army IC interrogation specialists and, as a result, 'As the SAF arrested other members of the Front, they all talked and told of others involved' and the plot was both unravelled and thwarted.[79] Despite Amb. Hawley considering Operation JASON a relatively lucky or 'close run' episode, the NDFLOAG was prevented from launching a second front in Oman, subsequently dismantled, and never posed a significant problem to the regime again, illustrating the important contribution of the UK IC personnel deployed to Oman in operational terms.[80]

A further UK personnel contribution came in the form of Field Surgical Teams (FST) that were deployed in rotation from the RAF and British Army (16th Parachute Brigade) to serve at RAF Salalah.[81] The FSTs performed a valuable service in support of operations by treating casualties and manning the newly built civilian hospital in Salalah, and as described by Brig. Graham: 'Thanks to these agencies [FST and improved SOAF helicopter capability] all but a tiny percentage of our wounded have survived.'[82] With the arrival of the FSTs there were professional trauma medical facilities available around the clock to support SAF operations. In the earlier stages of the war, operations were hampered by poor medical facilities and evacuation procedures. Previously the only medical facilities were at Bayt Al Falaj and serious cases of combat injury were often evacuated by air to British facilities in Bahrain up until the end of 1971, often having been taken off the Jebel over a period of many life-threatening hours potentially 'bleeding out' strapped to the back of a mule.[83] The other main benefit of the FSTs for the SAF was in terms of morale. As such, the 'knowledge of this [highly trained FST trauma surgeon capability] has had a markedly beneficial effect on the morale of everyone in the Government Forces'.[84]

The sum of British contribution to the Dhofar War in the operational domain was, therefore, greater than the constituent parts. Of many key inputs there were, however, several which stand out to illustrate the central UK operational role and contribution towards final war success.

Operation SIMBA was an audacious move orchestrated by the then CSAF, Brig. Graham, to reach behind enemy lines, take the fight to the insurgents, and reverse the 1970 SAF withdrawal to the Salalah plain. Launched in April 1972, the military operation involved landing a battalion group by helicopter to the exposed position of Sarfait, at the western frontier of Dhofar with the PDRY and approximately 5 km from the main insurgent base located at Hauf. The Sarfait operation has been described in some historical accounts as

MILITARY OPERATIONS AND TACTICS

effectively being merely an expensive folly which produced minimal results and put a whole SAF battalion at significant risk,partly because it was located well behind enemy lines, and could eventually only be resupplied with necessities including water by helicopter.[85] Scarce aviation assets were, therefore, put at risk as well as several hundred SAF personnel due to the constant threat of mortar and other weaponry trained on the position, which was liberally utilized. The position even had to be resupplied with the help of Iranian helicopters in February 1973 because of the strain on the SOAF's assets. Whilst this was the case, it was also a bold operational stroke against the insurgents and registered the offensive intent and capability of an expanded and more confident SAF. To successfully deposit several hundred troops well behind enemy lines and so close to the main insurgent centres of training support can be considered a significant psychological set-back for the Adoo. It also served to advertise this intent to the Jebali population and to increase the confidence of a revitalized SAF, which up until a few months prior to the mission was effectively trapped on the Salalah plain. The Sarfait operation was both tactically and operationally challenging, but from an overarching strategic perspective, it had clear benefits. It was important to show SAF resolve after the withdrawal to the Salalah plain in 1970 and to compensate for the underwhelming initial October 1971 SAF offensives. It accomplished this with an efficient helicopter-borne position assault, followed by a dogged long-term defence under near-constant insurgent bombardment, and being located behind enemy lines for much of the remainder of the war. As such, Operation SIMBA was an important British-instigated step towards the eventual Dhofar War victory.

Further to Operation SIMBA, the Battle of Mirbat was the key turning point in the Dhofar War. Although a tactical-level event, the battle represented the crossroads point where the advantage of the insurgents at the campaign level started to reverse in favour of Omani COIN forces and brought the prospect of victory into closer focus. This view diverges from the traditionally presented turning point narrative of the July 1970 coup being the primary factor in this regard and highlights the importance of the Mirbat action.[86] Unlike the limited immediate impact of the 1970 coup (including the relative failure of the 1971 offensives and scant subsequent progress towards a win), the undoubtedly heroic but at the same time partially luck-derived defeat of the insurgents at Mirbat in July 1972 was the true turning point in the campaign and not before, with significant insurgent casualties and a major cause of dissent within the organization.[87] The coup changed the long-term underlying parameters of the conflict in terms of leadership and overall war policy direction, but on a campaign or operational level, the impact of the single Mirbat event was fundamental. The insurgents were being progressively 'squeezed' by the increasingly successful strategy devised by Brig. John Graham of dividing the Jebel with reinforced lines to disrupt enemy communications, troop movements, and resupply. Due to both this and the successful military gamble of SIMBA and bold AQOOBA retaliation, in a change from their usual *modus operandi*, the insurgents resorted to conventional military tactics to try to strike a 'spectacular' face-saving blow against the SAF and the status quo and to regain the upper hand.[88] The attack was a disaster at both battle and campaign levels for the insurgents, and they were roundly defeated. The Adoo suffered up to forty casualties (between 26 and 38 attackers killed outright) out of approximately 200 attackers; whilst it is estimated as many as 100 insurgents perished in the action.[89] Instead of achieving its aims, the attack was a clear failure.[90]

During the attack, Mirbat was defended by some thirty local askaris, twenty-five DG soldiers, and the remainder of the Firqat Salahadin as well as the now well-publicized 'heroic' actions and 'superhuman courage' of the SAS detachment under Captain Mike Kealy.[91] Without taking anything away from the achievement of the SAS men, de la Billière does claim: 'To call Mirbat a close-run thing would be a masterpiece of understatement.'[92] From this perspective, the fortuitous presence of G Squadron SAS both in-country and in close proximity to Mirbat itself, as well as a break in adverse weather conditions, favoured COIN forces. A brief respite in the low monsoon cloud base and mists allowed the equally heroic SOAF low-level supporting attacks led by Sqn. Ldr. Bill Stoker, accounting for large numbers of the insurgent casualties, which led Brig. Graham to state that 'the jets, led by Bill Stoker had a field-day'.[93] The fighting prowess, bravery, and skill of the SAS men has been accused in the historical literature of being accentuated for ideological or political purposes, but this should not detract from the importance and impact of the action and the bravery of the men who took part.[94]

The win at Mirbat was largely achieved by British troops on deployment and UK airmen or soldiers on secondment or contract to the SAF; all under

MILITARY OPERATIONS AND TACTICS

Figure 5.1: Mirbat Fort, view from the Wali's Fort. © Stephen Quick 2022

the command of serving British senior officers. Without them, the battle would have been lost and SAF (and potentially the ruling status quo) discredited. It could be said that the Battle of Mirbat was the culmination and high point of British influence in the Dhofar COIN campaign, and the UK's historically decisive contribution towards the beginning of the end for the insurgency in the province. Although not perhaps the 'glamorized' event of SAS folklore as espoused by several traditional historical accounts of the war, with comparisons to the action which took place at Rorke's Drift in the Zulu Wars, the battle would not have been won without British input and its importance to the overall campaign cannot be overstated.[95] The SAS troops in situ defended valiantly, and the fortuitous availability of troops from G Squadron to relieve their comrades in the latter stages of the battle certainly helped to turn a potential defeat into victory. Graham commented: 'The BATT-men stationed in MARBAT [*sic*] fought superbly: there is no other word for it. We owe them a great debt.'[96] The role of the British SOAF pilots who flew in hazardous weather conditions to assist the defenders was also key. Without their strafing runs on advancing insurgent fighters, the battle may still have been lost.

Mirbat represented a decisive defeat for the PFLOAG, was a 'serious setback' for the insurgent cause and resultingly a major turning point in the war.[97] CSAF-controlled forces inflicted a morale-crushing defeat from which the insurgents never recovered, indeed Mirbat was '[a] bloody nose' and a 'severe defeat for PFLOAG' and therefore a major joint military success.[98] As well as likely over 100 casualties in a single day, the insurgents received their biggest military defeat of the entire campaign, a 'crushing psychological blow', and were unable ever to undertake a comparable large-scale conventional action for the remainder of the war.[99] The battle not only administered a blow to the Adoo from a military operational perspective but also a significant blow to their morale and for the wider insurgent cause. With the British-delivered defeat came recriminations, infighting, and the loss of faith in their leaders and cause for the idealistic young guerrillas who had been used to success.[100] The resultant adverse insurgent morale effect led to a post-battle revolt against the insurgents' leadership, and resulted in further attrition with the deaths of up to twenty-five men.[101] In an attempt to reassert their authority through fear, the Adoo leadership then set up 'kangaroo courts' and resultantly executed those scapegoats deemed responsible for the defeat, which further alienated the less committed comrades.[102] Further, the action had the effect of increasing levels of SEPs over the subsequent days, weeks, and months, with Jeapes noting: 'It was no surprise when August and September [1972] proved to be particularly good months for enemy surrendering to the Government.'[103] With the attrition of some 5% of the Adoo's full-time guerrilla force of approximately 2,000 men, and accounting for some 10% of total Adoo casualties from July 1970 to the close of 1972, the campaign-level success for the government, and scale of defeat for the insurgents, is clear.[104] The impact of the battle can also be appreciated in that as most of the Mirbat attackers were drafted in from outside (and to the west) of the Eastern Sector, so 'in one day, the SAF's victory reduced the need for an entire series of battalion operations into the Central and [further west] Ho Chi Minh areas.'[105] The effect on the SAF and the population was exactly the opposite, with Graham stating: 'Morale throughout SAF [as a result] and the Plains population is, I am told, skyhigh [sic].'[106] Mirbat can therefore be seen as the psychological and physical turning

MILITARY OPERATIONS AND TACTICS

point of the Dhofar War, was achieved primarily through UK input, and significantly contributed to the momentum towards eventual campaign success. Made possible by the campaign turning point achieved at Mirbat, the final Western Area operations (HADAF and HILWAH) to defeat the insurgents in western Dhofar involved diversionary attacks from both the SAF and Iranian forces based in Rakhyut. The closing operations were won through their keen management by the nominated Brigade Commander, Brig. John Akehurst, and CSAF, Maj-Gen. Ken Perkins, the latter taking command only a few months previously in February 1975. With the Iranian troops having secured the coastal town of Rakhyut in January 1975 and solidifying their advance positions to create the Damavand Line, the final phase of the war was entered. British operational planning put in place diversionary manoeuvres to confuse the insurgents. As such, the Iranians moved from Rakhyut towards the Sherishitti area in mid-October and a second diversionary operation was launched from the SAF position at Sarfait. Observing that the insurgents were fixated primarily on the feint manoeuvre by the Iranians, 'Akehurst [via Maj-Gen. Perkins] seized the opportunity to achieve the original objectives of "Simba", and directed the Sarfait garrison to drive on to the coastal town of Dhalqut, thereby severing the PFLOAG from Yemeni logistical assistance.'[107] With this spontaneous operational planning adjustment, UK commanders essentially disregarded months of meticulous planning to both seize and maximize the opportunity which presented itself.[108] At one stroke, the main communications and supply route from Hauf in the PDRY to insurgent forces and the Sherishitti base was cut, and within four weeks the latter was in COIN force hands via the Frontier Force as part of Operation HADAF.[109] The follow-up Operation HILWAH to clear the Darra Ridge, the final area of Dhofar physically still under insurgent control, was initiated towards the end of November, primarily via converging sets of SAF troops from Sarfait and further to the east, elements of which pushed on to Dhalqut, the last settlement to officially be recaptured in Dhofar. The main insurgent threat in Dhofar was therefore neutralized, with the survivors and remaining regular PDRY soldiers operating in Dhofar either surrendering or retreating over the border to safety.[110] After the hard fighting of the previous few months and subsequent collapse of insurgent resistance, Maj-Gen. Ken Perkins described the final mopping-up operations on the Darra Ridge as being conducted 'in a holiday atmosphere'.[111]

THE DHOFAR WAR

Figure 5.2: Mirbat Fort showing the gun pit where the 25-pounder artillery piece was fired at point blank range at the advancing Adoo by the SAS. © Stephen Quick 2022

MILITARY OPERATIONS AND TACTICS

It can therefore be observed that the general British contribution in operational terms towards achieving higher military strategy goals was pivotal and covered the entire war's duration. From the contribution made by British officers, that of the UK over other contributors (such as Iran or the Sultans themselves) or made by deployed British regular military units and specific impact of events as highlighted above, the UK role was decisive. This role contributed largely to containing the initial insurgent threat, preventing defeat for government COIN forces, and stabilizing then turning the campaign around to achieve the eventual insurgent defeat.

War Phases—Operations

Britain's primary military strategic aims for the Dhofar campaign were firstly to contain the insurgency and later to avoid defeat, and then to stabilize the campaign and expand COIN force capability eventually to defeat the insurgents. The UK's operationally focused contribution to achieving these overarching strategic aims is not just evident in general war-duration terms or in notable one-off operations but can be observed through four distinct campaign phases.

Phase 1 of the war (1964–1970) can be considered part failure and part success in terms of achieving strategic military aims. The initial insurgency was not contained from 1964 onwards due in large part to constraints imposed by Sultan Said, but the later avoidance of defeat was very much a result of UK operational input, which saved both Dhofar and greater Oman from insurgent domination. Due largely to Sultan Said's parsimony and a mostly ungenerous UK government attitude until 1970 and its knock-on effect on operational capability (allied to the post-PDRY formation upsurge in insurgent capability from 1968), much of the period can be considered a failure in operational terms. For the initial five years of the campaign up to the July 1970 coup, the SAF was unable to defeat the relatively small numbers of insurgents despite its experienced and competent CSAFs, British officers, and early numerical advantage. In terms of the overall UK contribution during Phase 1, bar 'Exchange of Letters' support, the UK government's unwillingness to be drawn into a 'Vietnam-like' commitment prevented substantial war assistance, which contributed to the poor SAF performance at the operational

THE DHOFAR WAR

level.[112] The war was not, however, lost and the input of British officers enabled the SAF to be professionally withdrawn to the Salalah plain's relative safety to regroup, and in effect allow Phase 2 to occur. Britain contributed to the strategic military outcome of avoiding defeat by controlling operations via the CSAF, HQ staff, and officers of SAF fighting units. Although direct UK military assistance bar the permanent RAF Salalah contingents was not yet in place, apart from small numbers of Indian and Pakistani officers, the SAF was officered only by UK personnel, and the command and control of operations was wholly under British control.[113] Both the SAF's and the regime's survival to 1970 was almost solely due to the cumulative impact of its British officers at the campaign level.

The initial NFR tour in late 1964 produced no contacts with the enemy and after one month the regiment was ordered home to the north after a presumed successful deterrent-based operation, and several months of relative quiet in Dhofar followed.[114] This presumption of success was put rudely into context by the May 1965 interrogation of Dhofari dissidents captured on a dhow off the coast of Iraq by the Iranian navy. Alongside a review of seized documents and weaponry, it was clear the scope of the insurgency was wider than initially envisaged, and that the deterrent-based NFR operation had not been successful. As a result, the SAF (MR) was redeployed in doubled numbers to Dhofar in May and this time engaged with the enemy and suffered its first casualty.[115]

After some successful operations, half the MR contingent returned to the north in June as the imminent monsoon facilitated a winding-down of military operations. Post-monsoon, the growing capability and morale of the insurgents was apparent through their first successful offensive actions against the SAF and the civilian Midway camp, with further evidence becoming apparent of significant external support via Saudi territory.[116] By this time, operation-level failures of the personnel and equipment-starved SAF meant control was maintained over the Salalah plain and northern deserts but not the Jebel, and the advantage was firmly with the resident no-Arab insurgents over the occupying outsiders from Northern Oman.[117] A stalemate situation had developed, with SAF forays onto the Jebel only ever temporary and seasonal, and the stage was, therefore, set for an extended conflict. In early 1966, the SAF (NFR) suffered its first deaths due to enemy action, with a British officer and two

MILITARY OPERATIONS AND TACTICS

Table 5.1: Key wartime operational-level contribution and influence

PHASE/ OPERATIONAL AIM	OPERATIONAL CONTRIBUTION/INFLUENCE	SUMMARY
PHASE 1 (end 1964–mid-1970) *Quell initial insurgency and later to avoid defeat to ascendant insurgents*	**British:** Supply, and COIN experience of CSAFs/UK seconded/contract personnel RAF personnel to man/protect RAF Salalah airfield (inc. RAF Regt. from 1969) UK control of SAF via chain of command/UK officers lead SAF troops on all ops **Other:** Omani and Baluchi SAF troops, plus limited numbers of Indian and Pakistani seconded military personnel	**Main aims only partially achieved** but—importantly—UK ops input ensures defeat avoided Sultan unwilling to spend on SAF—insists on repressive measures
PHASE 2 (Jul 1970–Sept 1971) *Hold Salalah position, consolidate and then expand COIN forces and prepare for large-scale offensive operations*	**British:** Consolidation of key Salalah defensive position Regular UK unit provision (SAS, RA, RCT, IC, FST), development and implementation of Watts Pan (SAS-run psyops, 'hearts and minds'-centred COIN approach and raising of Firqa militia units) First post-withdrawal battalion-plus size offensives launched by newly formed (Jan 1971) Dhofar Cmd. Large-scale (Oct) offensive plans devised by British CSAF **Other:** Sultan Qaboos supports UK SAF expansion plans and use of regular British units, e.g. SAS	**Operational aims eventually achieved**—Defence of Salalah, expansion of SAF, and organization of UK regular forces' assistance all British-controlled New COIN plan British-designed and implemented
PHASE 3 (Oct 1971–end 1974) *Launch offensive operations, reverse stalemate position and turn tide of war to government side*	**British:** Launch Oct 1971 offensives (JAGUAR/LEOPARD), establish first permanent SAF Jebel position (White City, Dec 1971) Key UK operational inputs of Op SIMBA (Apr 1972), Op AQOOBA (May 1972), Battle of Mirbat (Jul 1972), and Op JASON (Dec 1972)—tide of war turned	**Operational aims eventually achieved** due UK planning and management Operational success to 1972 mixed—some poor outcomes

(*continued*)

THE DHOFAR WAR

Table 5.1: Key wartime operational-level contribution and influence (*continued*)

PHASE/ OPERATIONAL AIM	OPERATIONAL CONTRIBUTION/INFLUENCE	SUMMARY
	UK-designed SAF expansion plan increases force numbers to approx. 10,000 by 1972 (from 3,000 in 1970) and further UK unit deployment (RE) Apr 1973 UK-run ops effectively clear Eastern Jebel area by mid-1973, and Hornbeam Line completed Jun 1974 (begun Dec 1973) **Other:** Iranian war supplies gift to Oman mid-1972—troops supplied from Nov 1972 (SF initially then later full battle group)—Iranian troops clear Midway Road by late 1973 UAE troops relieve SAF unit in N. Oman (Oct 1973), Jordanian Engineers arrive (Apr 1974)	Battle of Mirbat (Jul 1972) was campaign turning point—COIN forces in ascendancy from this point onwards
PHASE 4 (**Jan–Dec 1975**) *Defeat insurgents*	**British:** UK Cmdrs. change operational focus from COIN towards conventional actions Operation control of approx. 15,000 COIN forces to defeat Adoo by Dec 1975 UK Cmdrs. Plan and lead operations to retake Sherishitti Caves (Oct–Nov 1975) and clear Darra Ridge by 2 Dec 1975—Dhofar reported 'Secure for Civil Development', and Sultan declares victory 11 Dec 1975 **Other:** Key input of Omani and Baluchi troops of SAF to overall COIN win Iranians retake coastal town of Rakhyut (Jan 1975) and consolidate positions into Damavand Line Jordanian SF arrive in Oman early 1975 and supplies 31 Hunter jet fighter aircraft (Oct 1975) Iranian diversionary operations from Rakhyut towards Sherishitti (Oct 1975) and provision of naval gunfire support	**Aim achieved** Major personnel/materiel contribution to SAF by Iranians and Jordanians British-planned and commanded operations (including CSAF command over large-scale Iranian formations) led to defeat of insurgents by Dec 1975

soldiers of the same unit killed in the same week in the Wadi Naheez.[118] The increasingly confident insurgents subsequently almost achieved the elimination of Sultan Said by infiltrating the DF and conducting an assassination attempt at a guard of honour review in April 1966.[119] This event was followed in May 1966 by the first insurgent rocket-launcher attack, which caused several SAF deaths and highlighted the increasing sophistication of the weaponry and training available to the insurgents.[120] Not even an October 1966 Irish Guards and SAS operation to disrupt the Hauf insurgent base (involving an amphibious landing from the RN's new Landing Platform Dock—LPD—vessel, HMS *Fearless*) in Operation FATE was able to fully halt insurgent activities.[121] Although twenty-two insurgents were arrested and the town's use as a rebel base was temporarily thwarted, it remained the key insurgent stronghold until the end of the war.[122] The result of these operational shortcomings from 1964 was that by 1970, the military situation of the war had progressively deteriorated. The stalemate that ensued meant that the SAF were not able to defeat the insurgents, and all of Dhofar bar the coastal plain was effectively surrendered to rebel control by early 1970. So serious was the situation that 'increasingly disillusioned' British officers were reporting to London that the whole of Dhofar could be lost to the insurgents by late 1970.[123] That this did not occur, however, was due largely to the control and direction of operations afforded by British officers from the CSAF down. From the measured withdrawal to the relative safety of the Salalah plain under Brig. Purdon, to the sound military decision by Brig. Graham to relinquish the last exposed SAF position (held by a DR company on the Midway Road), because of the professional campaign leadership of British officers, withdrawal never became a rout. These UK-centred aspects enabled the SAF to retreat in an orderly fashion to the plain and prepare for the planned offensives in 1971. Although poor operational-level outcomes were apparent during Phase 1, a 1971 offensive would have likely been impossible without British input. Contrary, therefore, to the sometimes blinkered Dhofar War success narrative of earlier war accounts, as the outcome of quelling the insurgency was not achieved, the COIN campaign cannot be considered wholly effective nor successful from an operational perspective in the period up to 1970.[124] Despite effective UK-provided leadership and being well-trained, the SAF were hampered, largely due to Sultan Said's and the UK government's unwillingness to substantially increase war-related spending.

THE DHOFAR WAR

This situation was exacerbated with the UK withdrawal from Aden and subsequent PDRY, Chinese, and Soviet insurgent support, meaning the SAF faced an increasingly well-trained and armed enemy.[125] Post-formation of the PDRY, from the CSAF down, British officers with limited resources, therefore, prevented an SAF rout. A defeat to insurgent forces was avoided, allowing the SAF to regroup and prepare to re-engage on better terms.

With the development of a stalemate and a growing insurgent threat, the British-controlled operational priority in Phase 2 of the war (Jul 1970–Sep 1971) shifted from offensive to defensive operations. This enabled a regrouping of forces, with the SAF withdrawal to the relative safety of the Salalah plain being described by Brig. Graham as 'inevitable given the reluctance of Said bin Taimur to grant Corran Purdon the extra men, the modern weapons and helicopters ... for which he had pleaded'.[126] The securing and fortifying of the Salalah plain as completed by Brig. Graham did, however, enable a consolidation of forces, and following the 1970 coup, a British-led expansion of the SAF in both size and capability to prepare for large-scale offensive operations. In addition, the British role was expanded significantly through the deployment of numerous regular units from mid-1970 by the UK government to support Oman, and this further increased government COIN force capabilities.

The SAS were at the core of the new 'hearts and minds'-oriented COIN campaign launched post-coup (Watts Plan). SAS medical teams were deployed to towns such as Taqa and Mirbat to treat a population who had never had any modern medical support. The SAS spearheaded information operations and intelligence work and introduced the first fully functioning military intelligence cell.[127] The SAS were also instrumental in the operation to cement the Sultanate's governance over the virtually ungoverned enclave of the Musandam Peninsula via Operation INTRADON (known as Exercise 'Breakfast' in SAS and British military circles) in late 1970.[128] This was a bold statement of intent by Oman to protect its sovereignty and to counter subversive activities Sultanate-wide. In addition, the SAS raised, trained, and prepared the initial Firqa units for operations, a role key for the October 1971 offensives.

In a similar manner to Phase 1, the Phase 2 contribution to both failure and success was almost entirely down to British influence. The UK officer-planned expansion of the SAF began with the fourth SAF regiment (Jebel Regiment) in September 1970, and British military numbers were significantly

MILITARY OPERATIONS AND TACTICS

Figure 5.3: British soldiers returning to base on foot (Jebel area, west of Salalah).
© Sid Pass 1974

increased post-coup with the deployment of troops, including the SAS. UK personnel still had complete operational control, including over the first (limited) post-withdrawal offensive operations in January 1971. Phase 2 was not a war-winning period, but strong UK leadership, operational planning, and control meant the SAF line of defence in Salalah was held, enabling preparations for future large-scale offensive operations. This avoided the government stronghold of Salalah in Dhofar, then potentially the entire province, being lost to the insurgents. The key British operational role in Phase 2 was to ensure defeat was avoided, regroup, expand the SAF, and prepare for and lead offensive operations in 1971. The deployment of regular British troops also bolstered overall SAF capability and helped lay the foundation for future success.

The early stages of Phase 3 of the war (Oct 1971–late 1974) witnessed a further British personnel-led expansion of Omani COIN forces, with the increase of UK-deployed forces and SAF numbers. From October 1971, British officers and units led large-scale offensive operations, with 1972 witnessing significant UK-facilitated or conducted operations which helped turn the tide of the war. The period up to the end of 1974 then saw the UK SAF command integrate significant foreign troop contingents into Omani COIN forces, take the fight to the insurgents, and press towards a campaign win. In addition to the SAS, several hundred UK personnel were provided by the British government and in situ by late 1971 from units including the RA, RAF/RAF Regt. airfield and flight personnel, IC interrogators, FSTs, and even Veterinary Surgeon support (with RE elements subsequently deployed as part of Operation TENABLE from early 1973). British support increased but SAF numbers were also expanded via UK planning and by mid-1972 consisted of over 10,000 men, including the newly raised Firqa units.[129] As a result, the relative ratio of British troops to Omani and Baluchi personnel therefore decreased as part of COIN forces in Dhofar during this period. From 1973, allied foreign powers also started to deploy troops to Dhofar to assist the SAF, including Iranian and Jordanian forces. This development meant that towards the end of the war, UK troops accounted for only approximately 10% of allied COIN forces.[130] Resultantly, although absolute levels of UK personnel increased, from a relative perspective Britain's direct physical and numerical contribution to the war at the operational level was substantially less than other combined foreign COIN force allies.

Despite a significant growth in numbers and capability post-coup, up to 1972 there were many continuing challenges and other, newer issues which contributed to a continuing failure to defeat the insurgency. Central to these problems were the teething and other issues involved in the establishment of the tribal or SEP-constituted Firqa, despite the expertise of their SAS handlers. Whilst proving their worth later in the campaign, the Firqa were ill-disciplined and difficult to control with often selfish motivations which extended to power politics over their own tribal areas, and for the prospect of financial gain.[131] An example was the Firqat Salahudin, the initial raised multi-tribal unit which had to be disbanded 'due to internecine quarrels' by the British command as it could not work together, which effectively resulted in open mutiny.[132] The ill-discipline of the Firqa involved in Operation JAGUAR in late 1971 greatly frustrated the CO of 22 SAS, Lt. Col. Watts, and he resented that their performance and attitude did not match the professionalism and dedication of his own men.[133]

In part due to the issues concerning the newly raised Firqa, the much-vaunted post-coup offensives conceived by Brig. Graham and launched in October 1971 were also not the success hoped for. The showpiece operations to establish the first permanent SAF presence on the Jebel at Jibjat (White

MILITARY OPERATIONS AND TACTICS

City) during Operations JAGUAR and LEOPARD and the formation of small Adoo-blocking bases (including the Leopard Line positions) were underwhelming. Although starting well, the overall impact of the operations was minor and they were therefore considered somewhat underwhelming disappointments overall.[134] The immediate post-coup period and subsequent two years was, therefore, marred by considerable failure at the operational level. This reality was far from the high hopes of the post-coup era and runs counter to the traditional historic war accounts that contended largely that the Dhofar operation was a 'textbook' or model-type insurgency campaign.[135]

In 1972, however, the fortunes of the military campaign started to turn to the Omani government side, inspired by British-planned or led operations. In conjunction with substantially increased direct UK military aid, the failure of the insurgents to capture Taqa, and the successful SIMBA and AQOOBA operations, the high-profile defeat of the Adoo at Mirbat in July 1972 actually represented the war's key turning point.[136] Even at this point, victory was not certain and it would take the combined military inputs of Jordan and especially Iran to bring the necessary momentum to this late turning point to achieve further operational success by 1974. The year 1972 did, however, represent the period when the momentum of the campaign swung to the government side. In addition to the pivotal 1972 operational developments, Phase 3 also witnessed the effective completion of the Hornbeam Line, and therefore the ability to thwart insurgent supply lines from the west of Dhofar (and Hauf) as part of the CSAF-devised theatre 'block and clear' strategy. The Hornbeam Line grew out of the original Leopard Line positions, established in 1971 under the supervision of the Commander, Dhofar Brigade, Col. Mike Harvey. It was extensively reworked and expanded to become a permanently manned 35-mile cross-Jebel barrier north from Mughsayl, with added barbed wire and minefield deterrents and 'backed by five main patrol bases and artillery positions'.[137] The Hornbeam Line's construction was largely complete by June 1974 under the watch of CSAF Maj. Gen. Creasey and was a significant operational boon, as it all but cut off supplies from the western insurgent supply depots of Hauf in PDRY and the Sherishitti Caves to the eastern-based units. Phase 3, from October 1971 to late 1974, can therefore be considered inadequate in terms of military operational success up until 1972, but then turned around primarily via the bold UK-facilitated or -executed

THE DHOFAR WAR

operations later that year. The arrival of the first Iranian troops in 1972 and Jordanians from 1974 did significantly increase the momentum of the campaign turnaround phase by their sheer numbers. Whilst the war is sometimes described as an eventual international coalition or alliance to defeat the insurgency, the presence of the foreign troops was not only brokered by UK personnel but harnessing their operational effectiveness to maximize their benefit to the COIN campaign was ensured by the British SAF command structure.[138] This resulted in positive overall contribution to operations by not only securing the Midway Road, but by supporting the Sarfait garrison and manning the Hornbeam Line. Despite evidence, therefore, of cases of operational-level failure at the start of Phase 3 of the war, the aims of launching offensive operations, reversing the stalemate, and eventually turning the tide of the war were achieved, largely through UK planning and leadership.

The primary operational aim of Phase 4 of the war (late 1974–December 1975) reflected the prime military strategic goal of the Dhofar War overall, which was defeating the insurgents. From an unremarkable record up until 1972, with the turnaround in the campaign from this period, the momentum of success built up until the defeat of the insurgents was finally achieved in December 1975. In terms of the UK role in Phase 4 in achieving this, the change in focus from traditional COIN activities to conventional actions by British commanders and their operational command and control was key to all vital military episodes in the final stages of the war. From the post-coup period of the war, the focus of operations was on the execution of a more traditional UK-style COIN undertaking based on the Watts 'Five-Point Plan'. From late 1971, this evolved to include standard 'hearts and minds' elements but also, in response to insurgent actions (including the Mirbat attack), more conventional actions. The emphasis was consciously changed by British commanders from a primarily population-centric COIN approach to a wider conventional enemy-centric methodology focused on destroying the enemy on the battlefield.[139] Although the traditional COIN methods were largely retained in parallel, the overall war approach had been altered, and all major Phase 4 operations were, resultantly, large-scale conventional actions. The sheer volume of Iranian troop numbers contributed significantly to final operations from late 1974. Due, however, to the Artesh forces suffering high casualties, mainly because of poor levels of training and resultant general level of

MILITARY OPERATIONS AND TACTICS

performance in the field, they were consequently ordered by the CSAF Maj. Gen. Creasey to undertake more straightforward taskings—under his operational command—where their numbers and strong aviation support could be more effective.[140] These included advancing on Rakhyut and consolidating their advance positions into the Damavand Line, whilst the more technical taskings were allocated to SAF units.[141] The accumulated military experience of the senior British SAF commanders also heralded an inspired last-minute change in operational plans for SAF troops to march directly from Sarfait towards Dhalqut, thereby permanently cutting off all remaining PDRY-based supplies to the insurgents. Due to their limitations, the Iranians were allocated the less demanding task of a diversionary manoeuvre from Rakhyut towards Sherishitti. The physical clearing of the Sherishitti complex by SAF forces in Operation HADAF was completed by mid-November 1975 and followed by the clearance of the Darra Ridge in Operation HILWAH by the month's end. The seizure of Dhalqut was achieved in early December and was the final settlement in Dhofar to fall to government forces. With the stage-managed SAF entry to Dhalqut, Sultan Qaboos was notified by Maj-Gen. Perkins that Dhofar province was secured for civil development, enabling the ruler's victory announcement to the nation on 11 December 1975.

In terms of military influence, although Britain still supplied the CSAF and senior regimental commanders of the SAF, the arrival of Jordanian and especially Iranian troops meant a relative loss of UK military superiority and numerical strength at the war's operational level as per the 'sliding scale of influence' framework. From more recent Dhofar War historical narratives, it is to the Iranians that the accolade of securing the final victory in Phase 4 of the war often goes.[142] The importance of non-UK forces' contribution to Dhofar War operations is fully acknowledged. It is still likely, however, that none of the Phase 4 offensive actions would have been conducted as professionally, or with such flexibility and vigour, had they not been conceived, planned, coordinated, and commanded at all levels by British officers.

British personnel and units played decisive operational roles in all four campaign phases of the war. This included the 1970 coup and its aftermath, the new COIN approach, the 1971 offensives, the key 1972 campaign turnaround actions and momentum created from 1973 to 1975 by management of an increasingly multi-national COIN force. As such, the UK's contribution to

THE DHOFAR WAR

operations was the most significant in affecting the war's outcome. Whilst a relative UK decline in physical or numerical contribution to the war from 1973 can be observed, in absolute terms, British troop numbers did increase. Although non-UK influence on operations was important, for the first seven years of the decade-long war there were no Iranians or Jordanians present, and their main contribution was in crystalizing and accelerating the progress already made under UK operational control. It has been suggested that, from an operational perspective, it was primarily the bravery and dedication of the SAF's Baluchi and Omani soldiers that facilitated the overall insurgent defeat.[143] The actual fighting and 'boots-on-the-ground' contribution of thousands of such soldiers was undoubtedly a major reason for the campaign win. It was, however, as with the latent potential of the foreign military forces, the planning and execution of operations from the CSAF, through to Dhofar Command and the officers of the combat units involved, that was the key to eventual success. Overall control of operations was in British hands from the start of the campaign in 1965 and throughout all four phases until the COIN win was achieved.

Unlike operations per se, in the field of military tactics the UK's influence did not wane, and this was another key contributory factor in achieving the eventual COIN win. As highlighted in this book's introduction, tactics are essentially the physical ways by which operations are carried out and therefore how strategy is executed. Strategy is only as good as operations implemented to achieve strategic ends, and likewise these are only as good as the tactics used at 'battle' or 'fighting' level. As with overall war strategy, military tactics during the Dhofar War were predominantly under the control of the limited number of British SAF officers at combat unit level, and they were central to achieving operational outcomes in the war. Of the upwards of 15,000 combined COIN forces in Dhofar, the tactics of over 10,000 were directly controlled by British officers, and through embedded UK liaison officers and theatre-specific tactical procedural norms the remainder were highly influenced.[144] The fact that there were no Iranian or Jordanian troops in Dhofar for the initial seven years of the war, and that the decisive 1975 operations to defeat the insurgents were carried out by SAF units, illustrates the fact that British control of tactics was the most significant and consistent factor in this sphere. Whilst the contribution of non-UK foreign troops including the Iranians and Jordanians to the overall victory is certainly acknowledged, the view that the final insurgent

MILITARY OPERATIONS AND TACTICS

defeat should be largely credited to Britain and UK personnel from the tactical level up is appropriate.[145] Tactical control of SAF engagements or contacts was also almost completely a British role due to the skills and training of the embedded LSP and contract officers (and NCOs) at regimental army, SOAF, and SON level. With few exceptions, the only SAF personnel with the required military training and Omani dialect language skills to coordinate infantry contacts with supporting artillery and air or naval support operations were British officers.[146] SOAF tactics as part of the greater campaign effort were also wholly controlled by British flight officers, even after Iranian air force assets arrived in theatre. Despite the significant and important physical contribution of Iranian (and to a lesser extent Jordanian) flight assets, which operated according to their own internal procedures, these units operated as part of the UK-developed tactical framework and were under SAF operational command.

With regard to the tactical aspects of the Dhofar campaign, the principal British aims revolved primarily around forging SAF-wide tactically effective units to best support campaign operations, and the effective tactical integration of SAF and SAF-controlled combat units in action.[147] From the CSAF to the regimental officers of combat units, Dhofar COIN campaign actions were conceived, planned, and executed mainly by either seconded or contract British officers. The high quality of British training also produced a well-rounded and tactically capable officer, and frequently contemporary junior commanders had accumulated significant experience during the 1960s of COIN actions such as in the Brunei/early Borneo campaign or in Aden up to 1967. Added to this, the experience of other campaigns and the traditions of the old Indian Army and British regiments such as the Ghurkhas was an asset. This aspect helped in dealing with (for the older officers) leading indigenous troops or being stationed for long stretches of their careers in postings abroad, which meant there was a natural and seamless quality of leadership within the SAF. Many younger officers also had prior experience of the Middle East region, and some of Oman as well, and this even included British officers of UK units (for instance the SAS) who worked alongside the SAF. This situation was echoed by CSAF Brig. Purdon, who stated about the officers leading his Arab and Baluch soldiers: 'I greatly admired the splendid young British officers who led them from the front.'[148] This situation created strong, cohesive units which could perform well in arduous conditions.

British officer influence was also important in terms of language. UK officer language skills were invaluable for tactical control within all SAF entities, being able to communicate with largely non-English-speaking subordinates in Arabic or Baluchi dialects to the level necessary to effectively implement tactical orders. Such basic language skills were either taught prior to deployment for LSP army personnel or learned (often to a much higher standard) from years of service in the region by contract officers.[149] For inter-unit coordination, this important factor was reinforced when the decision was made to divide previously mixed SAF battalions. Battalions were divided into distinct Arab or Baluch units (in response to an outbreak of PFLOAG propaganda-driven anti-Baluch sentiments in 1971), which also resulted in Brig. Graham's orders for a purpose-raised all-Baluch SAF unit, the Baluch Guard, which was formed from Baluch askaris and later renamed the Frontier Force.[150] Cross-unit tactical coordination was therefore left primarily to junior British officers in the English language, whilst simultaneously directing their troops in the men's own dialects as a requirement of effective tactical command and control.[151] In addition, circumstances in Dhofar also dictated that all SAF coordination with the SOAF was conducted in English, therefore the junior British officers were vital to coordinating with pilots of aircraft in tactical support roles.

It can therefore be observed that British officers were not just well-trained to serve effectively at the tactical level and often had COIN and regional soldiering experience to their names, but their language skills made them invaluable in both liaison and tactical execution roles. The negative operational impact, especially of Sultan Said's policies, can be seen to highlight both the importance and contrasting positive role of British officers in this regard. Added to the situation where Dhofar COIN forces were under direct and total British officer tactical control for almost four-fifths of the war, the breadth of UK tactical influence on the Dhofar campaign is clear.

Forging SAF-wide tactically effective units was another key British aim, which centred around the development and integration of tactics within the force. Although carried out at the unit level, the general theatre-specific SAF tactical approach was developed by senior officers and implemented via its chain of command. Although comment in the historical literature points to a significant change of tactics from those of a traditional COIN nature to a more conventional warfare outlook as part of a 'coercion theory' approach, this

MILITARY OPERATIONS AND TACTICS

is not something unique to the Dhofar campaign.[152] Working at both ends of such a spectrum can also be observed in previous UK COIN campaigns. These include the use of large-scale sweeping military and police manoeuvres in Nairobi to round up insurgent suspects or sympathizers in urban areas and detaining or expelling many back to their home districts whilst platoon-level or smaller units pursued insurgents in the forested areas of the Abadares during the Kenyan Mau Mau campaign.[153] Conversely in the Aden campaign, whilst small units were conducting house search sweeps in the Crater district, a larger-scale tactical approach was employed in the Radfan in the more exposed rural environment. The development of COIN tactics also often mirrors those of the insurgents being countered. In other rural-based insurgencies largely in forested or jungle-type environments such as Malaya, Kenya, and Borneo, for example, the mainly small-scale enemy units were countered with smaller COIN units of company or platoon-size numbers or fewer and 'a degree of dispersion inconsistent with normal military practice'.[154] Due to the large-scale operating area in Dhofar, but also to the early ability of insurgent units to operate in well-equipped larger formations, more firepower and manpower were deemed necessary, so most Dhofari COIN manoeuvres and contacts were undertaken by SAF units of half (the standard operating unit in Dhofar) to full company size, alongside support elements such as artillery, as dictated by SAF high command.[155] An example of the Dhofari insurgents' gradual adoption of more conventional tactics over those of traditional guerrilla-warfare tactics was the Battle of Mirbat in July 1972, when a company plus equivalent-sized insurgent attack was launched against the town. In addition, with the traditional UK-style COIN approach introduced after 1970 such as 'hearts and minds', medical, information services, and an amnesty programme to help woo the Jebali population over to the government side, the tougher 'stick' elements of COIN tactics were also implemented. These measures included population control and free-fire zones, required to help defeat the insurgents in tandem with the 'carrot' approach elements. This was not a new phenomenon as can be observed in several previous UK COIN campaigns, with general tactical requirements dictated by the British command and implemented via the chain of command.

As British officers controlled the SAF chain of command almost exclusively for the entire war, the tactics employed by units in Dhofar were largely under such control from the CSAF (Brig. or Maj. Gen.) to half-company (Captain) level. From the start of the war, orders would be issued to commanders of subordinate units undertaking operations in Dhofar. Originally this was the role of the CO of the regiment serving on rotation in the province, and then from February 1971 it was that of the commander of Dhofar Brigade based at Umm al-Ghawarif camp near Salalah.[156] The general tactical approach was decreed by the CSAF and his staff, and their implementation at brigade or regimental level was the role of the British CO at each respective command level. Additionally, specific war zone and unit-level tactics were mainly the preserve of British officers. The CO of the resident Dhofar-deployed regiment, although limited by the general tactical guidance of SAF HQ, had devolved authority to operate tactically as deemed necessary. Likewise, when Col. Mike Harvey became the initial Dhofar Brigade Commander in February 1971, the responsibility of the translation of such guidance from a tactical perspective was his prerogative.[157] Furthermore, from a 'boots-on-the-ground' perspective, the CO of units operating under his command fulfilled the same role.

Within the infantry regiment, the primary combat unit of SAF, the unit command structure was under complete top-down British control. From the beginning of the war, units such as the MR and the NFR were single battalion-sized, unlike the case usually in the British Army where multiple, semi-autonomous battalions per regiment was, and is, the norm. This tradition continued with the introduction of later infantry units such as the Desert Regiment (DR) in 1970, followed by the Frontier Force (FF) and the Southern Regiment (KJ). Each battalion-sized regiment usually consisted of four rifle companies, each normally divided into two half-companies and commanded by a British captain, supported by Arab or Baluchi subalterns with platoons run by Arab or Baluchi staff sergeants.[158] The main role of the captains was to translate tactical directions to regimental subcommand groupings and ensure that they were followed. This is a key point because for at least half the war's duration, although Omani and Baluchi subalterns did exist in SAF infantry units, they were not academy-trained and were given field promotions only. This was done as per the policy laid down by Sultan Said, due to his fear of an 'Egyptian-style' coup staged by his own officers, as he preferred to exercise SAF authority mainly through British seconded and contract officers.[159] This meant there were few empowered Arab officers exercising command over

MILITARY OPERATIONS AND TACTICS

Omani troops, as all were field promoted (without formal officer training) and never beyond the rank of lieutenant.[160] The organization of SAF infantry regiments into half-company units was made therefore to ensure that a British captain could oversee tactical conduct in groupings of approximately sixty men.[161] Omani (and Baluchi for all-Baluch units such as KJA) officers were only commissioned as part of a training programme set up at Ghalla in 1971 under the watchful eye of the British DCSAF, Col. Colin Maxwell.[162] By 1972, there were approximately 100 Omani and Baluchi officers commissioned into the SAF or sent on established commissioning courses abroad.[163] Due, however, to the late start of this process in the Dhofar War, the majority of tactical command responsibility in the conflict remained with junior UK officers.

A note should also be added regarding SAF NCOs and basic infantrymen. In Western armies, the level of education and training traditionally meant certain tactical functions could be delegated to NCOs and in many cases to private or enlisted-level soldiers. In Oman at the time of the Dhofar War, this was usually not the case. Whilst they could still be efficient and courageous soldiers, such personnel usually had neither the technical training nor education to exercise effective tactical command, therefore this role was retained at British officer level. The near-complete control of tactics by British officers was only impacted from the autumn of 1972 onwards, almost eight years into the COIN campaign, with the introduction of Iranian and (from 1973) Jordanian troops.[164] Although, by necessity, unit-level tactics of non-UK foreign units were internally implemented, a measure of control was maintained in that the general COIN force-wide tactical approach to be adopted was dictated by the CSAF via Dhofar Brigade and through the use of embedded British SAF liaison officers.[165] In terms of campaign impact, the virtual single-handed tactical control of COIN forces for four-fifths of the decade-long war, allied to the 10,000 plus SAF and UK soldiers under direct British officer tactical command from 1972 (who carried out the decisive 1975 operations), were the most important tactical elements in achieving victory.

Further to forging SAF-wide tactically effective operational units, via the development and integration of the British tactical approach for the war, their efficient integration at the tactical level in action, and alongside non-SAF combat elements, was another key British aim. As such, the SAF depended on the tactical control skills of embedded British officers. This was historically the case within the Omani armed forces since the formation of the SAF and the start of the UK supply of LSP officers in 1958 via the 'Exchange of Letters'. This set the precedent for the SAF's UK officer structure throughout the war, although the tradition of ex-regular British officers working under contract as part of the former Muscat Armed Forces was also long established. The supply of junior LSP (and contract) British officers meant that the SAF benefitted from fully trained and qualified officers, both technically in standard British army infantry tactics and in the art of leadership. Because their subordinates largely lacked the requisite training, technical competence, and language skills (with troops largely illiterate on entry to the SAF), junior British officers often had to take on a higher level of direct tactical responsibility—and over an often diverse ethnic variety of soldiery—than would have been the norm in the British Army.[166] Due to the importance of such taskings and lack of alternatives, such officers in the main had to coordinate the technical art of artillery support whilst leading infantry manoeuvres.[167] This was often undertaken at the same time as calling for, and physically coordinating with, the individual pilots during air support from the SOAF including airstrikes. As highlighted by Maj. Gen. Creasey:

> The fighting capability of any sub-unit is [only] as good or bad as the standard of its British officer. Many of the local officers are experienced and brave leaders, but they lack the education to be able to carry out many essential [tactical] tasks in combat. The British officer in contact, must lead his company from the front, and also act as FOO [artillery forward observation officer], FAC [forward air controller] and MFC [mortar fire controller], and at times organise the evacuation by air of casualties.[168]

An extra facet to this situation which emphasizes the importance of British officers in control and execution of tactics is that English was the default language used for the SOAF. In addition to technical training challenges, by default, such officers had to control air support because of language issues. UK pilots operated in their native tongue in response to fellow countrymen commanding ground troops to effectively coordinate tactical air support. Key examples of such coordination between air and ground forces included Operation SIMBA, where a whole battalion was deposited behind enemy lines in coordinated waves via SOAF helicopters. Other examples include Operation

MILITARY OPERATIONS AND TACTICS

HIMAAR in February 1975 when a KJ (Southern) Regiment company was similarly airlifted to positions in the Wadi Ashawq as part of a seven-company operation to assault key insurgent ('9th June' Regiment) positions.[169] Similarly, effective fast jet support to ground forces coordination can be observed occurring during the Battle of Mirbat primarily between the SAS and British SOAF pilots. Such skilled synchronization was also evident during the final 1975 operations with the combined Hunter jet attacks in coordination with large-scale 5.5-inch field artillery bombardment of Hauf from the Sarfait garrison. As highlighted by Maj-Gen. Perkins, the use of British SAF forward observation parties (such as that commanded by Capt. Gordon Allen) were wholly 'responsible for the co-ordination of an artillery, air [support] and naval fire plan' to achieve the desired combined effects.[170]

Another key aspect of British control of tactics in the Dhofar War was the near-complete domination of British officers in the SOAF organization. Tactics were controlled at managerial level by the SOAF Commander, who was always a British officer, and down through the chain of command to pilot level. Even the maintenance of aircraft and arming for missions was undertaken by British personnel primarily from a private UK company, Airwork Ltd., which by 1974 had approximately seventy technicians working at RAF Salalah alone.[171] Likewise, the CO of RAF Salalah was a serving RAF officer and all coordination in terms of air traffic control, emergency support, and area defence was carried out at all times by UK forces.

As alluded to previously, unlike seconded British army officers, the RAF officers seconded to SOAF were not required to learn Arabic. Army officers from the CSAF down were required to attend language courses at the British Army School of Languages at Beaconsfield because they were to lead Omani and Baluchi troops, but it was not deemed necessary for RAF officers as there were only British personnel on the SOAF operational staff.[172] As English was the default language for SOAF operations it was therefore also standard for tactical air support for SAF units. This situation was, again, only challenged by the arrival of Farsi-speaking Iranian air assets as—because Iranian forces were under overall SAF (and therefore CSAF) command—standard theatre tactical procedures and processes had to be coordinated in English to operate effectively with both SOAF and SAF units in general.[173] As such, the integration of Iranian forces presented considerable challenges in terms of conducting joint operations but also down to the tactical level within units. Partly for this purpose, British officers such as Majors Johnny Braddell-Smith and Patrick Brook, and Captain Mike Lobb were inserted as liaison officers within Iranian units to try to smooth over any language issues or comprehension of orders when operating in tandem with SAF units.[174] Due to the challenges involved, the limited quality of Iranian officers, and the view of commanders including Maj. Gen. Creasey that the Artesh troops generally lacked even basic infantry skills, British officers on occasion even ended up effectively commanding smaller Iranian formations during manoeuvres to ensure tactics were carried out competently.[175]

Alongside liaison officers, the most important role for British interaction with non-UK troops from a tactical control perspective was with the irregular Firqa units. Initially via SAS troopers, as the SAF lacked the necessary expertise, but later through SAF officers as the Firqa organization became more tightly centrally integrated, the tactical management of such units was British-controlled.[176] This role ranged from planning and coordinating manoeuvres to leading from the front in action, arranging air or artillery support, or even arranging basic field necessities such as rations and ammunition. Despite recurring issues such as general unreliability, Firqa units 'have, on occasions, operated brilliantly and with outstanding courage and zeal' and as a result of this were to become indispensable to the overall campaign, due largely to UK tactical command and control, which maximized their overall effectiveness.[177]

For the duration of the Dhofar conflict, British control of SAF tactics was almost total. This aspect was a vital factor in unit-level success in the war, which contributed to the SAF's ability to achieve required end-states at the higher levels of warfare at both the operational and strategic levels. No other influence on Dhofar War tactics per se or tactical success matched that of the British personnel. Thus, whilst other factors including political or economic, or even operational execution aspects were subject to the 'sliding scale of influence' framework effect, in terms of military tactics, this was not the case. This is not to suggest that all military tactics utilized were successful or appropriate, but the key point is that they were for the most part under British officer control. This, in turn, meant tactical success was more likely due to the high skill and training levels of such individuals as compared to non-British

MILITARY OPERATIONS AND TACTICS

SAF officers and NCOs, and this situation only began to change late in the war, via the newly established Ghalla-based officer training unit.[178] In a similar manner, therefore, to the formation and execution of war strategy or operations, tactical control of units was largely in British hands from 1965 to the war's end in 1975. This was equally the case across SAF units, UK military forces, and through liaison officer influence in allied units from 1972. The ability of British officers to implement and control tactical procedures in units contributed to more effective operations and therefore was one of the main drivers behind the final COIN win. It would not be an overstatement to conclude that British officers were essentially the 'glue' which held together not just SAF intra-unit capability, but resultantly also the operational effectiveness of the wider COIN contribution.

It can therefore be seen that in the spheres of operations and tactics, both British influence and control were key aspects of carrying the result of the Dhofar War. Without British influence in these areas, the COIN campaign against the Dhofari insurgents would not have been won. Despite a relative loss of influence at the operational level due primarily to the arrival of thousands of non-British foreign troops to the Sultan's COIN coalition from 1972, through the control over operations by the British officer-dominated SAF chain of command, and the military authority of the CSAF over all UK regular and foreign troops, this aspect of influence never wavered. Alongside this, ubiquitous tactical control at all times was ensured, and the safeguarding of the quality and effectiveness of actions at the 'fighting' level was always fully in the hands of largely junior British officers. A joined-up and cohesive tactical-level picture benefitted larger actions at the operational level, especially in a small war like in Dhofar. Together, these aspects brought defeat for the insurgents both on the battlefield and in the wider campaign.

6 Non-Kinetic Military and Informal Support

Up to this point, this book has primarily covered two main types of British support. The first of these is political and diplomatic, and the second 'kinetic' military, or provision of 'fighting capability' at the strategic, operational, or tactical levels of warfare via either direct British forces or seconded military personnel. This chapter covers many types of key, but often overlooked, supplementary support functions provided by the UK or British nationals not directly employed by the state under the banner of 'non-kinetic military and informal support'. This includes 'non-fighting' military support such as provision of war supplies, military equipment, training, and personnel. Personnel provision includes British state military and civilian employees, but also those of UK origin working privately or for non-state organizations. Such support further includes economic aspects, and finally commercial UK technical support. Collectively, these elements can be considered on a par with kinetic military assistance in terms of achieving victory.

Whilst British influence was maintained over the whole Dhofar War timeframe in areas such as control of military strategy and tactical procedures, in the areas of 'non-kinetic military and informal support' this was less the case. As per the 'sliding scale of influence' framework, certain campaign support functions were subject to a significant reduction in UK influence, including the diversification of war supplies, finance, and military assistance to both Iran and Jordan, as well as to other Middle Eastern countries. Influence, however, in the above functions and especially to those relating to the largely UK-dominated areas of personnel provision and training remained central to efforts to win the Dhofar War from both a British state and non-state perspective. In addition, all non-UK war-related supplies provision and finance, for example,

NON-KINETIC MILITARY AND INFORMAL SUPPORT

was still required to be operationalized by the SAF command to be fully exploited in the war effort. Without such support, the capability of the COIN coalition would have been overstretched to the detriment of operational and potentially strategic goals. Had there not been British control and supply of these resources, the war would likely have lasted longer and may have been lost. As such, this chapter puts forward the premise that British influence was prime but acknowledges too that non-UK support was more important than credited in many of the historical Dhofar War accounts to date.[1]

Non-Kinetic and Informal Support Provision

Without Britain's large-scale and historically significant economic assistance to the Sultanate, the Dhofar War may well have been lost. Without such funding, a meaningful COIN response by the Omani government would not have been possible. Britain firstly supplied the lifeline of funds primarily through the long-term provision of annual subsidy payments, then through the 1958 'Exchange of Letters'. This enabled Omani forces to initially counter, and later expand in size and capacity to mount a concerted COIN response in Dhofar. The scale of British economic influence in Oman meant the Sultanate was effectively financially subsidized or in reality 'bankrolled' by Britain from 1861 onwards with the introduction of the Canning Award/ Zanzibar Subsidy, which provided up to 98% of Oman's annual budget up until the mid-twentieth century.[2] This was later reinforced through the financial assistance package established via the 1958 'Exchange of Letters' agreements and later upgraded in 1960 to further expand such assistance. Direct British support via the agreement was the basis for the reorganization of the Muscat Armed Forces into the SAF as well as the creation of the embryonic SOAF. These funds supported the development and expansion of new units of the re-designated Omani armed forces, including the Oman Regiment (OR), formerly the Muscat and Oman Field Force (MOFF), the Northern Frontier Regiment (NFR), formerly the Batinah Force (BF), and the Muscat Regiment, formerly the Muscat Infantry (MI), and these indirectly UK-funded units played key roles in the ultimately successful Dhofar War.[3]

Aside from capital, set-up, and army unit reorganization costs, the 'Exchange of Letters' also guaranteed the continuing development and effectiveness of

THE DHOFAR WAR

Table 6.1: Key Dhofar campaign non-kinetic and informal UK support contributions

UK CONTRIBUTION	NON-UK CONTRIBUTION	VERDICT
ECONOMIC/FINANCE FACTOR: Canning Award/Zanzibar Subsidy (from 1861) Financial advice/management (Bank of England, BBME, PD(O)) 1958 'Exchange of Letters'—£271k per year recurrent expenditure/£144k capital costs for SAF formation/£162k for SOAF creation and £68k annually for recurrent costs/£177k towards civil development programme and £14k annual costs 1960 'Exchange of Letters' upgrade (financial uplift)—over £1 million towards SAF reorg. costs/c. £900k towards recurrent costs/£280k for capital costs/approx. £165k annual civil development programme costs Financial costs of British LSP and regular UK military units (where not paid for by Oman, e.g. LSP relief of £500k 1973–74) as well as debt relief on military supplies (e.g. £850k in 1972)*	Omani Oil income from 1968 (1973 oil crisis income boost). 1974 sees quadrupling of oil income (to 200 million Rials) Gulf States financial assistance (inc. Saudi Arabia and UAE/Abu Dhabi)	British-dependent war finance from start of conflict to 1973. Useful UK cost/debt relief to 1973/74. Largely Omani oil funds predominate from 1973
PERSONNEL PROVISION FACTOR: **Civilian:** Private British civilians serving in Omani government during war e.g. Waterfield, Oldman (preceded by Innes, McLean, Chauncy, and Boustead) PRPG and Consul-General (later Ambassador) assistance **Military:** 'Exchange of Letters' provision of LSP officers and other ranks (x24) including every CSAF from 1958.** LSP numbers eventually exceed 40 (1960 'upgrade'—inc. additional 15 x junior officers).** Contract officers supplied via UK firm Airwork Ltd. All SAF regimental commanding officers seconded British officers (2i/cs usually UK contract officers) Deployment of RE, RA, and IC units to Dhofar including up to 2 x squadrons of SAS (approx. 120 men) Approx. 1,000 regular UK military personnel deployed to Dhofar by 1975	Civilian: Negligible Military: Approx. 10,000 Omanis/Baluchi (SAF) Approx. 3,000 Iranian forces Approx. 800 Jordanian forces Company of Abu Dhabi Defence Force (2 x deployments for guard duties)	British historical influence the strongest. Never matched from civilian perspective and UK military manpower figures only overtaken in Omani COIN force by other foreign troops in 1973

NON-KINETIC MILITARY AND INFORMAL SUPPORT

TRAINING FACTOR: Regular British Forces training teams despatched from Cyprus and Bahrain to train SAF units UK officers set up Ghalla SAF officer training wing SAS undertook new Sultan bodyguard training, SAF pre-deployment firearms training, Firqa formation	No equivalent training role	Complete British dominance
WAR SUPPLIES/ LOGISTICS FACTOR: UK main supplier of war materials for war duration (UK main arms exporter to Oman (bar 1972)) Pre-coup, most military stock items purchased from UK MOD via Kendall & Sons chandlery British loan supplies (e.g. RAF Wessex helicopters with crews) British officers i/c SAF departments—control force logistics from CSAF down	Large stores provision from Iran 1972 and double arms exports of UK to Oman 1972 Jordan gifts 31 Hunter jets and 12 25-pounder artillery pieces in 1975	Significant non-UK war supplies from 1972. UK was prime weapons exporter to Oman over lifetime of conflict (bar 1972) and UK officer control SAF logistics
TECHNICAL/MAINTENANCE SUPPORT FACTOR British command controls general SAF engineering/maintenance requirements UK company Airwork Ltd. supply engineers to maintain and arm all SOAF aircraft (inc. RAF Salalah).*** RE deployed (approx. 70 men) from 1973 past end of war (to 1977) for variety of technical, construction, and training tasks	LSP technicians supplied by Pakistani army Iranians maintain own extensive deployed equipment stocks (e.g. helicopters)	SAF technical maintenance and support provided mainly by British assets during Dhofar War

* J. Worrall, *Statebuilding and Counterinsurgency in Oman: Political, Military and Diplomatic Relations at the End of Empire* (London: I.B.Tauris), pp. 176 & 181.

** J.E. Peterson, *Oman's Insurgencies: The Sultanate's Struggle for Supremacy* (Lebanon: Saqi, 2007), pp. 102 & 148.

*** K. McCloskey, *Airwork: A History* (Stroud: The History Press, 2012), pp. 138–9.

the force, with £271,000 to be supplied annually to the Sultan's Army and £67,950 to his new Air Force for recurring costs.[4] This enabled continuity and investment, and leadership was guaranteed through British officers supplied on long-term loan by the UK government to lead the SAF at every command level. This put the UK in a highly influential position with regard to either controlling or at least influencing war policy, as well as maintaining a degree of psychological influence over the Sultan. The 'Exchange of Letters' arrangements also allowed the Sultanate's military forces to respond in a more effective manner to the insurgent threat when it arose in 1964 than would have been possible with the smaller, less organized, and 'semi-professional' force that existed previously. In 1960, after the Sultan's visit to London and talks with Edward Heath, the incumbent Lord Privy Seal (later Prime Minister), this agreement was updated. Britain agreed to provide nearly £1 million on an annual basis for the ongoing running costs of the SAF, plus a similar amount to contribute towards the further reorganization of the force.[5] UK-derived funds were also pledged to meet the majority of costs (£280,000 for capital expenditure and £165,500 annually for recurrent costs) for the much expanded civil development programme, which was a key consideration from the UK perspective.[6] In addition, the updated agreement provided for numbers of seconded military personnel numbers to exceed forty—up from the original agreed twenty-four—and to pay all costs for the fledgling Omani Air Force.[7] All such arrangements continued to be honoured with the onset of the Dhofar insurgency. Such provisions were all aimed towards enhancing the capability of the Omani military and subsequently the effectiveness of the COIN response, which developed into a both substantial and growing commitment.

British support to Oman was further expanded after the 1970 coup to include the deployment of regular military units for the first time including detachments of the SAS, RA, and RE. Despite most of the UK material support being paid for in full by the Sultanate, due to the (unsustainable) increasing absolute cost to Oman, Britain started absorbing up to 50% of LSP costs by 1973.[8] This development represented an even greater level of British assistance than ever before, and such costs, in addition to the financial burden of upkeep and operating both RAF Salalah and RAF Masirah, were substantial. Held by Britain on a ninety-nine-year lease, RAF Masirah was the more costly to run for the UK in part as it housed over 550 mainly military personnel

NON-KINETIC MILITARY AND INFORMAL SUPPORT

in contrast to fewer than half this number located at RAF Salalah.[9] The scale of funds transferred to Oman by the UK for both air bases and other financial assistance made the Sultanate almost completely dependent on Britain in terms of campaign funding. This was the case from the initial SAF deployment in 1964, at least up until the withdrawal of the UK subsidy to Oman in 1968, and, in reality, was the case fully up until 1973.[10]

In financial terms, the British contribution towards civil development remained paramount throughout the war and was in place from the 'Exchange of Letters' agreements. This important function of the 'hearts and minds' strand of the overall COIN campaign remained effectively reliant on British funding until approximately 1973, when the oil crisis-related boost to Omani income lessened the financial strain of the war on required development efforts. The civil development programme was also administered by UK personnel, so this key function, which was essential to the 'hearts and minds' aims of Operation STORM and towards overall COIN success, was also in British hands. Lt. Col. Martin Robb was a key player in the Dhofari civil development programme from 1974, which helped win back the Jebel population to the government side during the war. Robb continued this work as designated head of the Dhofar section of the new Omani governmental Civil Aid Department from early 1975.[11] He also had a seat on the British-instigated Dhofar Development Committee (DDC), which was chaired by HE Sheikh Braik, and had Brig. John Akehurst (Commander Dhofar Brigade), Mr. Robin Young OBE (Dhofar Development Department), Lt. Col. Bob Brown (Head of Dhofar Intelligence), and Lt. Colin McLean (Commander Firqat Forces) as committee members, set up to forge a coordinated inter-agency civil development approach.[12] In terms of the significance of the overall British-engineered civil aid effort, which culminated in the establishment of the CAD, Lt. Col. Tony Jeapes, Commander of SAS forces in Oman (1974–1976), stated:

> If the firqats' were the most important Government department to be created to win the war, Civil Aid must run them a close second. The Civil Aid Department was, I believe, the one new lesson the Dhofar Campaign provided in the study of counter-revolutionary war, yet it came about almost by default … It [the CAD] seldom had an executive staff of more than three or four but its impact on the war was enormous. CAD's fingers reached into practically every wadi on the jebel before the war was over.[13]

THE DHOFAR WAR

Overall British financial influence started to decrease from 1967 onwards as a result of the UK Treasury ending the long-established Zanzibar Subsidy payment in the late 1960s due to the advent of commercial oil exports from Oman and the resultant additional state income.[14] The oil revenue windfall ultimately gave the Omani ruler more options and made him less reliant on the British government for income, moving instead towards a traditional rentier-state funding model. Combined with the effects of the 1973–1974 Middle Eastern Oil Crisis, which resulted in a fourfold increase in oil prices between October and December 1973, this resulted in a quadrupling in oil income in 1974 to over 200 million Rials and a rise to over 300 million by 1975.[15] No longer being fully dependent on the UK for income gave Sultan Qaboos more room to manoeuvre in terms of spending. This he did with enthusiasm, from palace and luxury yacht-building, the purchase of an English manor house, a hotel, and even a German castle, to expensive military hardware.[16] In the midst of an expensive war, Qaboos even prioritized £2 million and £1.5 million respectively of this wealth towards the refurbishment of reception rooms at one of his palaces and ornamental furnishings ordered from luxury goods retailer Asprey's of London.[17]

In addition to the rise in oil income, Britain's financial influence over Oman, and therefore in economic terms over the Dhofar War, was further diminished by other sources of foreign aid. From 1972, Oman received welcome financial support from Middle Eastern neighbours including Saudi Arabia, the UAE, and Qatar.[18] This combined financial scenario made Oman by 1974 effectively financially independent from Britain for the first time (at least) since 1861. This gave the Sultan a freer hand on both important war-related procurement issues in conjunction with the fast-track civil development programme in the country. From being an impoverished, bankrolled state, 'Oman did not [now] have to choose between guns and butter, it could have both.'[19] With direct impact on the Dhofar War, the Sultanate's defence budget increased significantly, and by 1975 was double what the entire national budget had been in 1973, with Britain's influence in terms of economic leverage over Oman and the Dhofar campaign also simultaneously curtailed.[20]

Coupled with a rise in income came an increase in campaign costs, and therefore every saving possible contributed financially to the COIN win. From government revenue of just over 50 million Rials in 1971, 46 million was spent on the public sector, leaving a surplus; this was reversed in 1972, with 53 million Rials income versus 71.6 million spent, and in 1973, with 68.5 million Rials income versus almost 93 million spent, and in the 1975/6 financial year there was a budget deficit of over 100 million Rials.[21] With such pressures on the Omani budget and most significantly upwards of 50% of national income spent on the Dhofar War in 1972 alone, the situation led to Oman directly requesting UK intervention.[22] As a result, Britain eventually made financial concessions on such items as LSP costs and debts relating to UK-provided military supplies. In August 1972, the UK wrote off war-related charges of approximately £850,000, and up to £500,000 of costs relating to LSP were waived from 1973 to 1974.[23] Such finance-related UK state actions enabled the overall Omani—and therefore the Dhofar War—budget to stretch further. Britain's historic economic influence over Oman and the Dhofar COIN campaign is clear and was a key factor in ensuring the war's prosecution for its initial eight years. It also continued as an important, although less significant, factor in the end of the conflict in 1975. The support given by Britain to Oman from before the start of the war helped create a situation where the Sultanate had greater resilience than in the past and was financially able to conduct a military COIN campaign in the first place.

In addition to primary direct state-provided economic and financial support, British influence also provided secondary benefits which helped support the Sultanate and therefore the war effort towards a successful conclusion from a UK state-controlled and non-state actor perspective. Key British organizations had a significant effect on both providing and organizing Omani finances which assisted the wider military response. The BBME had a central role in Sultan Said's government administration from 1948, when it had been allowed to begin operating in Oman by the Sultan, and went on to have a key indirect role in the Dhofar conflict.[24] The BBME developed a strong influence with Sultan Said and his administration, eventually effectively administering the Sultan's privy purse and therefore acting as the de facto Treasury or central bank for the Sultan of Muscat and Oman's personal fortune, which was effectively one and the same as the country's wealth.[25] As such, the Sultan relied on the BBME to manage his financial affairs and it acted as an integral arm of the Omani state. The economic management of the early years of the Dhofar War, and even extending into Sultan Qaboos's reign, would not have been viable without this vital assistance in that the 'BBME continued to function as the central bank [of Oman] and managed the [country's] currency board, first established in 1972'.[26] The BBME was so influential that it administered the introduction of the Sultanate's new currency, the Sa'aidi Rial, and the phasing out of the Gulf Rupee in May 1970. Post-coup, the BBME fulfilled a similar, although diminished role as it had done previously until the creation of the Central Bank of Oman in 1974. It again, however, showed its influence and value to the Sultanate and the Dhofar campaign when it provided short-term loans in 1975 to stave off a financial crisis (facilitated by the spiralling war-related defence budget) in conjunction with a high-level commissioned study of the Sultanate's financial organization and status.[27] It also provided financial backing to the Omani government by extending credit to local companies receiving British exports, and to British companies contracted to undertake works for the Omani government, due in part to the financial mismanagement and widespread corruption of the latter, and in terms of governmental loans from other banks, hints of egregious corrupt practices.[28] This presented the situation where Oman's national finances were to a large extent, and further, for a majority of the eventually successful Dhofar COIN campaign, run by a private British company. Had Oman been left to default on its short-term loans, the potential resultant effect on the Dhofar War could have been far-reaching.

Unlike its modern independent status, the Bank of England (BoE) was an integral arm of the UK government apparatus at the time of the Dhofar War. Due to Sultan Qaboos's close partnership with the UK and allied to the lack of indigenous expertise, the British authorities, via the BoE, authorized and provided an important 'in-house' consultancy service to the Sultan. An experienced senior banking officer from the BoE served as the principal financial advisor to Qaboos from 1970 and all the way up to the creation of the Central Bank of Oman in 1974.[29] This arrangement afforded Britain significant oversight over economic policy and financial arrangements in Oman and, by default, over the war in Dhofar. The arrangement also contributed significantly to Oman's ability to conduct its affairs of state and thereby manage the economic aspects of the ever more costly war. This highlights another situation where strong British influence over Omani finances is clear. In this case, direct senior and high-level influence over Omani financial policy and planning by seconded BoE personnel from an arm of the British government apparatus is clear.

NON-KINETIC MILITARY AND INFORMAL SUPPORT

Another actor of significant UK economic influence on the Dhofar War was the majority-British-owned oil company PD(O). It had operated in Oman in one guise or another for decades and had become increasingly important over time to Sultan Said. This was initially through the raising of the Muscat and Oman Field Force (MOFF) in 1952, which reported to the Sultan but was created to protect PD(O) assets and personnel from potential tribal clashes. MOFF was fully paid for by the oil company but armed, trained, and officered by the UK government, before subsequently being incorporated into the state's military forces as the re-designated Oman Regiment (OR) in 1957.[30] This, as with BBME and Airwork Ltd. (with its RAF-related revolving door recruitment policy), is an example of the substantial links between the UK government and private business in overall financially related British dealings and influence in Oman. The central importance of PD(O) to Sultan Said personally, his regime, and to the country as a whole was cemented when the company discovered oil in July 1964.[31] When the necessary production facilities were completed, Oman's initial oil export took place in July 1967 when the container ship *Mosprince* departed the Sultanate for Japan.[32] From this point, PD(O) became intertwined with the fortunes of the Sultanate and indeed 'became part of the social and economic structure of Oman'.[33] From a negligible oil income before this point, its contribution to the Omani exchequer grew fortuitously to over £50 million in 1972, as the Dhofar War cost some £20 million to prosecute in the same year.[34] Despite the steep rise in cost of carrying out the Dhofar campaign in terms of GDP, Oman in part avoided a full economic crisis precisely because of the funds being secured from oil exports, and their substantial rise after the 1973 oil crisis. The by now Shell-backed PD(O) would continue contributing to the Omani national coffers throughout the Dhofar War and beyond, despite the Sultanate taking over a 60% share in the concession by 1974.[35] Largely as a result of the onset of oil income, the UK Treasury ended the old Zanzibar Subsidy payment, in effect making the ruler largely financially dependent on the workings and management of a private (partially now) UK-owned oil company and a British bank, so much so that 'By the late 1960s, two key business figures also dealt regularly with the Sultan: Peter Mason, the manager of the BBME in Muscat, and Francis Hughes, the managing director of PDO.'[36] The finances available for the Dhofar campaign and the management of such were, therefore, largely under

THE DHOFAR WAR

control by British individuals, and partially also even by the UK government at least until 1967, and were subsequently highly influenced by such actors throughout most of the war.

Although oil exploitation and therefore hydrocarbon-based income had begun under the reign of his father, this was expanded under Qaboos's rule. It was vital to help pay for the expansion of the SAF to conduct the Dhofar COIN campaign, as well as the necessary social and infrastructure development of the country post-1970. PD(O)-derived oil revenues, alongside the military and economic aid of Britain and later Oman's other allies, were key factors in achieving eventual campaign win as the cost of prosecuting the war increased to upwards of half of the Sultanate's GDP by 1971.[37] By 1969, oil income was forty times that of the total national income of the early 1960s, and was further boosted by oil price increases arising from the 1973 oil crisis.[38] Due primarily to oil income, Oman's national budget increased nearly fourfold from 1973 to 1974 and up to fivefold by 1975 (65.5 million Rials in 1973 to 325 million Rials in 1975), and this increased oil-facilitated national income, alongside the security-related benefits of the UK-devised and executed military campaign, enabled a large programme of internal investment.[39] As such, PD(O)'s indirect contribution to the war in Dhofar was, therefore, highly significant.

It can be observed, therefore, that the British government, as well as private UK institutions, helped to keep Oman solvent, even whilst the cost of the war in Dhofar was claiming ever higher levels of national wealth. Although the financial management, both during the conflict and in the post-war years, has been criticized (with cases even identified of misappropriation of funds by UK personnel), UK financial provision, via widespread government supplier credit cover provided via the Treasury's Export Credits Department, and expertise were central to Oman's ability to prevail in the COIN campaign.[40]

Alongside economic assistance, Britain was also instrumental in terms of personnel provision, which was central to conducting and winning the Dhofar War. This can be seen primarily in the guise of UK state civilian and military personnel, but also from a private British (both civilian and military) citizens' perspective. In the latter case, the most important were in terms of individuals contracted to work directly for the Sultanate. Key UK state-related civilian influence was exercised up to 1971 by the resident UK Consul-General in Oman, and in turn by the British Political Resident Persian Gulf (PRPG),

NON-KINETIC MILITARY AND INFORMAL SUPPORT

based in Bahrain. Such individuals were the 'eyes and ears' of the UK FO and government and helped develop and implement regional-wide as well as Oman-specific policy which had a direct bearing on the Dhofar War. It has also been suggested in war accounts that the UK FO and its emissaries were at least responsible for encouraging, if not assisting directly, in the organization of the 1970 coup, with all the previously described repercussions for the COIN campaign and eventual result.[41] After the British withdrawal East of Suez in 1971, these roles were defunct, the PRPG position was dissolved, and the Consul-General's position was upgraded to that of Ambassador. (Later Sir) Donald Hawley took up the role in 1971 and served throughout the war period until the last few months of 1975, when he handed over to Jim Treadwell. British diplomatic representatives were influential in assisting the Omani war effort and supporting the SAF, for instance with Hawley helping navigate the diplomatically tense Operation AQOOBA raids episode through the permitted use of UK contract officers only.[42] These representatives also undertook such a facilitation role whilst concurrently advancing UK interests in Oman in terms of trade, for example.[43] It is clear Hawley was heavily involved not only in diplomatically communicating on issues, but also being 'hands on' in many aspects of the war. These included, for example, being involved in UK military personnel provision, anti-propaganda efforts, and even specific operational aspects of the war including deconflicting RAF Salalah air operations and Iranian anti-aircraft guns in its vicinity and even start dates for military action.[44]

As a secondary-level influence, it can be observed that private British civilian personnel historically had an even more important role within Oman, its governance, and on the Dhofar War itself. During Sultan Said's reign, many of the most influential governmental jobs were held by British citizens, including the Director and Development Secretary of the Dhofar Development Board (Messrs. Pelly and Heber-Percy), a Petroleum Affairs Secretary (Maj. Hirst), and the Sultan's influential Private Secretary, former Royal Navy officer Jim MacLean.[45] Whilst this waned during Sultan Qaboos's reign, it remained strong and cumulatively played an important role in the run-up to, the conduct of, and eventual winning of the Dhofar War. The Sultan's top government and military administration historically involved a large expatriate British component, which had both an indirect and direct bearing on the

THE DHOFAR WAR

Table 6.2: Key British persons of influence in Oman during Dhofar War

PRPG (BAHRAIN)	CONSUL-GENERAL/ AMBASSADOR TO MUSCAT	SULTAN'S MILITARY SECRETARY/ DEFENCE SECRETARY	CSAF	DEPUTY CSAF
Sir William Luce (1961–66)	J.S.R. Duncan (1963–65)	P.R.M. Waterfield (1958–70)	Col. A.D. Lewis (1964–67)	Col (later Brig.) C.C. Maxwell (1958–76)
Sir Stewart Crawford (1966–70)	D.C. Carden (1965–69)	H.R.D. Oldman (1970–73)	Brig. C.W.B. Purdon (1967–70)	
Sir Geoffrey Arthur (1970–71)	D.G. Crawford (1969–71)	Position dissolved when Hugh Oldman retired in 1973— replaced by Omani Defence Minister and (British) Director-General of Defence Administration, R.F. Semple	Brig. J.D.C. Graham (1970–72)	
N/A from 1971 onwards as post dissolved due to withdrawal 'East of Suez'	D.F. Hawley (1971–75)		Maj. Gen. T.M. Creasey (1972–75)	
	J. Treadwell (1975–79)		Maj-Gen. K. Perkins (1975–77)	

Dhofar COIN campaign, from both a military and governmental perspective. To 1970, the Omani Military Secretary was Brig. Pat Waterfield, a UK citizen and former British army officer working privately for the Sultan.[46] If one discounts the Sultan himself, this represented a situation where the top defence-related job in the whole of the independent state of Muscat and Oman was held by a British citizen. This situation continued in 1970 via Col. Hugh Oldman in the re-titled position of 'Defence Secretary'. Although technically independent, both men had long associations with Oman and indeed the latter had actually served as the third CSAF as a regular British army officer seconded to Oman in the early 1960s.[47] Alongside others, including the Sultan's Private Secretary, Jim MacLean, and his Minister of Foreign Affairs Neil Innes, and with all bar a single one of his government ministers UK citizens, such influence greatly enhanced the deep and enduring linkages with the UK authorities and general Dhofar COIN campaign policy.[48]

The British-oriented advisory organization to the ruler, allied to the fact that Sultan Said effectively retired to his Salalah palace in the late 1950s, meant that the influence of his UK advisors was extensive. As an example, during the early phase of the war, the UK seconded CSAF, Col. Tony Lewis, operated his British-officered SAF units through receiving orders from the Sultan's Muscat-based British Military Secretary, who himself only spoke to the Sultan in Salalah once per week via radio telephone to receive his own orders.[49] This situation clearly indicates the potential for Britain to influence, manipulate, or control the Dhofar campaign, and indeed some Omanis even adhered to the rumour that the Sultan was actually dead and Britain was secretly running the country.[50] This situation was further reinforced by the presence of the PRPG, as well as the Commander British Forces Gulf (CBFG), based in Bahrain up to 1971, and through the resident British Consul-General in Muscat (later upgraded to Ambassador), with whom the CSAF and the Military Secretary were in regular work-related and social contact.

In addition to these influential personnel, there were other high-profile Britons in Oman such as the long-time personal advisor to the Sultan, Maj. Leslie Chauncy.[51] He was a previous (post-war) UK Consul-General to Muscat and returned in a private capacity to serve the Sultan in 1961. Chauncy also arranged UK-based schooling for the then Crown Prince Qaboos, as well as a host family in rural Suffolk in preparation for attendance of the Royal Military Academy Sandhurst and further service with the British Army.[52] Chauncy also accompanied Qaboos on his global educational trip prior to returning to Oman, thus completing the Crown Prince's anglicization and basic training for future high office. This, in turn, acted as a UK insurance policy to both mould future succession to fit with British interests and provide a replacement for the incumbent if necessary. In addition, from a developmental perspective, noted soldier, explorer, and diplomat Sir Hugh Boustead was seconded by the British government to Sultan Said in the late 1950s as his primary development advisor. With a modest annual budget of approximately £250,000 and a tenure lasting only three years, Boustead and subsequently his successors had both a thankless and nigh on impossible task due to the Sultan's general disinterest in such matters.[53] Although producing results in terms of Omani development that were lower than hoped for by UK authorities, the example does, however, illustrate another aspect of London's influence over Omani internal policy and social and economic development.[54]

The influence of British military personnel in Oman and on the Dhofar COIN campaign was also one of the most important factors in securing the 1975 insurgent defeat. The prime UK influence was via British state military personnel, in the guise of seconded officers. A secondary level, but still important contribution was that made by private UK citizens as SAF contract officers. There were even cases of those (including Hugh Oldman) who served in both capacities, starting as LSP, then returning to work on private contract, with the infamous Timothy Landon perhaps the most influential example in terms of the war's outcome.

From its conception, the head of the SAF during the Dhofar War was always a British seconded officer. This was a result of the original 1958 'Exchange of Letters' between the British and Omani governments. The first incumbent was the experienced wartime officer and former SAS and Special Operations Executive (SOE) member, Col. David Smiley. Although loyally working for the Sultan and his interests, the incumbent of the CSAF position remained technically under orders from the British army command and ultimately therefore the UK government; with loyalty lying with his 'Queen and Country'.[55] An example of this is when ex-SAS soldier Maj. Johnny Cooper was released in 1963 by then CSAF Col. Hugh Oldman on fictional compassionate leave from his role as the second-in-command of the Muscat Regiment to undertake deniable covert operations in North Yemen, commanding British mercenaries, in full knowledge of the British government, and when returning some three years later was 'pardoned' by the Sultan's Military Secretary, Briton Brig. Waterfield, and returned to his previous role and to service in the Dhofar War.[56] A further illustration of how dominant British influence was in the SAF is Brig. Corran Purdon's recollection of the scene when he arrived to take over as CSAF in 1967, where he was met on arrival by a coterie of Britons including the Military Secretary, the incumbent CSAF, Deputy CSAF,

NON-KINETIC MILITARY AND INFORMAL SUPPORT

and Commander SOAF.[57] Purdon further highlights how nearly all staff officers at the SAF headquarters were either seconded or contract UK personnel, emphasizing the almost complete (direct British state or UK-national) control or influence over the SAF, the conduct of the Dhofar campaign, and ultimately forging the eventual victory.[58]

Britain's primary, state-level contribution to the Dhofar War in terms of personnel was the LSP officers sent to serve in the SAF as part of the 'Exchange of Letters' agreements. Under the terms of the original agreement, Britain eventually agreed to supply twenty-four officers (twenty-three officers in place by October 1958) ranging in rank from colonel to captain.[59] These British officers would remain as serving UK military personnel but would also serve the Sultan of Oman in his armed forces, and under its distinct chain of command. The seconded colonel (subsequently upgraded to brigadier, then to major-general) supplied would act as the CSAF and would serve the Sultan and his interests directly, originally working through the (British) Omani Military Secretary. These arrangements were expanded upon throughout the war, with an increase in British LSP officers and NCOs to Oman to fifty-two by June 1970, to eighty-seven in 1971, and increased substantially further to 194 individuals by 1974.[60] This meant that the SAF leadership largely comprised British seconded military personnel throughout the war.

As such, Britain not only supplied the CSAF, but all the key regimental unit heads and many of the junior officers who served in the SAF's key infantry units. This had a significant effect on the Dhofar conflict as the theatre strategy was conceived by the CSAF and his British staff but enacted through the seconded chain of command. The commander of forces on the ground in Dhofar was also always a British officer, initially the CO of the resident SAF battalion on rotation, and then became a fixed staff officer position in January 1971 when the new senior officer, HQ Dhofar (Col. Mike Harvey), took command.[61] Later this position was upgraded to a brigadier-level command and filled by Brig. Jack Fletcher in 1972 and finally by Brig. John Akehurst in August 1974, illustrating the near-total dominance of the Dhofar War theatre's SAF command by UK officers. In addition, regimental officers in all combat units were almost exclusively British, with the CO and second-in-command of each infantry regiment a seconded officer and a UK officer on contract, respectively. This organization had the effect of securing a direct and unbroken British controlled (either private citizen or army personnel) chain of command from CSAF to junior regimental officer level within the SAF.

Bar small numbers of junior loaned Indian and Pakistani medical or technical officers, due to the both numerically limited and unstructured Omani officer corps, the SAF officer leadership was almost fully dependent on British LSP and UK contract officers under Sultan Said, and therefore for over half the war's duration.[62] An indication also of the value placed on their services as rendered during the war subsequently by Sultan Qaboos is that the service heads and senior staff officers of the Omani military remained British long after the war officially ended in 1975. Officers such as Brig. Peter Thwaites (formerly CO of MR), Lt. Gen. John Watts (former CO 22 SAS and author of the instrumental 'Watts Plan'), and Gen. Sir Tim Creasey (CSAF 1972–1975) all returned in senior roles in the 1970s and 1980s within the Omani military command structure in either a contract or seconded capacity.[63] The top Omani service heads were not fully Omanized until 1990, when the final senior British officers (Air Marshall Sir Erik Bennett and Rear-Admiral Hugh Balfour) left their posts and handed over responsibilities to Omani officers.[64] This situation of dominance by British personnel, especially from a military or security perspective, endured throughout the war, and continued long after its conclusion also as:

> Until the Dhofar rebellion ceased to represent a direct threat for the regime, in the early 1980s, all the high-ranking army officers and the vast majority of sensitive positions in the Security, Immigration, Police and Intelligence departments were held by British staff. In 1985 almost 1,500 British citizens served in the Omani army.[65]

In addition to general factors discussed, the specific example of Timothy Landon was a special case of the influence of British personnel over the Dhofar War. As such it is necessary to discuss Landon's case in some depth as an illustration of the true extent of British influence both on and within the Omani regime. Landon was a notable example of British military personnel influence, not only returning as a contract officer after LSP service, but later occupying a central and highly influential role in the Omani administration as a civilian. Landon became a high-ranking advisor to the new Sultan after the 1970 coup and later became known as the 'White Sultan' due to his status as one of Qaboos's closest confidants, eventually rising to brigadier rank within

NON-KINETIC MILITARY AND INFORMAL SUPPORT

the SAF.[66] Landon's example also serves to illustrate the important, and sometimes blurred division that existed between UK state support via LSP and the influence of private British citizen contract officers, with no other Briton arguably having more indirect impact on the trajectory and outcome of the Dhofar War. Landon's impact on the Dhofar War and Oman in general was largely due to his influence on the planning and eventual execution of the 1970 coup. Starting as a seconded junior infantry officer in the SAF's Muscat Regiment, he eventually specialized in intelligence-related matters as a Desert Intelligence Officer, and as one of few British officers who could speak the Jebali language, he quickly established himself as a prominent intelligence fixture in Dhofar, serving in this capacity from 1968 to 1970.[67] Becoming a close associate of Bareik bin Mahood, the son of the Wali of Dhofar, Landon also had access to Crown Prince Qaboos as one of the few people allowed to visit him, by orders of the Sultan, in his accommodation near the main palace in Salalah where he was kept under virtual house arrest.[68] This was largely due to the personal influence he had with Qaboos as a fellow cadet at Sandhurst and with whom he is said to have shared a study and protected from the widespread bullying of 'foreign' officers which created a lasting bond between the two men and also 'created a debt of honour' which benefitted Landon throughout his time and career in Oman.[69] Landon was a key player in the organization of the coup by acting as a go-between alongside Bareik between Qaboos and other influential personnel such as the Military Secretary, Hugh Oldman, and various trusted military officers such as the Desert Regiment's Lt. Col. Turnhill and Malcolm Dennison, the senior SAF intelligence officer.[70] As such, Landon was likely part of the small group of individuals who planned Sultan Said's overthrow; indeed, as famed explorer and former SAS and SAF soldier Ranulph Fiennes states: 'whilst Tim was telling me what to do, and I really liked Tim, I didn't realize that he was planning to get rid of my boss. And the only reason he could do that was because he was a good friend at Sandhurst of Qaboos.'[71] Landon is also said to have accompanied those who entered the palace on 23 July 1970 to remove Sultan Said from power and place Qaboos on the throne.[72]

After the coup, Landon remained a close confidant of Qaboos, and his career blossomed as a result. He left the British Army, and became the Sultan's aide-de-camp, then equerry (on contract to the SAF), then subsequently his most trusted personal advisor. Landon's promotions and financial success followed as Qaboos increasingly took to his new role and reinforced his position. Landon was involved in a wide portfolio of matters from ministerial-level appointments, setting up of government departments (including the external intelligence service), military procurement, and liaison with business contacts, as well as Omani allies such as Iran and his erstwhile employer, the British government via the UK Ambassador, the CSAF, and others, and even the Sultan's itinerary.[73] Landon's sway in government can be illustrated by his national 'gatekeeper' role in terms of the country's finances and departmental budgets, where he was, for example, influential in helping to restructure Omani debt and loans with both local and foreign banks such as BBME and Union de Banques Arabes et Françaises (UBAF).[74] This was due to his trusted status and less to do with his knowledge of economics. Importantly, he was instrumental in introducing non-British individuals to the Omani economic scene, including Robert Anderson and American companies as well as the individuals labelled the 'Muscat Mafia' who became powerful advisors in their own right to the Sultan, and it was stated: 'There is now little doubt that he [Landon] is the "Mafia's [sic] man in Oman".'[75] Despite his relative inexperience in military matters, Landon also had a level of influence over the conduct of the war. This is illustrated through his involvement in behind-the-scenes decision-making on issues as wide as cross-border actions by SAF in the PDRY, the potential use of seconded Sudanese troops in Dhofar, and even attempts to introduce napalm into the SOAF's inventory despite it being a potential 'emotive and political hot potato'.[76]

Landon therefore became very influential, and was trusted completely by Qaboos. It was stated that he 'occupies a powerful position in the government; Landon sometimes refers to himself as a Minister! [sic]' and was essentially 'the most powerful man in the kingdom after its ruler'.[77] Britain's first Ambassador to Oman, Donald Hawley, stated: 'Col. Landon acts on behalf of the Sultan, and in many matters his office is The [sic] Palace office in Muscat', adding that 'he is feared and disliked by many Omanis, both officials and ministers.'[78]

Landon reportedly also received a fixed income from Oman's oil revenue via Qaboos for his key assistance in relation to the coup.[79] In addition, his position allowed him influence over arms deals whilst Oman was expanding its military capability; British assessments believed that after his initial almost

NON-KINETIC MILITARY AND INFORMAL SUPPORT

'missionary zeal' towards Qaboos and Oman, his integrity slipped somewhat and he joined the widespread practice of benefitting personally from government contracts and expenditure and has 'used his position to benefit likewise'.[80] Through his association with Oman and Sultan Qaboos and business deals often on behalf of, or with the ruler, Landon eventually amassed a fortune of over £500 million as an arms and oil broker to become one of the largest landowners and wealthiest individuals in the UK.[81] Later, when he left Oman, he remained registered as an official 'counsellor' at the Omani Embassy in London (travelling on an Omani diplomatic passport), worked as an arms dealer, and was involved in lucrative, albeit somewhat questionable oil deals between Omani companies and South Africa and Rhodesia (now Zimbabwe) which potentially circumvented sanction regimes.[82] In addition, Landon was even received at 10 Downing Street to discuss the issue of the successor to General Tim Creasey as the Sultanate's Chief of Defence Staff in 1984, with Landon having been promoted to the Omani military rank of brigadier.[83] All such activities were highly lucrative and Landon was named the UK's 98th richest person in the *Sunday Times* newspaper in 2002.[84] As a result of this wealth generation, he purchased stately homes, grouse moors, was able to marry into European royalty, and additionally was awarded an honorary knighthood.[85] On top of this, Landon even reportedly received a yearly birthday gift of £1 million from the Sultan up to his death due to cancer in 2007.[86]

As one of the most influential Britons in Omani affairs during the Dhofar War and beyond, Landon 'embodied' the small group of prominent UK citizens who held favour in the Sultan's court.[87] Although an exceptional case, and despite often being in disagreement with UK officials in his later contractor role and being deemed of only average intellect, he was considered 'no fool and shows on occasions an instinctive grasp of the essentials of a problem', making him a useful, if somewhat problematical, point of contact for UK officials seeking access to the upper levels of the Omani administration.[88] In short, his inexperience, lack of judgement, and somewhat arrogant demeanour was tolerated by UK officials, as: 'We would probably not enjoy our access to the Sultan's and Omani thinking with another in his place.'[89]

Landon's case illustrates the breadth and depth and sometimes blurred issue of UK influence on Omani affairs and the circumstances leading to the overall Dhofar campaign win. The sentiment was not lost on Sultan Said. It was reported that shortly before his death in 1972 whilst living in exile at London's prestigious Dorchester hotel, the former Sultan was asked if he held any regrets about the turn of events. 'Yes,' he replied. 'I should have had Landon shot.'[90]

Another example of key British ex-military influence in Oman is the case of Anthony Ashworth. He will be mentioned only briefly as his appointment and ongoing influence illustrates the power and influence of Tim Landon; although he did contribute to the Dhofar War effort as a Foreign Office 'information' or intelligence officer, his main impact came later. A former cavalryman like Landon, Ashworth was moved from the Beirut to the Muscat Embassy with full knowledge of the then Foreign Secretary, James Callaghan and was seconded to work with Sir Graham Bell on his key report on future Dhofar development in 1974.[91] Impressed with his information management skills, Landon recruited him to the Sultan's employment, officially as an advisor to the Minister of Information.[92] Over time, Ashworth carved himself a unique role where he controlled all external press relations, had power over ministers, and essentially forged and protected with vigour the external image of Oman. Journalists were 'groomed' with free visits to the Sultanate to write favourable articles, others who did not stick to the official narrative were persuaded to rewrite pieces or were sometimes banned from the country.[93] A close advisor to the Sultan, like Landon he was both feared and disliked by many, in Ashworth's case as a behind-the-scenes 'gatekeeper' who had the Sultan's authority and therefore the power to control the narrative from ministers and the media in Oman for over twenty years, and was often referred to within Oman simply as 'God'.[94]

Although of secondary importance to direct state LSP assistance, the provision of UK SAF contract personnel, mainly in the form of officers with service in the UK or British Indian army or colonial police forces, was another war-winning factor. These personnel were largely recruited, alongside its engineering support role for SOAF, through Airwork Ltd., a private British company with established links with the UK military and government.[95] Numerically, the contribution of such personnel was significant, as throughout the Dhofar War there were consistently more UK SAF contract officers than seconded LSP, with figures between 50 and 100% greater with, on average, up to 300 contractor officers deployed in theatre from 1970, serving predominantly in the army and air force.[96] Whilst seconded LSP officers were considered 'the professionals', those on direct contract often provided valuable experience and were

NON-KINETIC MILITARY AND INFORMAL SUPPORT

the backbone of the officer corps commanding units above platoon level.[97] As such, these personnel provided the everyday authority and command within SAF units, and ensured continuity in knowledge and service which could not necessarily be provided by LSP officers. This was because junior seconded officers usually just served approximately nineteen months in theatre, with those above major for up to three years only.[98] From the senior contract officer (DCSAF, Col. Colin Maxwell) down, such personnel tended to stay longer in Oman, often accumulating more wartime service than their LSP colleagues, and as such provided vital continuity as well as military knowledge and experience of the country and specific Dhofar theatre. As an example, Maxwell served in post for eighteen years and throughout the whole war, whilst LSP CSAFs tended to serve two or three-year assignments only.[99] Combined, this synergistic arrangement between officer designations ensured that almost every SAF command position was in British personnel hands, including, importantly for combat operations, the second-in-command of each infantry regiment, who by convention was a contract officer. It also ensured near-complete British control over military policy, operations, and tactics which enabled flexibility to best utilize personnel of either designation in the war. Contract personnel also proved vital for when LSP were not permitted to take part in activities which may have potentially harmed UK interests. Brig. Graham was shown a secret UK government directive by Amb. Hawley which forbade use of LSP officers outside Oman, so actions such as the Operation AQOOBA airstrikes on Hauf in PDRY territory and similarly such manoeuvres in 1974–1975 were carried out by contract pilots only, and the orders for the retaliatory strikes in 1972 were also signed off by the contractor DCSAF to avoid Brig. Graham contributing to directly violating the protocol.[100] Ex-SAS contract personnel also led a Mahra Firqa force in cross-PDRY border guerrilla operations including the raid on the Sinau fort, located approximately 80 miles across the border in PDRY territory.[101] Firqa forces in general were also largely trained and led on operations by ex-SAS SAF contractor personnel from 1972, when responsibility for such units transferred to the Sultan's forces.[102]

Although contract personnel were not supplied directly by the UK government, they were largely trained ex-officers of the British armed forces and the former had strong links with Airwork Ltd, the primary contracting agency for such personnel. In addition, therefore, to the important task of keeping the

SOAF's fighter and assorted transport aircraft flight and combat-ready, the company also had key recruiting role in the Sultanate, acting as main agents for the supply of SAF contract personnel.[103] Airwork had significant links to the British military and government through domestic flight training contracts and numerous contracts abroad, including in Saudi Arabia, which transpired due to at least tacit UK governmental support.[104] Its Omani contract was relatively small in terms of its overall business and in the Middle East in particular. The company's relationship, however, with elements of the British establishment meant a relatively high level of UK indirect influence on the control of personnel supply, as well as SOAF combat capability to the war effort.[105]

It can therefore be seen that a large proportion of the SAF military chain of command from the CSAF and DCSAF, to HQ staff officers to regimental COs and officers before, during, and for a significant period after the Dhofar War were seconded British personnel or UK contractor citizens. That the war was won in Oman is testament to these British leaders at all levels within the SAF regardless of contractual status, as well as civilian personnel serving as UK state representatives in Oman and the region, or those UK citizens engaged in Sultanate government service on private contract. As highlighted in Qaboos-era briefing notes for contract military personnel, the situation is summed up succinctly: 'The SAF are [sic] commanded by a seconded British Army officer' and 'The army is [led and] trained predominantly by British army officers in British military techniques adjusted to meet local needs and customs, and the air force is manned by RAF and contract pilots and maintained by British engineers.'[106]

British officers were not, however, the only foreign personnel serving in the SAF. There were also numerous administrative, technical officers, or medical personnel of junior rank seconded from both India and Pakistan. In addition, later in the war, the SAF and the COIN campaign in general were bolstered by further foreign troops from Iran, Jordan, and the UAE. In the early days of the war, the SAF's medical officers were usually Indian personnel who played a significant practical as well as morale-boosting role within the force.[107] Medical facilities in general were few and far between and were as primitive as the means of evacuation off the Jebel for the seriously wounded (mule-back), meaning survivability of such wounds was negatively affected. Soldiers from India and Pakistan were also seconded and served as stores clerks and technicians in vehicle maintenance workshops, for example, which are important roles in any armed force. Such personnel, while contributing valuable service to the SAF and the overall war effort, were both junior in terms of leadership and relatively few in number, and the main non-British contributions, and therefore the overall war, were from Iran, Jordan, and to a lesser extent the UAE, from 1972.

Although not joining COIN forces in Oman until 1972 and 1974 respectively, Iranian, and Jordanian forces especially, provided the manpower and equipment to allow large-scale SAF offensives and shorten the war. By 1975, such forces contributed over a third of total SAF combat forces in Dhofar.[108] As such, they provided much-needed manpower directly for offensive operations or to release SAF troops for combat duties in Dhofar which Britain could or would not provide. An example of the former was the full reopening and securing of the strategically important Midway Road from three unbroken years of insurgent control by Iranian forces in December 1973. Additionally, in December 1974, a large Iranian force moved south towards Rakhyut, which cleared resistance in the area and re-took the town for government forces. This ended five years of insurgent control with facilities in the town providing the PFLOAG's regional administrative centre. Iranian and Jordanian troops were also used to patrol and keep a government-controlled presence on the Midway Road, which released SAF units for the front line farther west in the province. A similar role was also fulfilled by UAE troops in October 1973, when two rifle companies of the Abu Dhabi Defence Force (ADDF) were deployed to northern Oman (primarily Sohar) to relieve Oman Gendarmerie troops on static guard duties so that the latter could undertake front-line deployments in Dhofar (a similar ADDF deployment occurred from November 1974).[109] Although largely symbolic, this deployment underlined the growing regional advocacy for Qaboos, which translated into practical support for the Dhofar War effort.

Such non-UK foreign troop deployments played an important role in assisting the SAF and Oman to eventually prevail in the Dhofar War. As a result, some historical accounts purport that non-UK forces, and especially the Iranians, were actually the prime movers in enabling the war to be won. Examples include comments such as that 'Iranian firepower thwarted PFLOAG's regular attacks on the forces garrisoning the [Midway] road [in 1973] and accomplished an important mission that Oman's overstretched forces could not', and the Dhofar War result being 'actually an international victory', as

THE DHOFAR WAR

opposed to a largely British-facilitated outcome.[110] Whilst this was the case to a certain extent, and non-British military forces enabled the war to be concluded earlier through force of numbers, and although working under their own internal commands, all such forces were still under CSAF operational control.[111] These forces were therefore utilized in Oman and Dhofar as the CSAF—as a British LSP officer—saw fit.[112] Questions of quality regarding the training, ability, and effectiveness of the Iranian troops (for instance on the Midway Road) meant they were often utilized specifically by the CSAF on less important or potentially sensitive duties where sheer numbers of troops would tell.[113] As such, they were often deployed away from key operations where more reliable SAF and British forces could better control proceedings and their outcomes. An example of this is the December 1974 Sherishitti Caves operation, where the Iranian forces were diverted by the CSAF to another task (to capture Rakhyut) due to high casualties and fears they were not up to the task.[114]

Often overlooked, the contribution of the SAF's Omani and directly recruited Baluchi soldiers and NCOs (as distinct from seconded Pakistani personnel) was also a significant factor in the Dhofari insurgent defeat. Without their input, the war quite simply could not have been won. Indeed, it has been stated that 'the main "element of victory" [in Dhofar] was actually the SAF [itself]'.[115] In terms of personnel numbers, the SAF was substantially increased in size after the 1970 coup and tripled in size in less than two years to over 10,000 men.[116] Mainly Baluchi and Omani in origin, these troops helped even the odds when deployed against approximately 2,000 full-time or front-line insurgents and up to 4,000 supporting PFLOAG ad hoc militia by 1971.[117] By 1975, when Iranian, Jordanian, and regular British forces had joined the campaign, Omani and Baluch SAF troops still comprised approximately half of Omani COIN forces, and the impact of such troops should not be overlooked.[118] Up until 1970 and therefore for the first five years of the war, excluding the British seconded or contract officers, these men effectively comprised the entire COIN ground fighting force in Dhofar, and some historical accounts credit them also with being primarily responsible for defeating PFLOAG from 1971 to 1975.[119]

Whilst there is no doubting the contribution of such troops, especially in the early years of the war, and their dedication and sacrifice towards achieving victory, the reality is more nuanced. In all military campaigns, soldiers need

NON-KINETIC MILITARY AND INFORMAL SUPPORT

to be effectively led. In Dhofar, this was the role of the British seconded and contract officers and NCOs of the SAF, wherever embedded. The British role in the war was to galvanize such latent potential and ability offered by the Omani and Baluchi soldiers of the SAF and forge it into effective fighting units to the benefit of the SAF's overall capability. This was done not only with SAF units but also with the Firqa and was replicated within deployed regular UK forces. This process was often difficult and was not, as initially with the Firqa, always successful, but the victory was achieved eventually in 1975 due primarily to such British leadership. With the rise in overall non-British numbers from 1972, the UK's relative wartime numerical contribution to operations reduced significantly as per the 'sliding scale of influence' framework. British officers, however, remained in command of the SAF from the CSAF down to all combat units. Such forces were ultimately, therefore, under the command of UK personnel. In this respect, the Dhofar War was not a UK campaign as such, but it was certainly a British, or British-inspired win.

Another area of unparalleled non-kinetic military support provided by Britain was in the sphere of training. Whilst other countries provided equipment, supplies, and even troops to be utilized in the Dhofar War, it was the martial training provided by British personnel which converted the raw military personnel numbers available into combat, and therefore war-winning performance. New SAF recruits, whether Omani or from Baluchistan, were trained in British-run establishments; primarily the Ghalla training depot, located near Muscat. Here, new recruits underwent basic military training and were turned into operational assets under the watchful eye of the establishment's UK officers and NCOs. Although British officers had always overseen in-house training in the SAF's individual regiments and units, to train sufficient troops during the post-coup SAF expansion phase, extra professional UK expertise was required. This came in the form of regular British military personnel or units brought in to cope with the increased training demands to prepare the new troops for combat.[120] The Ghalla-based SAF soldier training depot was expanded and boosted by visiting instructional teams of Royal Marines and British army units from the closest UK military bases at Bahrain and Sharjah (to 1971) and the sovereign base areas located on the island of Cyprus, in addition to a number of Jordanian officers.[121]

Under the rule of Sultan Said, the selection and formal training of Omani or Baluchi SAF officers was not permitted, but this changed under Qaboos.

167

As highlighted previously, Omani and a small number of Baluchi officers did exist, but all were field commissions to junior rank only, and they were not allowed to command troops directly. This was primarily because of Sultan Said's fear of a military coup against him by local officers, as had happened elsewhere in the Middle East, including Egypt. Post-coup, under Sultan Qaboos, the British plan to increase Omani and Baluchi organic officer capability was implemented. To address the non-British officer training requirement, and as part of the Omanization plan put into place and managed by Col. Maxwell as DCSAF, an officer training wing was also established at Ghalla in 1971 and run by a British officer, Capt. David Baxter.[122] Although operated with minimal facilities and 'under pretty austere conditions', the new and very basic Omani Sandhurst equivalent quickly proved successful.[123] Similarly, while not permitted under Sultan Said, a conventional career structure for new Omani officers was mapped and established. By 1972, approximately 100 officers of Omani or Baluchi origin had either passed out as commissioned officers or were based abroad attending high-profile foreign military training academies.[124] Although the new British-devised and implemented Omani officer training programme under the DCSAF could be considered war-related progress, a boost for force morale and vital for SAF development in the longer term, the number of Omani officers trained and serving in the SAF was relatively small. Such efforts had limited effect at the strategic or operational level of leadership, again emphasizing the British influence over the Dhofar COIN campaign. British officers therefore provided virtually all the key trained SAF officer manpower for the duration of the Dhofar War.

Once dispersed to their allocated regiments, the in-unit professional training for recruits and latterly for junior officers was also the responsibility of the unit's British officers. Responsibility for teaching tactics, unit procedures, and diffusing the knowledge gained from professional military experience was carried out in units under the control of UK officers and was 'necessarily a long-term measure' due to the absence of engrained or widespread modern military knowledge.[125] This was especially important for pre-deployment training, as highlighted by ex-SAS soldier (later Sir) Ranulph Fiennes as the officer commanding the MR's Recce Platoon in the late 1960s. He remarked: 'The resulting drills were not, so as far as I know, present in any military textbook. They stemmed from common sense reactions to the emergency

NON-KINETIC MILITARY AND INFORMAL SUPPORT

situations likely to occur in Dhofar.'[126] This applied for existing members of units such as an infantry regiments, but especially to new members who had never served in Dhofar or a live combat situation.

On balance, the most important in-unit training role with impact on the Dhofar conflict was that undertaken by the SAS regiment. In addition to the urgent and vital task of training the new Sultan's bodyguard, SAS forces undertook training with SAF infantry regiments in northern Oman before Dhofar deployments to sharpen their tactical and weapons skills before engaging in combat operations.[127] This meant standard SAF infantry units were trained in skill sets by the most accomplished and highly trained soldiers in the UK military in preparation for COIN operations. Even more important was the role of the SAS in training and later leading the Firqa units. By the end of the Dhofar War, these numerous individual and tribally homogenous units numbered some 1,800 individuals; all trained and led in operations by members of the SAS under the official BATT pseudonym, then later under direct SAF operational control.[128]

At the tactical level, the SAS men allocated to the Firqa lived with and worked alongside their trainees in basic settings and moulded such units with patience and skill, as the SAS had done in previous COIN campaigns such as in Brunei/Borneo and Malaya with indigenous tribesmen. The SAS provided everything required for the Firqa units, ranging from basic military skills training to weapons instruction. On operations, the SAS even provided their rations and ammunition and, most crucially, leadership. The natural skills of the tribesmen were honed into effective units via SAS training and mentoring and then employed to the benefit of the COIN campaign and often to a higher level than standard SAF troops.[129] Whilst the problems and frustrations created by the Firqa due to ill-discipline and self-interest are well-documented, they were also invaluable to the COIN campaign.[130] They created a bridge between the insurgents and the SAF which non-Jebalis could simply not replicate. In terms of operational impact, the Firqa were the 'most important Government department to be created to win the war', and the central British role, via the SAS, in facilitating this is clear.[131] To turn individualistic, illiterate tribesmen via tailored, non-orthodox training, and patience into a war-winning organization by the SAS was a key British war effort contribution and would have been impossible without such highly experienced SF personnel. This is illustrated in that when responsibility for the Firqa transferred to the SAF in 1972, it was ex-SAS soldiers on private contract to the SAF who largely continued this training and liaison role.[132] UK influence over the creation and training as well as leading the Firqa forces was, therefore, total. Without the SAS's ability to mould effective units from SEPs and their kinsmen, it is likely that the war would have lasted longer, without a sizeable weakening of insurgent resolve and grip on the Jebel and its population.

In addition to the factor of key personnel supply, the most important contribution in terms of war materiel provision for the duration of the conflict came from the British state, and principally via the UK Ministry of Defence (MOD). As a secondary-level effect, private UK companies also had a central role to play, especially earlier in the war, in material provision. Other countries such as Iran also provided significant amounts of supplies in the latter years of the war, but the SAF, and therefore UK control of logistics was required to operationalize and utilize such materials. As such, the overall UK role from this perspective was the most important of any nation's influence on the winning of the Dhofar War. Britain provided the bulk of Omani war supplies for the first seven years of the decade-long conflict (largely through sales), which enabled the Dhofar campaign to be fought in the first place. This also enabled defeat to be avoided and the military line held for future successes starting with the return to offensive operations in 1971. Britain provisioned Oman to the greatest extent possible without being detrimental to its interests. This self-imposed limitation was even sidestepped on occasion for the war effort with, for example, the entire British army reserve war stock of ammunition being utilized to support UK objectives in Oman as part of the SAS's Operation STORM.[133] Although not the whole spectrum of war supplies, as an indication of the dominance of British provision of such materials during the war, it can be seen that Britain was virtually the only supplier of arms to Oman until 1971, the largest provider each year for the Dhofar War except for 1966 and 1972, and with the largest cumulative supply figures for any country.[134] British provision of arms to Oman for the Dhofar conflict was therefore greater than all other countries combined.

As a secondary-level effect, Britain also had significant influence over Oman and the Sultan from a commercial business perspective, which affected control over aspects of the early Dhofar campaign. Charles Kendall was the Director

Table 6.3: Arms exports to Sultanate of Oman during Dhofar War
(sipri tivs—millions)

YEAR	UK SUPPLIED	IRAN SUPPLIED	JORDAN SUPPLIED	OTHER (SPECIFY)
1965	1	N/A	N/A	N/A
1966	N/A	N/A	N/A	2 (USA)
1967	7	N/A	N/A	N/A
1968	5	N/A	N/A	N/A
1969	36	N/A	N/A	N/A
1970	15	N/A	N/A	11 (Canada)
1971	35	N/A	N/A	24 (Italy), 1 (USA)
1972	3	6	N/A	2 (Saudi Arabia)
1973	57	6	N/A	8 (Canada),
1974	36	N/A	N/A	13 (Italy), 9 (Netherlands), 8 (UAE)
1975	70	N/A	50	34 (USA), 14 (Netherlands), 13 (Italy), 1 (Switzerland)
TOTAL	265	12	50	140

Source: SIPRI Arms Transfers Database: https://www.sipri.org/ [accessed 22 April 2023]

of London-based Kendall & Sons (chandlery) and was also described as 'Oman's only "diplomatic representative" overseas', being appointed as the Sultanate's official Consul in London by Sultan Said in 1964.[135] Further to this, Kendall's acted as the primary supplying agent to the Sultanate for defence sales procurement and regularly liaised with the UK MOD and the Omani Military Secretary on such issues.[136] Archival documents show large-scale sales of equipment to Oman via Kendall's (and extensive communication between the company, the FCO Arabian Department, MOD, and Omani Defence Department) for both general and more specific Dhofar War use.[137] This illustrates the importance of Kendall and his firm both to Oman and for Britain in supplying the SAF with military equipment, enabling the war to be prosecuted from 1965 and potential defeat at the hands of the Adoo to be avoided. This importance also

THE DHOFAR WAR

made a return to the offensive in 1971 and future defeat of the insurgents a possibility, and all long before subsequent non-UK foreign supplies were available to Oman. This situation also highlights the integral nature of the secondary-level impact of the private sector on the ability of Britain to provide war supplies to Oman. As such, it emphasizes the close and sometimes blurred nature of the role of a private UK entity with governmental agencies in terms of such provision. The combined effect of primary governmental and secondary private company UK entities in terms of war supplies provision to Oman was, therefore, key and had a direct influence on the Sultanate's capability to both conduct and win the Dhofar COIN campaign.

Concerning war-related equipment and materials, it was not just in terms of arms sales or provision that Britain assisted Oman during the Dhofar campaign. There was also the loan of UK state assets, made available for theatre service, in addition to formally deployed units. Two key examples of such provision were the loan of RAF helicopters and the use of Royal Fleet Auxiliary (RFA) ships for helicopter operations in support of the key SAF Sarfait position in western Dhofar and Hornbeam Line construction. In early 1973, the RN positioned an RFA vessel off Dhofar to enable its helicopter landing pad and maintenance facilities to be utilized by the aircraft delivering supplies to sustain the beleaguered Sarfait position.[138] The troops of the Sarfait garrison were completely dependent on such helicopter-borne supplies for survival since the position was established in 1972. Due to the urgent need for such supplies, including all water and ammunition requirements, helicopters were on round-the-clock duty to supply the garrison, with the attendant operational wear and tear and potential combat damage. The use of the RFA platform was like a localized offshore base and was a significant source of British support to the SOAF and therefore to Oman during the war. Likewise, the loan of British helicopters was also a great boost to SOAF capability. Prior to the 1974 loan, the SOAF was only able to operate three Italian-made Augusta Bell 205s, as ordered with the permission of Sultan Said in 1969 and delivered after the coup.[139] Four UK RAF Wessex helicopters plus their pilots and support crews were loaned to the SOAF, which both almost doubled the supply availability to help sustain the Sarfait position and assisted with Hornbeam Line construction efforts by British Royal Engineers.[140] The Hornbeam Line was an integral part of the practical theatre 'blocking line' strategy, and the Sarfait position

NON-KINETIC MILITARY AND INFORMAL SUPPORT

had symbolic value. Although difficult, and indeed hazardous to supply, withdrawal from the position near the PDRY border was not a realistic option due to its symbolic value of the SAF's capability and resolve. Sultan Qaboos also actually later refused Maj. Gen. Creasey's request to withdraw from the position as 'face', in terms of his standing and dignity, was at stake.[141] The position at Sarfait was subsequently to prove vital in the final anti-insurgent operations in late 1975 via deception manoeuvres undertaken by the garrison and the final clearance of the Darra Ridge, which completed the enemy's defeat and sealed victory. The loan of the helicopters therefore both assisted the war effort from a practical standpoint, but also helped uphold the Sultan's prestige and authority, which was of intangible benefit. Both such examples highlight the extra lengths the UK state went to in order to support Oman, both overtly and covertly throughout the Dhofar War, and often at potentially significant political risk.

Although the UK was the major supplier of war materials to Oman for the majority of the Dhofar conflict, from 1972 other countries did begin to contribute significantly to the COIN effort in this regard. Resultantly, some historical accounts highlight that the Omani win in Dhofar was more of an international or coalition victory as opposed to a campaign conducted solely (or even mainly) by UK forces themselves.[142] The supply of such non-British-derived materials was key, but viewed in their totality, UK war supplies provision remained the most important factor in ultimately achieving victory. Important alternative sources include Jordan gifting twelve 25-pounder artillery pieces to Oman in June 1972. Iranian supplies of weapons and ammunition also first arrived in Oman, via sixty Iranian Air Force C130 transport aircraft, in August of the same year.[143] Significantly, in 1975 Jordan also supplied Hunter aircraft to the SOAF (initially with loaned pilots) which, although arriving late in the campaign, were eventually, and with the engineering assistance of British Airwork personnel, a considerable boost to SOAF's attack capability. These aircraft were successfully utilized in the late-1975 final operations after being formed into British-piloted squadrons, including conducting aerial attacks on the Hauf insurgent supply and training base.[144] Other countries also provided war supplies, including Saudi Arabia and the UAE. Even the USA provided a level of support through provision of claymore mines as well as TOW missile launchers, including a package of missile projectiles and US

THE DHOFAR WAR

Figure 6.1: British soldiers being transported by an RAF Wessex helicopter on the Jebel (the Mughsayl coastline can be seen in the far distance). © Sid Pass 1974

army system training instructors, although this was blocked until 1975 due to the USA's 'own supply reasons', or perhaps more likely related to negotiations regarding occasional landing rights at RAF Masirah.[145] Despite this, the Iranian and Jordanian assistance was the largest non-British support in this respect in Dhofar.

It was not just direct provision of war materials to the SAF that contributed towards the campaign but those provided by foreign forces themselves. Whilst the construction of the Hornbeam Line from September 1972 (largely with scarce UK-supplied materials) by the SAF and British military engineers took approximately two years to complete, when the Iranian combat engineers built the Damavand Line in 1975, with all materials flown in direct from Iran, construction was completed in under twelve months with no expense spared and engineered to a superior standard to the Hornbeam Line itself.[146] Another example of plentiful Iranian supplies was the construction of the airstrip at Manston in western Dhofar in 1973, where the task was completed in only three months.[147] This strategically situated new base provided a second operational airbase in Dhofar where substantial Iranian flight assets, including heavy

NON-KINETIC MILITARY AND INFORMAL SUPPORT

lift helicopters such as Chinooks and fighter jets, could be fully utilized in relation to Dhofar operations. In addition to these material contributions, the Iranians also provided the capability of additional AB-205 helicopters with a squadron sent in February 1973 to assist in re-supplying the Sarfait garrison.[148] Iranian naval forces were also deployed in support of SAF operations, with a task force located in the Arabian Sea which operated off the Dhofari coast. These naval forces, and especially the escorting frigates, were to provide much-needed naval gunfire support for Operation HADAF in 1975 to help clear enemy forces, with hundreds of 4.5-inch shells fired onto land in support of operations.[149]

While the contribution of all these countries in terms of war materials was helpful to the Dhofar COIN campaign efforts, they must be viewed in context. While such contributions feed into the 'sliding scale of influence' framework of specific areas of diminishing British Dhofar War-related influence, it should also be remembered that the war had started in 1965. It was, therefore, almost solely British-supplied weaponry and materials which sustained the COIN campaign up to the 1970 coup and beyond, to enable the first offensive operations on the path to victory to be launched in October 1971. The materials supplied by other nations would have been rendered irrelevant if the lifeblood of supplies for the campaign up until that time had not been provided by Britain and the war lost prior to the involvement of Iran and Jordan, for example. British domination of war materials diminished in a relative sense, but not absolutely. Later non-British foreign supplies helped shorten the war and were to the serving CSAF (Brig. Graham) 'heartening beyond my expectations', but, in essence, UK-derived supplies had enabled the war to be fought and sustained from its start in 1965 and eventually won a decade later.[150]

The war materials supplied by the UK or other foreign allies of Oman in the Dhofar conflict were ultimately only as useful as their eventual operational utilization via the SAF's logistical command. Excellent and costly supplies lying dormant on a remote airstrip were of no real benefit, and provision only of such materials was insufficient on its own to contribute effectively to the war effort. The large-scale 1972 Iranian 'CAVIAR' provision of war supplies, for example, had to be taken under SAF logistical control and utilized, and the latter part of the equation was not provided by the Iranians and was almost entirely a British role. From the CSAF through to HQ staff officers, the logistics chain to the operational end users in SAF units was controlled principally by British officers. This organization provided the necessary materials to the combat units to fight and sustain themselves and therefore contributed significantly to the ability to prevail. An illustration of the importance of British logistical control and supply was the forward SAF base located at Sarfait. Established in 1972, then deep inside enemy-controlled territory, it was completely supplied, down to 100% of required water provisions, under SAF logistical control and delivered by air transport, primarily via helicopter in hostile territory. Even though Iranian helicopter support was utilized from 1973, without this general UK-controlled logistical support, the constant resupply of the high priority and exposed position of Sarfait would not have been sustainable. A further example was the logistical chain of command utilized for the final 1975 operations in the Western Area. When the major change in plans occurred after the successful Capstan feature diversion manoeuvre launched by the Sarfait garrison, it was to British officers only that the CSAF turned for immediate and urgent advice on feasibility to enable the operation to go ahead. As the incumbent CSAF, Maj-Gen. Perkins, stated:

> [To] discuss reallocation of air and logistics support [with Brig. Akehurst] I called in Air Commodore Erik Bennett, Captain Philip Brooke-Popham, my naval commander, Colonel Stuart Green, my Chief of Staff, and Lieutenant-Colonel Bugs Hughes, who was Dhofar Brigade gunner; all had been waiting close at hand.[151]

Even though many of the supplies distributed were sourced from countries other than the UK towards the end of the conflict, nevertheless from 1972, the British-controlled SAF logistical organization enabled such supplies to be fully operationally utilized and therefore contributed greatly to the overall Dhofar War victory.

The British contribution to technical support for the Dhofar War is another key war-winning factor which is often overlooked. This is most clearly observed in the control by British operatives of technical support to assist the operational capability of Oman's aviation assets. At the primary (state) influence level, RAF Salalah was run by serving RAF personnel throughout the Dhofar War and was a result of the 1958 'Exchange of Letters', and meant the UK

NON-KINETIC MILITARY AND INFORMAL SUPPORT

was obliged to both maintain and run the airfield. This entailed physical repairs such as to the runway or buildings that were controlled by the RAF, also technical support including firefighting assets, air traffic control and airfield defence; the latter task undertaken by the RAF Regiment. All airfield support functions were, resultantly, administered and carried out by the RAF and therefore by default the UK government, and this was available to the SOAF to use as required for Dhofar War operations. This arrangement became even more important once SOAF Strikemaster aircraft were relocated, post-coup, from Bayt Al Falaj, adjacent to Muscat, some 900 km west to RAF Salalah. As a result, RAF support functions were, from this time, not just indirectly supporting the war in Dhofar but were now directly supporting it with SOAF fighter squadrons based at RAF Salalah. This was a function expanded with the formation of the SOAF Hunter squadrons in October 1975, formed from the thirty-one Hawker Hunter fighter aircraft gifted to Oman by Jordan.[152]

In addition to UK state support, at the secondary level, the maintenance of aircraft and combat preparation was British-controlled but not, however, by the RAF. This was undertaken by the ubiquitous private UK company, Airwork Ltd., which combined this with their higher-profile contracted personnel provision service.[153] Airwork's technical services provision was illustrated with the company's previous air force flight training and aircraft maintenance contracts in many previous UK overseas territories such as Aden (even after British withdrawal in 1967), Kenya, and Uganda.[154] Airwork Ltd. also controlled the maintenance of the SOAF transport and fighter aircraft fleet and was responsible for making them operationally ready. Airwork essentially acted as an extension of the SOAF, but as a private contractor. Such works included regular maintenance, control of airframe flying hours and combat damage repairs as necessary. Slower transport aircraft and helicopters were as much at risk as high-speed jets to enemy fire and Strikemaster tactics made them particularly vulnerable, including attack runs utilizing Sura rockets and 30-mm cannon in amongst high-sided valleys and wadis. Another key role was arming fighter aircraft for combat, with Airwork personnel attaching aircraft missiles and loading ammunition for combat sorties. Without Airwork's input, translation of latent capability into effective actions would have been substantially reduced. In short, the prosecution of the air war was made possible by a private UK company closely aligned with the British military and political establishment.

As highlighted previously, Airwork Ltd. had significant links to the British military and government through existing (UK and abroad) contracts which were likely facilitated through official channels: 'British companies [often] received significant support from the [UK] government in securing "firm-to-government" deals with foreign states.'[155] In addition to this factor, large numbers of Airwork staff were ex-RAF or British military personnel from other services employed via a substantial 'revolving door' recruitment model.[156] Similarly to other examples such as their contracts in Saudi Arabia in the 1960s, Airwork's relationship with the UK government resulted in significant overall British influence on the control of both personnel and SOAF combat capability in Dhofar.[157] It can therefore be observed that from a technical support perspective, British input and influence had a significant bearing on the operational capability of COIN forces during the Dhofar War and therefore to eventual success.

Limiting Support and Maximizing Ongoing Influence

As highlighted at the start of this chapter, alongside the aim to provide the necessary non-kinetic military and informal support to Oman to defeat the insurgents, the other key aim was to limit British support whilst maximizing ongoing influence in Oman. The UK government achieved both of these aims. The UK approach to Oman and the Dhofar War prior to 1970 was a limited form of assistance, described as parsimonious by Brig. Purdon when he stated:

> We simply could not convince the British Directorate of Military Operations, nor the Defence Staff, that if they gave us what we asked for straight away—very little at that time—we could [quickly] crush the rebellion. They had to support SAF with far more aid and consequent expense later. The old principle of 'Firm and Timely Action' had to be learned yet again at the expense, as always, of lives and limbs.[158]

After 1970, with potential defeat looming, this minimalist approach was modified, with supplies and UK military support increased to boost COIN

NON-KINETIC MILITARY AND INFORMAL SUPPORT

force capability. Whilst support was increased, it remained relatively restricted in an attempt to achieve the difficult balance of limiting support to the minimum necessary to achieve required war outcomes. In addition, British influence in Oman was also consciously sacrificed by UK authorities to achieve the greater strategic goal of defeating the insurgents.

The UK was, from the outset of hostilities, effectively the sole backer of Oman in the Dhofar War and had to provide supplies to enable the COIN campaign to be sustained. To mitigate the impact on British taxpayer funds, however, Oman was charged for nearly all materials and loan personnel at commercial rates. In essence, everything supplied by the UK to Oman 'came with a price tag', and the UK authorities even charged for the charter flights to deliver such paid-for supplies to their Omani customer.[159] This applied to ammunition and other war materials sourced through Kendall's of London, but also for both contract and seconded personnel. This arrangement permitted the UK to assist an ally but in a way that limited costs over and above the financial arrangements and already substantial funds supplied to Oman as part of the 'Exchange of Letters' agreements. With such agreements in place up until 1970, allied to the ending of the Zanzibar Subsidy, Britain was able to both limit costs relatively successfully and support its ally's war. The problem lay in the fact that the war, for the reasons outlined previously, was slipping into a stalemate situation. The SAF was withdrawn in its entirety back to the Salalah plain and actual defeat in 1970 was considered a real possibility. As a result, under a new Conservative government in 1970, Britain redoubled its efforts to support Oman with materials as well as more seconded personnel and especially regular UK military forces, so that by the end of the war there were upwards of 1,000 such military personnel serving in Oman.[160] This could be viewed as a failure of the British policy to limit involvement but can also be considered exactly the opposite. The diplomatic efforts undertaken by British representatives to help secure tangible support for Oman and the Dhofar War (primarily from the Middle Eastern region) were notable. This largely British-inspired initiative provided thousands of troops, especially from Iran and Jordan, as well as weaponry and other military supplies, and financial resources, including (by 1973) over £30 million worth of aid from Saudi Arabia, nearly £15 million in aid from the UAE, and £600,000 equivalent from Qatar.[161] All these factors contributed to the COIN campaign and eventual insurgent defeat, and simultaneously acted to limit UK war involvement as well as support expectations from the Omanis themselves. Whilst increased war support was provided by the UK authorities from 1970 onwards, and British diplomatic efforts helped secure important war-related supplies and personnel from COIN allies, the overall UK commitment to Oman and the war remained limited. British forces, except the standard RAF airfield deployed personnel located at RAF Salalah and RAF Masirah and some SAS and RE elements, all departed Oman by early 1976. The limitation of the size and timescale of British support was therefore successfully capped. As a result, Britain managed to avoid an open-ended commitment in Oman, or the feared possible 'mini-Vietnam' scenario on the Arabian Peninsula.[162] The avoidance of such an outcome should, therefore, be considered a key element of British success.

Although a degree of loss of influence on political, diplomatic, and economic fronts was accepted in the Sultanate due to the necessity of not damaging the fragile, yet necessary outward appearance of the reality of Omani self-determination, Britain was able to maintain significant economic 'informal' influence in the country throughout the Dhofar War and beyond. Due largely to the deliberate policy of discreet nation-building assistance, the UK did experience a reduction in overall economic influence in Oman as per the 'sliding scale of influence' framework, as such actions loosened its long-standing virtual trading monopoly.[163] This situation was compounded by the largely discreet UK diplomacy-facilitated and substantial aid provided by Iran and Gulf partners in the latter stages of the war and the rise in oil prices due to the 1973 Yom Kippur War and subsequent OPEC-instigated oil crisis. Sultan Qaboos also diversified his circle of advisors away from mainly British (official or private capacity) to aid his administration and country. This led the way for those such as the 'mafia-like' cabal of Arab advisors (including the increasingly more powerful Barouni, Omer, and Shaker) to assert more influence, which directly affected the Dhofar campaign on issues of governance, procurement, and the awarding of contracts, and led to the general sidelining of sensible and measured British assistance, support, and advice.[164] Despite this reduction in economic influence, due mainly to its investment of money, expertise, and other assistance, Britain was able to maintain its status as Oman's most important overall backer and trading partner throughout the Dhofar

NON-KINETIC MILITARY AND INFORMAL SUPPORT

War years and beyond.[165] Britain also remained, both historically and in absolute terms throughout the war, the largest supporter of Oman. This is illustrated by Oman's purchase of the British-built Rapier missile defence system and twelve Jaguar ground attack fighters costing over £80 million in 1974.[166] Although UK advisors considered these items strategically unnecessary and unaffordable for Oman (with CSAF Maj. Gen. Creasey viewing it largely as a status symbol issue), the purchase was eventually made.[167] Sultan Qaboos had explored the possibility of obtaining French Mirage jets instead, but when they saw he was set on purchasing such items, UK officials worked to make sure that the contract did not go to a rival vendor and incumbent CSAF Maj-Gen. Perkins was instructed by the Sultan to effectively stop procrastinating and to proceed with the purchase in 1974.[168]

After 1970, Oman was not exclusively a British market as in the past. UK companies did still benefit, however, from large-scale export, civilian development, and infrastructure, banking services, and more visibly large-scale military procurement contracts, and firms such as Taylor Woodrow and Cable & Wireless succeeded in gaining significant contractual awards.[169] These commercial agreements, which saw, for instance, an over 90% increase in UK exports to Oman during January–October 1975 to £81.9 million (and consequently a higher value of export trade than with Egypt, twice as much as with Qatar, and only just less than with Kuwait) over the same time period in 1974 benefitted both British companies and therefore, indirectly, the UK Exchequer.[170] Such large-scale commercial linkages were to continue post-war, with twelve additional Jaguar aircraft sold to Oman in 1981, and thirty Scorpion and twenty-seven Chieftain Tanks both purchased and in service by 1985.[171] Although no longer a virtual monopoly, Britain remained Oman's most important trading partner. This was especially the case with military sales, which illustrate the enduring UK economic influence in Oman. Furthermore, UK influence in general was also maintained in terms of the SAF's British seconded military personnel as senior command positions were occupied by such personnel well into the 1990s despite the concerted Omanization programme begun in 1971. The last UK SAF service head did not leave his post until 1990, with the departure of Air Vice-Marshal Bennett as the seconded SOAF Commander, in addition to Rear-Admiral Balfour as SON commander.[172]

In terms of non-kinetic military and informal support-related supplies and functions, the British can, therefore, be considered to have had a major influence on the sustainability, robustness, and outcome of the COIN campaign. It can also be seen that in certain areas of support-related functions, the UK's influence did reduce during the Dhofar War as per the 'sliding scale of influence' framework. These 'reductions' included in terms of financing for the Omani state and the provision of personnel to assist the war effort but were mainly, however, in relative terms only. Britain's non-kinetic and informal support function role did not diminish absolutely but the contribution from other nations merely increased in relative terms. There were also other areas of such support where the British remained the primary provider. These areas included the provision of SAF leadership, SAF training, and in the sphere of technical support, especially for SOAF. It was not therefore necessarily the amount of support given which was the key factor, but its quality, importance, and 'replaceability'. The UK also managed to achieve the difficult balancing act of both successfully containing or limiting its overall wartime commitment to Oman, whilst simultaneously contributing decisively to the overall COIN win. Although necessarily and consciously diminished in areas such as diplomatic or economic leverage, Britain was also able to maintain strong and beneficial links to the Sultanate throughout the Dhofar War and beyond, primarily through economic, but also through military ties. As a result, no other country provided or was able at the time to provide the level of assistance to Oman across the highlighted non-kinetic and informal support functions. Britain effectively bankrolled the SAF (including SOAF) throughout the war years but had also virtually created the force and moulded it into an effective organization since the initial 1958 'Exchange of Letters' agreements. It also, in a formal and informal manner, supplied the military and civilian (government and private capacity) expertise to effectively run the Dhofar COIN campaign and provided the training to the SAF to make it both capable and effective. The UK also remained the key provider of war supplies to Oman and remained the Sultanate's largest supplier of military provisions during the war, providing more than the combined value of arms exports of all other countries.[173] UK personnel also ran the SAF logistics organization which operationalized not only British military supplies but also those supplied by COIN allies, and the private UK

NON-KINETIC MILITARY AND INFORMAL SUPPORT

company Airwork Ltd. provided the technical maintenance of the SOAF air fleet (and therefore a substantial component of the SAF's operational capability) throughout the conflict.

Britain was historically and practically the most important partner to Oman in the Dhofar War. As such, in overall terms, it played the most important role of any nation from a non-kinetic and informal support perspective in winning the COIN campaign.

7 Conclusion: 'Cut from a Different Cloth'

The Dhofar War was a British win achieved on behalf of the Sultanate of Oman. It was a win accomplished under a veil of almost total secrecy from both the British public and further afield until 1970. Then, whilst UK involvement was more widely publicized after the accession of Sultan Qaboos, elements remained top secret including the large-scale covert SAS component up until the official end of the war in 1975, and beyond. It can be regarded as a win via the facilitation of the insurgent defeat by military and other means, as well as the attainment of the UK's primary goals pertaining to the conflict. This was accomplished despite never realizing the traditional military minimum required ten to one COIN force to insurgent ratio (up to 15,000 COIN forces versus a maximum of 5,000 Adoo) success marker.[1]

The Dhofar War was therefore both a victory for and facilitated by the UK, from a primary (state) as well as that of a secondary (private UK citizen or organization) perspective. It was distinct from other post-World War Two UK COIN campaigns because Britain did not solely conduct the Dhofar War, but UK influence and contribution can be considered as the main factors behind its eventual win. As such, it was very much a British-inspired and facilitated victory, and one also for the UK in terms of achieving war aims from political, diplomatic, military strategy, operational and tactical, and non-kinetic and informal support-related perspectives. It is equally clear also that Britain's influence over Oman and the Dhofar War declined in several ways over the conflict's duration as per the 'sliding scale of influence' framework, yet in the key areas of military strategy, operational command and control, tactics, and several essential non-kinetic and informal support functions, it did not diminish. The UK's influence in these areas remained firm throughout and

CONCLUSION: 'CUT FROM A DIFFERENT CLOTH'

was the fundamental reason for overall success. Primarily through its politicians, civil servants, and seconded military personnel, but secondarily through its private citizens or organizations, Britain set the required war end-states via its aims and was the main driver in achieving them. In this, perhaps rarely, it can be observed that the hard-nosed business of national interests and aims was genuinely mixed with a tangible component of altruism, sentiment, and notion of historical responsibility.

The COIN campaign should certainly not be described as 'model', as often portrayed by early historical accounts, as there were both mistakes and multiple areas and instances of clear failure.[2] Later accounts utilized previously unavailable archival materials to challenge the 'ideal' or potentially 'best ever' (COIN) campaign narrative or provide alternative explanations for the success or otherwise of the war such as the Iranian military or non-British financial or war material supply.[3] Many of the latter, however, do not necessarily hold up to full scrutiny, and the wider and more holistic aims-based British success perspective as portrayed by this book has been largely neglected. In doing so, the magnitude of the success achieved in Dhofar has been overlooked and the ubiquitous British role often progressively negated, downplayed, or in some cases virtually written out of history.[4] Whatever the operational shortcomings, more conventional warfare tactics over largely 'hearts and minds'-oriented activities utilized towards its end, the contribution of non-British allies to the cause, and the fact that the war lasted over a decade, history records that the Dhofar COIN campaign was eventually a win. Furthermore, it was a rare Cold War-era success against Communist-led insurgents, and this was largely as a result of the overarching combined British support provided to Oman. The win was achieved during a period of history when failure in COIN campaigns against insurgent forces was more often the norm, including earlier British losses in Palestine in 1948 and Aden in 1967.[5] The British role has even been described as potentially the 'most clear-cut counter-insurgency victory' since the Malayan campaign in the 1950s.[6]

Where the 'sliding scale of influence' framework identifies a reduction of British influence in areas such as politics and diplomacy, operations, and support, this was often in relative and not absolute terms. This meant that British influence and support rarely reduced in real terms, only that Oman became, by design, more resilient and independently capable, boosted by the support of other nations such as Jordan and Iran, from 1972 onwards. The war had, however, begun in 1965 and it was firstly the British contribution which prevented a potential impending defeat by 1970, and secondly laid the foundations for a campaign turnaround and eventual victory. In addition, although a reduction in British influence over Oman and the Dhofar War is apparent in several areas from mid-1970 onwards, in the key areas which affected the strategy, leadership, and execution of the COIN campaign, British influence remained paramount. Other reasons to account for the Dhofar War success such as other foreign military interventions, the SAF soldiery itself, or the Sultan's leadership are rightly fully acknowledged as important but are ultimately of secondary importance. Without the Jordanian and especially Iranian contribution, the war would have probably lasted longer, and the UK would likely have reluctantly been forced to play a more overt and larger, direct military role. Without such non-UK assistance, the win, however, would likely still have been eventually achieved, albeit at greater cost in terms of British and Omani (as well as Baluchi) 'blood and treasure'. The insurgency had effectively already been broken, and the momentum towards the overall victory set by mid-1972 through actions 'firmly based upon the traditional pattern of British counter-insurgency'.[7]

The key external assistance from November 1972 was merely the 'icing on the cake' in accelerating the insurgent defeat, as by this time the fundamentals to enable the win were already in place through UK efforts, the COIN forces were already in the ascendancy, and the assertion that Britain merely prevented the war from being lost does not hold up to full scrutiny.[8] The war was won by leveraging the wide experience and skills of the often (and sometimes highly) COIN-experienced British officers in SAF leadership positions and UK civilians employed in the Omani regime, backed by key British governmental support from 1965. The change in Omani leadership resulting from the 1970 coup certainly contributed to a turnaround in the COIN campaign in terms of fundamentals such as funding and development policy, but it was not the key turning point of the war. Sultan Qaboos had a central role in social and economic policy, and an insightful, progressive view of changing the very circumstances within Oman and Dhofar which were the main reasons for the initial insurgency. Apart from funding the campaign adequately, however, and in allowing his British military commanders to conduct the war largely as they saw fit, his strategic or

CONCLUSION: 'CUT FROM A DIFFERENT CLOTH'

operational role in winning the war was, essentially, limited. The change in Sultan merely allowed Britain to conduct the war more according to how it considered, through extensive experience, such a war should be fought, free of many of the restrictions imposed by the previous ruler. The war and the UK role should also be seen as an overall victory yet tempered by significant elements of failure. It was not all plain sailing, and this aspect of the war should be fully acknowledged and not glossed over. There was early failure to defeat an initially weak, nationalist-only insurgency, and there was failure in that the war was almost lost by late 1970/early 1971 and the initial SAF offensives were disappointing to all. This leads towards the fact that the war could, and should, have been won earlier and not only after a full decade of fighting.

The main conclusions of this book are firstly that despite the large Jordanian and Iranian military contributions, substantial funding sourced primarily from other Gulf monarchies, and the positive aspects of leadership and likewise encouraging changes which came with Sultan Qaboos's accession, without the British input and custodianship of the campaign, the war would likely have been lost. The fact that the Dhofar War was not lost, and that despite a decade-long expensive and hard-fought conflict the win was eventually achieved, is primarily the result of British influence and input. Because Britain achieved all its goals relating to the Dhofar War, the undertaking should also be considered a victory both by, and for, the UK. Although it took longer than hoped, the result was the right one for both Britain and the Sultanate's governing status quo. Secondly, the British role did change significantly during the war. As can be observed through the 'sliding scale of influence', the role changed from one where the UK was both the main supporter of Oman and lead actor in prosecuting the war, to one where it took a more 'hands-off', managerial, or 'consultancy-type' approach. Thirdly, it should also be noted that the Dhofar War was substantially different from previous classical-era UK COIN campaigns. In a largely unique approach at the time, Britain's role was primarily limited to providing the leadership and resources to win, and, importantly, was the driving force behind the strategy and overall conduct of the campaign to this effect.[9] As such, it represented a crossover from an older colonial-style approach to a more covert-natured modern consultancy or limited support-based role utilizing remote warfare techniques including emphasis on

THE DHOFAR WAR

'partnered operations', training, intelligence, and use of SF troops.[10] As a result, the Dhofar War should indeed be considered *sui generis* in terms of post-war British COIN in that it was not a wholly or sovereign UK-run campaign as such, but was, nonetheless, largely a British-facilitated win. It was, in essence, both a victory for, and one facilitated by, the UK and was fundamentally a case of 'British covert action, [largely] in pursuit of British interests'.[11]

The primary contribution of this book is to offer a new historical interpretation and explanation of the role of the UK in its conduct and the eventual victory over the insurgents. As such, this book puts forward a distinct narrative in which the role of the British is clarified in terms of influence on, and contribution to, the COIN win. This narrative puts forward the view that for many reasons the Dhofar War should not be considered a fully UK-conducted campaign as such but was most certainly a British win. This historical reinterpretation moves away from newer historical war narratives which act to either over-emphasize the non-UK contribution to the COIN campaign or downplay the British role. This book reverts more to the spirit of the traditional orthodox historical narrative, but still makes a clear and original distinction from its often tactically focused and narrowly UK-centric emphasis. This book's second key contribution to the Dhofar War literature is in providing a more detailed and holistic assessment of the British role. This book both contests and revises the binary view prevalent that depicts a supposedly pre-eminent and UK-centric British military role on the one hand, whilst other accounts champion the purported decline of the UK's influence on the campaign.[12] The 'sliding scale of influence' framework highlights the more nuanced reality that the British role was a combination of both elements and that it was not static throughout a decade of war. Instead, it evolved throughout the COIN campaign, and indeed diminished in several respects. This can be observed for instance in terms of political and diplomatic influence, or that of relative numbers of troops provided to the campaign. Conversely, the framework also importantly highlights key areas where UK influence and contribution did not diminish. As control of military strategy, operations and tactics, and vital areas of non-kinetic and informal support were always under British control, the UK influence remained strong and was the most important driver of what was a historic victory. The 'sliding scale of influence' framework therefore highlights that throughout the decade-long Dhofar COIN campaign, the

CONCLUSION: 'CUT FROM A DIFFERENT CLOTH'

British role changed over time from a position of almost pre-eminent influence to a substantially diminished role in certain areas as per the three distinct yet overlapping phases highlighted in this book's introduction. The concept reinforces the idea that whilst the UK's influence declined relatively in some aspects of economic, political, and military spheres, through the CSAF and senior leadership of the SAF, Britain was always effectively in control of military direction, management, and conduct of the COIN campaign. The UK government, military, and civil service bureaucracy was collectively, therefore, the mastermind behind a campaign which produced a rare Cold War COIN win against Marxist insurgents. This was further reinforced by British citizens or organizations not directly part of the UK state apparatus.

This book also acts to respectfully contest enduring historic narratives such as the simplistic division of the Dhofar campaign into unsuccessful pre-1970 and successful post-coup periods, and the supposed key turning point of the war being the July 1970 coup.[13] Whilst it was undoubtedly a key moment in the war and had the effect of boosting the flagging COIN campaign and profoundly altering the fundamentals of governance and campaign support, it was not the key pivot point. This book puts forward the more considered perspective that success for the Omani government side was not to fully occur until after the Battle of Mirbat in 1972, approximately two years after the much-heralded coup that brought Sultan Qaboos to the throne. By the time Operation SIMBA was successfully launched in April 1972, the Operation AQOOBA retaliation had played out in May and then the defeat of the insurgents had occurred at Mirbat in July, for cumulative reasons the tide had already turned. The arrival of the Iranian and later Jordanian contingents merely helped quicken the win and share the laurels of the largely British input in many spheres for the previous seven years. As archival documents suggest, 'If any one incident ... can be taken as an example of the turning point in the Dhofar war [sic]—Marbat [sic] would be it'.[14]

This book also provides the more holistic view that the Dhofar War was an amalgam of success and failure. Aspects of British-inspired failure are highlighted, including the inability to thwart the growing insurgency in 1965, and the underwhelming 1971 UK-led Operation JAGUAR and LEOPARD SAF offensives. In seeking a modicum of balance, the level of campaign success is also clarified, and the magnitude of the win confirmed. It is reinforced not

THE DHOFAR WAR

from the highly UK-centric military operations or tactically oriented emphasis of much of the traditional historical literature, but in evidence-based relative and strategic terms, and in its status as a rare COIN win in the Cold War era.[15] As such, the achievement is put into perspective when the case is compared to contemporary unsuccessful Cold War COIN campaigns conducted by other European powers or the USA in Algeria, Mozambique, Guinea, and Vietnam, to name but a few examples.[16] Whilst certainly not without fault or numerous elements of failure, the overarching British contribution to this rare COIN win should be acknowledged and the campaign recognized as a relatively small but well-fought campaign of which the UK input was both key and decisive.[17] Without such input to the Dhofar War, it would likely have been lost. Furthermore, such input enabled the campaign to be brought to an eventual successful conclusion. With hindsight, despite its limited size, the Dhofar War should be lauded as both one of the relatively few successful, and, overall, one of the most effective COIN campaigns undertaken by any nation, and as this book demonstrates, it can justifiably be considered a 'British' win.[18] Elements such as these should bestow the Dhofar War case with extra facets of academic interest, but also act to raise its profile within the public consciousness.

The idea is also advanced by this book that the Dhofar COIN campaign was in many ways unique as well as being a stepping-stone to a new type of anti-insurgent approach. The Dhofar War was a hybrid COIN campaign, and was the 'first of type' illustrating a new British approach to such undertakings. As such, it was a crossover campaign which saw the gradual phasing out of the older colonial-type COIN model, amalgamating aspects of previous Imperial-era large-scale British campaigns primarily in UK-held territory with newer, more modern approaches emphasizing a more hands-off, low-key, or consultancy-type approach. These include the concept of 'remote warfare', which includes the primary use of SF troops, the training of indigenous capability, and small operational footprint in the foreign territory concerned.[19] In a related manner, this book also clarifies the extent of the key British military influence of technical or wholesale campaign management, as well as the emergence of what was effectively a new UK way of conducting anti-insurgency operations towards a 'consultancy-type' of COIN engagement. The Dhofar campaign was neither a full British colonial COIN operation as

CONCLUSION: 'CUT FROM A DIFFERENT CLOTH'

undertaken in Malaya, Kenya, Cyprus, or Aden, nor a fully 'light-touch' remote warfare-type operation. It came somewhere in between these parameters. Aspects of colonial-type influence were retained, such as the CSAF always being a serving British military official and all Omani combat units being led by UK officers. Oman was, however, a sovereign country, the SAF was an Omani organization, and latterly the war was financed primarily by the Sultanate's oil-derived income and not by UK funds. In the history of UK COIN, the Dhofar campaign in effect represented the changeover point from colonial or Empire legacy campaigns with Britain wholly in control of the territory, government, and security forces to one where limited assistance was provided to a sovereign ally. As such, by design or accident Britain managed to find the 'sweet spot' in Dhofar in terms of how to successfully counter armed insurgency, which few other countries have.

Dhofar was a markedly small war and COIN campaign as compared to many of those undertaken by Britain in the post-World War Two era, and further in the later Cold War era in Vietnam, Angola, Mozambique, and Afghanistan, for example. Peterson goes as far as to state that 'Dhufar [sic] was a very small war, even in the context of "small wars".'[20] Despite this, and its several unique characteristics, there are, however, relevant general COIN-related lessons which can be extracted from the Dhofar case. This study outlines the impact of the past, and of historical knowledge and capabilities on COIN operations. In turn, this illustrates the consequences of hard-won COIN lessons being learned and fully incorporated, and the negative resulting consequences when they are not, as the pre-coup phase of the Dhofar campaign under Sultan Said illustrates. There have been significant changes in factors affecting COIN apparent since the 1970s. These can be seen in terms of geopolitics, civil and military technology, the extent of global media coverage, and even the impact of social media. These do not, however, invalidate time-honoured and still relevant principles as used to good effect in previous British-conducted campaigns including that undertaken in Dhofar. These include clear political objectives, effective 'hearts and minds' activities, selective use of (minimum) force and clear, unified civil and military command structures, allied to an overall approach where political initiatives take primacy over military equivalents.[21] Other British-illustrated COIN principles would be to make the overall strategic calculation to either quit whilst ahead as in Malaya (with independence granted by Britain in 1957 after resistance was largely defeated), cut one's losses when things become unsalvageable, as per UK actions in Palestine, commit unreservedly to the 'long haul', as per the British approach in Northern Ireland, or indeed to not get involved or commit politically and militarily in the first place, especially in theatres without vital strategic or economic importance. By way of illustration, Peterson states: 'Perhaps the biggest difference between Dhufar [sic] and Vietnam was that, in political terms, the former was eminently winnable whilst Vietnam was inevitably unwinnable.'[22] The unsuccessful and, in both human and economic terms, costly campaigns from Vietnam up to the 1970s, Afghanistan in the 1980s, and over two decades of war and COIN later in Iraq and Afghanistan together illustrate a degree of loss of both institutional memory and from the British perspective a readily available corporate expertise on such issues gained from multiple decades of cumulative COIN experience in UK political and military circles. Over time, leaders at all military levels from the tactical up are promoted to staff roles then eventually retire from active duty, and different political, strategic, or operational military priorities emerge. In the UK case, the hard-won corporate knowledge gained from decades of COIN experience in UK political and from regimental to Chief of Staff levels in military circles reaching their zenith in Dhofar (and subsequently provided wide utility in the long war in Northern Ireland), was either depleted, lost, or ignored by new generations of leaders. This book's conclusions highlight lessons that could (or should) be re-learned in terms of COIN policy or doctrinal approach by UK military and political leaders from their predecessors. These are the predecessors who facilitated a both impressive and rare Cold War COIN victory in Dhofar and have this achievement sealed in the historical record. The win was achieved by utilizing a post-colonial but nevertheless highly integrated approach where control was fully maintained in areas such as military strategy and operational command. This approach was key to achieving the overall victory.

Such contributions and conclusions also illustrate that the surge in academic and public interest seen in both the classical COIN era and subsequently in the early 2000s because of the Afghan and Iraqi campaigns should be maintained. This is because despite the periodic return to large-scale conventional warfare such as that tragically witnessed in Ukraine, insurgency will not fade away into the history books. True inter-state wars are now a relative rarity

CONCLUSION: 'CUT FROM A DIFFERENT CLOTH'

with irregular and 'grey zone' warfare becoming the norm and not the exception. As such, anti-insurgent actions and especially 'consultancy' or remote warfare-type roles will likely continue to be the new norm in this brave new world. Studying the Dhofar War and the various facets of the COIN campaign undertaken is important to selectively learn from going forward and, in the aftermath of failures in the Middle East, to get 'back to basics' on how anti-insurgent actions can be successfully prosecuted. The twin principles of 'control', be it of strategy, operations, or logistics, and from an overall campaign perspective, and that small is not only beautiful, but also a necessity, are key considerations. A more junior and perhaps inexperienced COIN partner can significantly benefit from a fully integrated and 'hands-on' experience like that provided by the UK loan service or contract personnel in Dhofar serving within the SAF. This can serve to 'stiffen the backbone' of the COIN effort and provide the knowledge, experience, leadership, and 'joined-up' fighting capability, especially in the initial phases of a campaign. The Omani SAF, with its mix of Arab and Baluchi soldiers, never melted away, never deserted, or turned on its COIN partner. It was a well-led, motivated force which 'stuck to its guns', did its job, and helped to deliver a rare COIN win. As such, it could be suggested that a combination of 'hands on' in terms of leadership and control, yet still relatively detached 'consultancy-like' approach in terms of overall commitment such as regular forces, is perhaps the most effective method employed for COIN in general. This approach was tried and tested in Dhofar. The Dhofar War represented a COIN win where most other modern examples failed, and this was not achieved by accident. It represented the synthesis of multiple decades of experience by British forces garnered through wars and COIN campaigns across the globe, from desert to jungle, from sparsely populated rural backwater to densely populated urban area, and untrained agitator to highly trained, motivated, and armed Marxist insurgents.

The Dhofar War was unique in many respects but in terms of time-honoured principles it ticked almost every required box. Unlike the large-scale and expensive COIN failures of the early twenty-first century, the premise that 'less is often more' when assisting COIN allies is a key takeaway from the Dhofar case. As a result, why Britain was relatively successful both historically, and specifically in Dhofar, whilst other contemporary era anti-insurgent actions were less so, is an interesting and potentially important perspective which deserves further study. As an example, out of approximately twenty COIN wins achieved globally from 1945, Britain can claim ownership of up to six.[23] The Dhofar War was, therefore, one of the success stories of UK COIN as it resulted in a clear and decisive military victory. As such, this idea of key fundamentals is not only potentially important in terms of lessons to apply for the political decision-makers as well as military forces of the UK, but for those of other countries to successfully undertake future COIN operations. From the British perspective, through elements of the post-2020 UK Integrated Security Reviews and via the introduction of the Integrated Operating Concept (IoC), there are positive developments in this direction.[24] Highlighting and incorporating key issues such as persistent and forward deployed engagement with partner nations through training, advising, technology transfer, and importantly through embedded forces, it can be seen that the lessons of history are to a degree potentially being re-learned.[25] It remains to be seen to what extent such hard-won historical lessons will be incorporated to benefit future COIN forces as the world transitions into a multi-polar system in which they are more likely to be called upon than in any other period of history.

Postscript

When the Sultanate of Oman celebrated its fiftieth National Day on 18 November 2020, it was with a new Sultan, HM Sultan Haitham bin Tariq Al Said, on the throne. The former Sultan, Qaboos bin Said, died in January 2020, having ruled since the British-backed coup in July 1970 when his father was forced to abdicate. The 2020 transition carried out the final wishes of Sultan Qaboos, penned by him and placed in envelopes secreted in various locations in the Sultanate for safekeeping, and resulted in a smooth transition of power. There is perhaps an element of irony that Qaboos chose his cousin, the son of his uncle Tariq, as heir. Tariq had originally planned to overthrow his brother, Sultan Said, and take power in the 1960s, and also resigned as Qaboos's Prime Minister in 1971, due in part to their problematic personal and later working relationship.[26]

That Oman successfully reached its fiftieth National Day and is working towards the Sultanate's Vision 2040 Plan for national development, this

CONCLUSION: 'CUT FROM A DIFFERENT CLOTH'

achievement, in a similar manner to the outcome of the Dhofar War, can be viewed as being fundamentally facilitated by the UK. As a result, it was not necessarily due to the 'founder of Oman's modern renaissance' as has been described by some commentators.[27] Britain's influence and support saved the Omani governing status quo from an insurgent defeat in the late 1960s. The UK facilitated the coup which brought the twenty-nine-year-old Qaboos to power in 1970 when the war was being lost against formidably backed insurgents, returned his uncle to Oman from self-imposed exile to serve as Prime Minister, and sealed the victory against the insurgents in 1975. That Oman celebrated its milestone fiftieth National Day well into the twenty-first century with an Al Said still on the throne as a stable, prosperous, intact, and sovereign state is largely due to the enduring historic influence and legacy of the UK's long-standing involvement in the Sultanate.

If viewed from a longer-term historical perspective, the crowning of HM Sultan Haitham is not really a surprise. The event was part of a long historical association between the Sultans of Oman and Great Britain. The actors play their parts and enter and leave the stage over time, but the longer-term strategic interests, national respect, and friendship dating back over 300 years remains. With the fiftieth anniversary of the Dhofar War victory in 2025, the words of the treaty between the British East India Company and the Sultan of Oman in 1800 remain apt; that the friendly relations between the two countries should 'endure till the end of time or the sun and moon cease their revolving careers'.[28]

Notes

1 Introduction

1. Marc DeVore, 'The United Kingdom's Last Hot War of the Cold War: Oman, 1963–75', *Cold War History*, 11 (2011), 1.
2. Jonathan Walker, *Aden Insurgency: The Savage War in Yeman 1962–67* (Barnsley: Pen and Sword, 2014), pp. 286–87.
3. Walter C. Ladwig III, 'Supporting Allies in Counterinsurgency: Britain and the Dhofar Rebellion', *Small Wars & Insurgencies*, 19 (2008), 63. Ranulph Fiennes, *Where Soldiers Fear to Tread* (London: New English Library, 1976), p. 9.
4. Ian F. Beckett, *Modern Insurgencies and Counter-Insurgencies: Guerrillas and Their Opponents since 1750* (London: Routledge, 2001), p. 230. Ian Beckett and John Pimlott, *Counter Insurgency: Lessons from History* (Barnsley: Pen and Sword, 2011), pp. 42–43. Tony Jeapes, *SAS Operation Oman* (London: HarperCollins, 1980), pp. 11–14. Thomas R. Mockaitis, *British Counterinsurgency in the Post-Imperial Era* (Manchester: Manchester University Press, 1995), pp. 92–93. Marc R. DeVore, 'A More Complex and Conventional Victory: Revisiting the Dhofar Counterinsurgency, 1963–1975', *Small Wars & Insurgencies*, 23 (2012), 144. Daniel Marston and Carter Malkasian, *Counterinsurgency in Modern Warfare* (London: Bloomsbury, 2011), p. 175.
5. David A. Charters, 'Counter-Insurgency Intelligence: The Evolution of British Theory and Practice', *Journal of Conflict Studies*, 29 (2009), 63.
6. DeVore, pp. 1 & 22.
7. Sergey Plekhanov, *A Reformer on the Throne: Sultan Qaboos Bin Said Al Said* (London: Trident Press Ltd, 2004), p. 126.
8. Fred Halliday, *Arabia Without Sultans* (Harmondsworth: Penguin, 1974), pp. 350–52. Abdel Razzaq Takriti, *Monsoon Revolution: Republicans, Sultans, and Empires in Oman, 1965–1976* (Oxford: Oxford University Press, 2013), pp. 132–33.
9. Jeapes. John Akehurst, *We Won a War: The Campaign in Oman 1965–1975* (Salisbury: M. Russell, 1982). John Peterson, *Oman's Insurgencies: The Sultanate's Struggle for Supremacy* (London: Saqi, 2007).

NOTES

10. Takriti. James Worrall, *Statebuilding and Counterinsurgency in Oman: Political, Military and Diplomatic Relations at the End of Empire* (London: I.B.Tauris, 2014).
11. TNA—DEFE 25/186—Muscat and Oman—General-Secretary of State for Defence (Secret) Memorandum, 'SAS Assistance to the Sultanate of Oman', 4 Sep 1970. TNA—DEFE 24/1856—Middle East/Africa: Muscat and Oman—DMO Briefing Notes for Chiefs of Staff Meeting Wednesday on 15 July 1970, 14 Jul 1970.
12. Peterson, pp. 486–87.
13. Ian Beckett, *The Roots of Counter-Insurgency: Armies and Guerilla Warfare, 1900–1945* (London: Blandford Press, 1988), p. 6.
14. Beckett, p. vii.
15. David Kilcullen, *Counterinsurgency* (Oxford: Oxford University Press, 2010), p. 1. Beckett and Pimlott, p. 1.
16. Kilcullen, p. 1.
17. Beckett, p. 6.
18. Paul Dixon, '"Hearts and Minds"? British Counter-Insurgency from Malaya to Iraq', *Journal of Strategic Studies*, 32 (2009), 353.
19. Hew Strachan, 'British Counter-Insurgency from Malaya to Iraq', *The RUSI Journal*, 152 (2007), 8. Dixon, p. 362.
20. Mackubin Owens, 'Strategy and the Strategic Way of Thinking', *Naval War College Review*, 60 (2007), 111.
21. Richard K. Betts, 'Is Strategy an Illusion?', *International Security*, 25 (2000), 5.
22. Owens, pp. 115–16.
23. DeVore, pp. 1–2. Geraint Hughes, 'Demythologising Dhofar: British Policy, Military Strategy, and Counter-Insurgency in Oman, 1963–1976', *Journal of Military History*, 79 (2015), 423–25. Mockaitis, p. 72. Beckett and Pimlott, p. 32. Halliday, p. 346. Robert Alston and Stuart Laing, *Unshook to the End of Time: A History of Britain and Oman, 1650–1970* (London: Gilgamesh Publishing, 2012), pp. 255–56.
24. Khalid Al Kharusi, 'The Dhofar War 1965–1975' (University of Central Lancashire, 2018), p. 40.
25. Tony Lewis, 'The Story of the Sultan of Oman's Armed Forces 1964–67', *The Journal of the Sultan's Armed Forces Association*, 7 (Feb 1988), 31–40 (pp. 35–36).
26. DeVore, p. 22.
27. Lewis, pp. 35–36.
28. Corran Purdon, *List the Bugle: Reminiscences of an Irish Soldier* (Vancouver: Greystone Books, 1993), p. 244. Ladwig III, p. 70.
29. DeVore, pp. 10–11.
30. TNA—DEFE 24/575—'Oman'—CSAF's Assessment of the Military Situation in Dhofar as at 14 February 1972, 17 Feb 1972. John Graham, *Ponder Anew: Reflections on the 20th Century* (Kent: Spellmount, 1999), p. 361.
31. Ibid., p. 350.
32. LHCMA, KCL—THWAITES COLLECTION—Purdon to Thwaites, 16 Feb 1969.

33. John E. Peterson, 'Guerrilla Warfare and Ideological Confrontation in the Arabian Peninsula: The Rebellion in Dhufar', *World Affairs*, 139 (1977), 285. DeVore, p. 163.
34. Lewis, p. 40. David French, 'Nasty Not Nice: British Counter-Insurgency Doctrine and Practice, 1945–1967', *Small Wars & Insurgencies*, 23 (2012), 744. MEC—GRAHAM COLLECTION—Briefing Document, Col. M. Harvey 'Dhofar Background', 27 Jun 1971.
35. LHCMA, KCL—THWAITES COLLECTION—Purdon to Thwaites, 16 Feb 1969. TNA—DEFE 24/575—'Oman'—CSAF's Assessment of the Military Situation in Dhofar as at 14 February 1972, 17 Feb 1972.
36. Ibid.
37. Geraint Hughes, 'A "Model Campaign" Reappraised: The Counter-Insurgency War in Dhofar, Oman, 1965–1975', *Journal of Strategic Studies*, 32 (2009), 301.
38. DeVore, p. 20.
39. TNA—FCO 8/1688—'Attachment of SAS Division of UK to Armed Forces of Oman'—Ackland to Parsons, 1 Feb 1971. Peter de la Billière, *Looking for Trouble: SAS to Gulf Command* (London: HarperCollins, 1995), p. 271.
40. Nikolas Gardner, 'The Limits of the Sandhurst Connection: The Evolution of Oman's Foreign and Defense Policy, 1970–1977', *The Journal of the Middle East and Africa*, 6 (2015), 50.
    Calvin H. Allen and W. Lynn Rigsbee, *Oman Under Qaboos: From Coup to Constitution, 1970–1996* (London: Frank Cass, 2002), p. 36.
41. DeVore, p. 20.
42. Geraint Hughes, '"Amateurs Who Play in League Division One"? Anglo-Iranian Military Relations During the Dhofar War in Oman', *British Journal for Military History*, 4 (2017), 103. Peterson, p. 331.
43. Gardner, p. 45.
44. Ibid., pp. 47 & 56.
45. Worrall, pp. 202–03.
46. Alston and Laing, p. 249.
47. Peterson, p. 420.
48. John Beasant and Christopher Ling, *Sultan in Arabia: A Private Life* (Edinburgh: Mainstream Publishing, 2004), p. 130.
49. UAE NA—FCO 8/2020—'Summary of main points discussed in the meeting between DMO and CSAF, 12 Jul. 1973', Loose Minute (meeting minutes) meeting between DMO and CSAF, 12 Jul 1973. Gardner, pp. 55–56.

2 The Dhofar War: Origins, Players, and Timeline

1. K. Perkins, 'Oman 1975: The Year of Decision', *The RUSI Journal*, 124 (1979), 38.
2. Ian Gardiner, *In the Service of the Sultan: A First-Hand Account of the Dhofar Insurgency* (Barnsley: Pen and Sword, 2007), p. 16.

NOTES

3. DeVore, p. 3. Marc Valeri, *Oman: Politics and Society in the Qaboos State* (London: C. Hurst & Co., 2017), p. 55. The Gulf Committee, 'Dhofar: Britain's Colonial War in the Gulf' (London: The Gulf Committee), p. 7.
4. Takriti, p. 8.
5. Akehurst, p. 12. Halliday, p. 275.
   Sultanate of Oman NRAA—Records of Oman 1966–1971 (Cambridge Archive Editions, 2003) Vol. 6: Diplomatic Dispatch—G. Arthur (British Residency Bahrain), 20 Apr 1971.
6. Ladwig III, pp. 65–66. Halliday, pp. 274–75.
7. Halliday, p. 276.
8. Allen and Rigsbee, p. 24. Halliday, pp. 276, & 287.
9. Simon Anglim, 'The Oman Djebel War, 1957–9', https://thestrategybridge.org/the-bridge/2014/12/1/the-oman-djebel-war-195759 [accessed 8 July 2020].
10. Takriti, p. 36.
11. Jim White, 'Oman 1965–1976: From Certain Defeat to Decisive Victory', *Small Wars Journal*, 1 (2008), 3.
12. Ibid., pp. 3–4. Halliday, p. 314.
13. S. Monick, 'Victory in Hades: The Forgotten Wars of the Oman 1957–1959 and 1970–1976. Part 2: The Dhofar Campaign 1970–1976', *Scientia Militaria: South African Journal of Military Studies*, 12 (1982), 5.
14. Purdon, p. 244. John McKeown, 'The Dhofar War and Its Significance' (Cambridge, MA, 1981), p. 47.
15. Peterson, pp. 186–87.
16. Takriti, pp. 54–55. Peterson, pp. 476–77 and 186–87.
17. Takriti, p. 60.
18. John Beasant, *Oman: The True-Life Drama and Intrigue of an Arab State* (New York: Random House, 2011), p. 132.
19. Alston and Laing, p. 219.
20. Peterson, p. 476.
21. Lewis, p. 36.
22. 'Dhofar: Britain's Colonial War in the Gulf', ed. by The Gulf Committee (London: The Gulf Committee, January 1972), p. 13.
23. Halliday, p. 318. Peterson, p. 477.
24. Lewis, p. 36.
25. Peterson, pp. 198–99.
26. Worrall, pp. 54 & 280.
27. Jan Morris, *Sultan in Oman* (London: Arrow Books Ltd, 1990), p. 27.
28. Marston and Malkasian, p. 177.
29. Monick, p. 5.
30. 'Dhofar: Britain's Colonial War in the Gulf', pp. 14–15.

31. TNA FCO 46/609, 'Defence Planning of UK Armed Forces in Muscat and Oman', Note by the Defence Operational Planning Staff, 30 Jul 1970. Valeri, p. 57. LHCMA, KCL—THWAITES COLLECTION—'Operation Lance', *Guards Magazine: Journal of the Household Division* (Summer 1970), 65.
32. Christopher Paul *et al.*, 'Paths to Victory: Detailed Insurgency Case Studies' (Rand National Defense Research Inst Santa Monica CA, 2013), p. 275. Valeri, p. 57.
33. Ladwig III, p. 70.
34. Peterson, p. 222.
35. Ibid., p. 224. LHCMA, KCL—THWAITES COLLECTION—'Operation Lance', *Guards Magazine: Journal of the Household Division* (Summer 1970) p. 65.
36. Peterson., pp. 225 & 479.
37. DeVore, pp. 10–11.
38. 'Dhofar: Britain's Colonial War in the Gulf', p. 17.
39. MEC—GRAHAM COLLECTION—Briefing Document, Col. M. Harvey 'Dhofar Background', 27 Jun 1971.
40. Graham, p. 375. MEC—GRAHAM COLLECTION—'Point Summary on Development of SAF for Lecture at Anglo-Omani Society, June 1996'.
41. DeVore, p. 163.
42. The Sultan's Armed Forces Association Newsletter No. 15 (March 1975), 'The Dhofar War July–December 1974 (General)'.
43. TNA FCO 8/2459, 'Political Relations Between Oman and Jordan', Clark to Wier/Green, 18 Sep 1975.
44. Akehurst, p. 173.
45. Ladwig III, p. 76. Allen and Rigsbee, p. 75.

3 Politics and Diplomacy

1   TNA FCO 8/33, 'Persian Gulf: Political Affairs (Ext): Bilateral: UK Policy In', Crawford to Brown, 31 Jan 1968.
2   AGDA FCO 8/2215, 'Political Situation in Oman', Diplomatic Report 379/74, 'The anatomy of Oman' (D. Hawley), 31 Oct 1974.
3   LHCMA, KCL—THWAITES COLLECTION—'Brief on Muscat and Oman', P. Rooke, Jun 1965. TNA FCO 8/2020, 'Military Assistance from UK to Oman'—Annex A to DP 20/73(C), 5 Oct Akehurst, pp. XV, 3, 16. TNA FCO 49/10, 'Steering Committee Meeting on 11 May: Defence Expenditure in the Middle East', Defence Expenditure Study no. 6. Long Term Policy in the Persian Gulf, 7 Jun 1967. Worrall, pp. 221–24. Alston and Laing, pp. 276–77.
4   TNA FCO 49/10, 'Steering Committee Meeting on 11 May: Defence Expenditure in the Middle East', Defence Expenditure Study no. 6. Long Term Policy in the Persian Gulf, 7 Jun 1967. Graham, pp. 308–09. TNA FCO 8/2020, 'Military Assistance from UK to Oman'—Annex A to DP 20/73(C), 5 Oct 1973.

NOTES

5   Worrall, p. 205. Akehurst, p. 3. Fiennes, p. 9.
6   TNA FCO 8/2020, 'Military Assistance from UK to Oman'—Annex A to DP 20/73(C).
7   Julian Paget, *Counter-Insurgency Campaigning* (London: Faber and Faber, 1967), pp. 66 & 96.
8   Beckett, p. 218. DeVore, p. 20.
9   Ian Cobain, 'Britain's Secret Wars', *The Guardian*, 8 Sep 2016. Fiennes, p. 9.
10 TNA FCO 49/10, 'Steering Committee Meeting on 11 May: Defence Expenditure in the Middle East', Defence Expenditure Study no. 6. Long Term Policy in the Persian Gulf, 7 Jun 1967.
11 TNA FCO 8/1688, 'Attachment of SAS Division of United Kingdom to Armed Forces of Oman', Ackland to Parsons, 1 Feb 1971.
12 Sultanate of Oman NRAA—Records of Oman 1966–1971 (Cambridge Archive Editions, 2003) Vol. 6: D. Hawley diplomatic report 'Impressions of Oman: The First and the Last', 5 Aug 1971.
13 Worrall, p. 58.
14 Clive Jones, *Britain and the Yemen Civil War, 1962–1965: Ministers, Mercenaries and Mandarins: Foreign Policy and the Limits of Covert Action* (Eastbourne/Portland, OR: Sussex Academic Press, 2010), p. 191.
15 TNA FCO 49/10, 'Steering Committee Meeting on 11 May: Defence Expenditure in the Middle East', Defence Expenditure Study no. 6. Long Term Policy in the Persian Gulf, 7 June 1967.
16 TNA AIR 20/10377—(COS Committee) Review of the Emergency in Malaya from Jun 1948 to Aug 1957.
17 TNA—CAB 158/70—'Cabinet Joint Intelligence Committee (A): Likely Developments in the Persian Gulf and their Probable Effects for British Interests', 7 June 1968.
18 Called Operation DHIB in UK military parlance. Geraint Hughes, 'A Proxy War in Arabia: The Dhofar Insurgency and Cross-Border Raids into South Yemen', *The Middle East Journal*, 69 (2015), 92.
19 Hughes, p. 301.
20 TNA FCO 49/10, 'Steering Committee Meeting on 11 May: Defence Expenditure in the Middle East', Defence Expenditure Study no. 6. Long Term Policy in the Persian Gulf, 7 Jun 1967. TNA FCO 8/2020, 'Military Assistance from UK to Oman'—Annex A to DP 20/73(C).
21 Interview Correspondence Response, Goodall, R., 17 May 2019. Colin Richardson, *Masirah: Tales from a Desert Island* (Durham: The Pentland Press Ltd., 2001), pp. 224–26.
22 Jones, p. 191.
23 Douglas Porch, *Counterinsurgency: Exposing the Myths of the New Way of War* (Cambridge: Cambridge University Press, 2013), p. 266.
24 Richardson, p. 87.
25 Ibid., p. 243. TNA—CAB 186/11—Joint Intelligence Committee (A) (JIC(A)): reports 1–16—JIC, 'The Outlook for Oman', 1 Mar 1972. TNA FCO 8/2020, 'Military Assistance from UK to Oman'—Annex A to DP 20/73(C), 5 Oct 1973. AGDA FCO 8/2478, 'Future UK Military Assistance to Oman'—Annex A to DP 15/75(C) (Draft).
26 Fiennes, p. 57.
27 Interview Correspondence Response, Goodall, R., 17 May 2019.

28 Worrall, p. 207. TNA FCO 8/2020, 'Military Assistance from UK to Oman'—Annex A to DP 20/73(C), 5 Oct 1973.
29 Valeri, p. 75.
30 Worrall, p. 227.
31 Jones, p. 191.
32 Halliday, pp. 332–33.
33 MEC—Granada TV 'End of Empire'—Archive list of interview transcripts; the Rt. Hon J. Amery (Roll 4, p. 5), Feb 1983. Mockaitis, p. 11.
34 Worrall, pp. 49–51.
35 Abdel Razzaq Takriti, 'The 1970 Coup in Oman Reconsidered', *Journal of Arabian Studies*, 3 (2013), 156.
36 Hawley was told by the Omani Minister of Works that Omer was smuggled out of Libya prior to Qadhafi's revolution in a piano as he was a CIA asset. AGDA FCO 8/2215, 'Political Situation in Oman' Memo 'Call on Minister of Works' (Hawley), 12 Dec 1974.
37 Allen and Rigsbee, p. 36. AGDA FCO 8/2027, 'Diplomatic representation of Oman in UK', Clark to Tatham, 19 Sep 1973, Hawley to Wright, 7 Oct 1973, Wright to Hawley, 23 Oct 1973. AGDA FCO 8/2465, 'Economic Situation in Oman', Treadwell to Lucas, 4 May 1975. AGDA FCO 8/2215, 'Political Situation in Oman', Diplomatic Report 379/74, 'The anatomy of Oman' (D. Hawley), 31 Oct 1974.
38 Worrall, p. 214.
39 Replaced in 1970 with the first British Ambassador to Oman (Donald Hawley), 'Sir Donald Hawley (Obituary)', *The Telegraph*, www.telegraph.co.uk/news/obituaries/1578238/Sir-Donald-Hawley.html [accessed 11 November 2020]. AGDA FCO 8/2215, 'Political Situation in Oman', Diplomatic Report 379/74, 'The anatomy of Oman' (D. Hawley), 31 Oct 1974. TNA—FCO 8/2687—Oman—Annual Review 1975, Review summary page, 1 Jan 1976.
40 Alston and Laing, pp. 305–06. Interview Correspondence Response, Goodall, R., 17 May 2019.
41 Keith McCloskey, *Airwork: A History* (Stroud: The History Press, 2012), p. 98.
42 Worrall, p. 209. Allen and Rigsbee, p. 75. DeVore, p. 20.
43 TNA—FCO 8/2687—Oman—Annual Review 1975, Review summary page, 1 Jan 1976.
44 TNA—FCO 8/2687—Oman—Annual Review 1975, Treadwell to PM (Callahan), 1 Jan 1976.
45 Worrall, p. 214.
46 Sultanate of Oman NRAA—Records of Oman 1966–1971 (Cambridge Archive Editions, 2003) Vol. 5: Crawford to Wier (Bahrain), 3 Aug 1970. UAE NA-FCO 8/1669, Annual Review of Oman—Crawford to PRPG, 4 Jan 1971. Allen and Rigsbee, pp. 75–77.
47 Valeri, p. 159.
48 Allen and Rigsbee, pp. 74–77.
49 Peterson, p. 466.
50 Mockaitis, p. 93. Jeapes, p. 14.
51 Ibid., p. 14.
52 John Pimlott, *British Military Operations 1945–1985* (London: Bison Books, 1984), pp. 15–17.

NOTES

53 Paul *et al.*, pp. xv, 51, 64 & 274. Jeapes, p. 14.
54 Paul *et al.*, p. xv.
55 Worrall, p. 155.
56 Ibid., p. 227. Alston and Laing, p. 277. TNA FCO 8/1688, 'Attachment of SAS Division of United Kingdom to Armed Forces of Oman', Ackland to Parsons, 1 Feb 1971. TNA DEFE 11/854, 'Oman'—Minute, Mason to Prime Minister (UK Military Assistance to Oman), 13 Mar 1975. Akehurst, p. XV.
57 Francis Owtram, 'Oman and the West: State Formation in Oman since 1920' (University of London, 1999), pp. 68–69.
58 Alston and Laing, p. 277.
59 Worrall, pp. 221–22.
60 Ian Skeet, *Muscat and Oman: The End of an Era* (London: Faber and Faber, 1974), p. 38. Alston and Laing, pp. 9–11.
61 Donald Hawley, *Oman and Its Renaissance*, Revised edn (London/New Jersey: Stacey International, 1990), p. 59.
62 Valeri, p. 50.
63 Wendell Phillips, *Oman: A History* (Beirut: Librarie du Lebanon, 1971), p. 205. David Neild, *A Soldier in Arabia* (Surbiton: Medina Publishing Ltd., 2015), pp. 40–41. Anthony Parsons, *They Say the Lion: Britain's Legacy to the Arabs: A Personal Memoir* (London: Random House, 1986), p. 132.
64 Simon Anglim, 'The Oman Djebel War, 1957–59', https://thestrategybridge.org/the-bridge/2014/12/1/the-oman-djebel-war-195759 [accessed 8 July 2020].
65 Peterson, p. 102.
66 Ibid., pp. 102–04.
67 Ibid., p. 104. David Smiley, *Arabian Assignment* (London: Leo Cooper, 1975), pp. 13–14.
68 Ash Rossiter, 'Britain and the Development of Professional Security Forces in the Gulf Arab States 1921–71: Local Forces and Informal Empire' (University of Exeter, 2014), p. 141.
69 Plekhanov, p. 70. Beasant, p. 171.
70 James F. Goode, 'Assisting Our Brothers, Defending Ourselves: The Iranian Intervention in Oman, 1972–75', *Iranian Studies*, 47 (2014), 446. AGDA FCO 8/2215, 'Political Situation in Oman', Diplomatic Report 379/74, 'The anatomy of Oman' (D. Hawley), 31 Oct 1974.
71 Ibid. Neil Innes, *Minister in Oman: A Personal Narrative* (Cambridge: The Oleander Press Ltd., 1987), p. 279.
72 Plekhanov, pp. 85–88. Allen and Rigsbee, p. 28. Beasant and Ling, p. 89.
73 DeVore, p. 151.
74 Beasant, p. 167.
75 Graham, p. 344. Peterson, pp. 479–80.
76 Graham, p. 328.
77 TNA FCO 8/1688, 'Attachment of SAS Division of United Kingdom to Armed Forces of Oman', Ackland to Parsons, 1 Feb 1971.

78 Ibid.
79 Ladwig III, p. 76. Allen and Rigsbee, p. 181.
80 Takriti, p. 223.
81 Mockaitis, pp. 74–76. White, p. 8. The Sultan's Armed Forces Association Newsletter No. 31 (June 1983), 'The Sultan's Armed Forces March 1970 to September 1972 (Major-General J.D.C. Graham)'.
82 DeVore, p. 2.
83 Takriti, p. 169. Hughes, p. 438.
84 John Newsinger, *British Counterinsurgency*, 2nd edn (Basingstoke, Hampshire: Palgrave Macmillan, 2015), pp. 145–46.
85 Goode, p. 446.
86 Rory Cormac, *Disrupt and Deny: Spies, Special Forces, and the Secret Pursuit of British Foreign Policy* (Oxford: Oxford University Press, 2018), pp. 190–91.
87 Worrall, p. 73.
88 Ken Perkins, *Khalida* (London: Quartet Books, 1991), p. 213.
89 TNA DEFE 24/1856—Middle East/Africa: Muscat and Oman—ACDS to Minister for Defence, 16 Jul 1970.
90 TNA DEFE 24/1856—Middle East/Africa: Muscat and Oman—Addendum to DMO Brief no 42/70 'Qaboos' Imminent Bid for Power in Muscat and Oman', 15 Jul 1970, and Minute J. Gibbon (Head of DS11), 'Muscat and Oman', 8 Jul 1970.
91 AGDA FO 1016/793, 'Muscat and Oman: Political Situation', Draft Memo (Secret): 'Points for Action Immediately After Qabus's [*sic*] Succession' (undated).
92 TNA DEFE 24/1856—Middle East/Africa: Muscat and Oman—DMO Briefing Notes for Chiefs of Staff Meeting Wednesday on 15 July 1970, 14 Jul 1970.
93 Under instructions from his late father, Graham's son released documents only after Qaboos's death clearly implicating British personnel in the coup. Matthew Campbell, 'The Soldier Who Overthrew the Sultan of Oman in a Very British Coup', *The Sunday Times* (22 November, 2020).
94 Peterson, p. 239.
95 David Benest, 'Ponder Anew: Brigadier John Graham & the Dhofar War 1970–1972', *The Strategy Bridge* (2015) [accessed 12 September 2017], p. 2. https://thestrategybridge.org/the-bridge/2016/1/1/ponder-anew-brigadier-john-graham-the-dhofar-war-19701972?rq=benest
96 Ibid.
97 The Journal of the Sultan's Armed Forces Association—Issue No. 41 (March 1992), 'Obituaries—Brigadier Peter Thwaites'.
98 Cormac, p. 191. AGDA FO 1016/793, 'Muscat and Oman: Political Situation', Telex no. 155 Bahrain to Consul-General, 21 Jul 1970.
99 Worrall, p. 73.
100 Takriti, pp. 171–72.
101 '23-11-2009', in *BBC Sounds* (Radio 4), ed. by Mike Thomson (UK: BBC, 2009).
102 Ladwig III, p. 71.

NOTES

103 Graham, p. 371.
104 MEC—GRAHAM COLLECTION—Statement copy 'The Case for Oman', dictated May 1972, 4 Sep 2009.
105 Graham, p. 372.
106 MEC—GRAHAM COLLECTION—'Point Summary on Development of SAF for Lecture at Anglo-Omani Society, June 1996'.
107 Worrall, pp. 128.
108 Alston and Laing, p. 249.
109 Ibid.
110 Parsons, p. 105.
111 DeVore, p. 11.
112 Ladwig III, p. 76. Sultanate of Oman NRAA—Records of Oman 1966–1971 (Cambridge Archive Editions, 2003) Vol. 6: D. Hawley diplomatic report 'Impressions of Oman: The First and the Last', 5 Aug 1971.
113 Ibid. Worrall, pp. 155–57.
114 Ibid., p. 155. Alston and Laing, pp. 249–50.
115 Graham, p. 372.
116 Al Kharusi, p. 164.
117 Worrall, p. 58.
118 Jones, p. 191.
119 Worrall, p. 2255.
120 UAE NA—FCO 8/2022, 'Extracts from Intelligence Reports', Introduction to Oman Intelligence Report no. 56 (16–29 Dec 1973), Registry no. 35 Archive, 10 Jan 1974. UAE NA—FCO 8/2020—Summary of main points discussed in meeting between the DMO and CSAF on 12 Jul 73, 12 July 1973.
121 Graham, p. 372. Goode, p. 447.
122 Goode, p. 454.
123 Ibid., pp. 453–54.
124 Worrall, pp. 221–26.
125 Graham, pp. 319–20, 29.
126 Gardner, p. 45.
127 TNA—PREM 15/215, '1973–1974 Middle East Record of a Conversation Between the Prime Minister and the Sultan of Oman at 5:15 on 11 September 1973 at No.10'.
128 Allen and Rigsbee, p. 35.
129 Worrall, p. 106.
130 Gardner, pp. 48–49. Allen and Rigsbee, p. 35.
131 AGDA FCO 8/2215, 'Political Situation in Oman', Diplomatic Report 379/74, 'The anatomy of Oman' (D. Hawley), 31 Oct 1974. Gardner, pp. 49–50.
132 UAE NA—FCO 8/1856—Military Assistance to Oman from UK—Memorandum prepared by D. Hawley, Muscat, 26 Feb 1972.

133 AGDA FCO 8/2215, 'Political Situation in Oman', Diplomatic Report 379/74, 'The anatomy of Oman' (D. Hawley), 31 Oct 1974.
134 AGDA FCO 8/2005, 'Political Situation in Oman', Memorandum, 'How Oman is Governed' (D. Hawley), 11 Jul 1973.
135 Ladwig III, p. 65.
136 Worrall, pp. 221–29.
137 Lewis, p. 32.
138 Worrall, pp. 106–07.
139 Takriti, p. 224.
140 Graham, p. 342.
141 Ladwig III, p. 72.
142 Ibid., pp. 72–75.
143 Jeapes, pp. 140–42. TNA—CAB 186/11, JIC 'Outlook for Oman (Delicate Source)', 1 Mar 72, Part 2, Main report.
144 Ladwig III, p. 65.
145 Halliday, pp. 274–5.
146 M. Robb, The Anglo-Omani Society/Sultan's Armed Forces Association Lecture: 'Civil Aid in Dhofar: The Key to Peace', London, 15 Jun 2023.
147 Peterson, pp. 392–93. M. Robb, The Anglo-Omani Society/Sultan's Armed Forces Association Lecture: 'Civil Aid in Dhofar: The Key to Peace', London, 15 Jun 2023.
148 Ibid.
149 MEC—GRAHAM COLLECTION—Briefing Document, Col. M. Harvey 'Dhofar Background', 27 June 1971.
150 Peterson, p. 428.
151 Hughes, p. 292.
152 Akehurst, p. 12.
153 Graham, pp. 340–41.
154 Beckett, p. 230.
155 TNA FCO 8/1688, 'Attachment of SAS Division of United Kingdom to Armed Forces of Oman', Ackland to Parsons, 1 Feb 1971. TNA DEFE 11/854, 'Oman'—Minute, Roy Mason to Prime Minister (British Military Assistance to Oman), 13 Mar 1975.
156 TNA FCO 8/2006, 'Annual Review of Oman 1972', Letter, Parsons to Le Quesne, 12 Feb 1973. TNA FCO 8/1688, 'Attachment of SAS Division of United Kingdom to Armed Forces of Oman', Ackland to Parsons, 1 Feb 1971.
157 Ibid. Ladwig III, pp. 75–6.
158 Akehurst, pp. ix-x. Peterson, p. 486.
159 Paget, pp. 74 & 104.
160 Newsinger, p. 193.
161 DeVore, p. 10.
162 Peterson, p. 329.

NOTES

163 Ibid. TNA—CAB 186/11, JIC 'Outlook for Oman (Delicate Source)', 1 Mar 72, Part 2, Main report.
164 Ladwig III, p. 76. DeVore, p. 20.
165 TNA—DEFE 11/854—Oman, COS Committee Defence Planning Staff, 'The Progress of Operations in Oman', 26 Feb 1975. DeVore, p. 21.
166 UAE NA—FCO 8/2022—Introduction to Oman Intelligence Report No. 56 (16–29 Dec 1973), Registry Archive 10 Jan 1974. UAE NA—FCO 8/2021—Extracts from Correspondence: Muscat and Oman: Cooperation between armed forces of Oman and United Arab Emirates. Wright to Lloyd-Jones, 2 Aug 1973, and Pridham to MODUK, 5 Aug 1973.
167 DeVore, p. 163.
168 Peterson, p. 328.
169 Alston and Laing, p. 277. Worrall, p. 227.
170 Ibid.
171 TNA—WO 386/17, 'Joint Investigation into Internal Security Incidents in Crater—20 Jun 67 (Final Report)'. TNA—DEFE 11/533, 'Aden', Report on the Mutinies Within the South Arabian Forces on 20 June 1967 and the Action Taken to Control Them by British and South Arabian Forces', 26 Oct 1967.
172 As highlighted by the various press cuttings collected by Graham during his secondment as CSAF and available to view in the MEC, Graham Collection, Boxes 7 and 8, e.g. 'Britons lead Sultan's thrust against rebels' in the (London) *Times*, 12 May 1972.
173 TNA FCO 8/1688, 'Attachment of SAS Division of United Kingdom to Armed Forces of Oman', Ackland to Parsons, 1 Feb 1971.
174 J.E. Peterson, 'The Experience of British Counter-Insurgency Campaigns and Implications for Iraq', *Arabian Peninsula Background Note—APBN-009* (2009), p. 9.
175 Michael Crawshaw, 'The Evolution of British Coin', ed. by Ministry of Defence Joint Doctrine Publication (JDP 3–40) (2012), p. 20.
176 Sultanate of Oman NRAA—Records of Oman 1966–1971 (Cambridge Archive Editions, 2003) Vol. 6: Arthur to British Residency Bahrain, 26 Apr 1971.

4 Military Strategy

1 Akehurst, p. 65.
2 Purdon, pp. 242–43.
3 Hughes, pp. 279–81.
4 Plekhanov, pp. 126–27.
5 TNA—DEFE 24/575—'Oman'—CSAF's Assessment of the Military Situation in Dhofar as at 14 February 1972, 17 Feb 1972. Hughes, pp. 284–85.
6 DeVore, pp. 144–45, 151–53. Beckett and Pimlott, pp. 31–32. Jacqueline Hazelton, 'The "Hearts and Minds" Fallacy: Violence, Coercion, and Success in Counterinsurgency Warfare', *International Security*, 42 (2017), 112. Perkins, pp. 38–39.

7   D. de C. Smiley, 'Muscat and Oman', *Royal United Services Institution. Journal*, 105 (1960), 34.
8   Purdon, p. 243.
9   Ibid., pp. 188–91.
10 Michael J. Gunther, 'Combined Omani-British Strategy During the Dhofar Rebellion (1963–1982)' (King's College London, 2019), pp. 286–87.
11 Pimlott, p. 50.
12 Purdon, pp. 188–91.
13 Ibid., pp. 99–117.
14 Ken Perkins, *A Fortunate Soldier* (London: Brassey's Defence Pubishers Ltd., 1988), p. 59.
15 Graham, p. 362.
16 Billière, pp. 204–08. TNA—WO 305/4293, 'Borneo Operations Feb–Jul 1965', Various patrol reports.
17 Jeremy Jones and Nicholas Ridout, *Oman, Culture and Diplomacy* (Edinburgh: Edinburgh University Press, 2013), p. 191. Plekhanov, p. 126.
18 Valeri, p. 54., 126–27.
19 Plekhanov, p. 121.
20 Beasant and Ling, p. 174.
21 Ibid. Beasant, pp. 211–12.
22 Pauline Searle, *Dawn Over Oman* (London: George Allen & Unwin, 1979), p. 3.
23 Peterson, p. 477.
24 Lewis, p. 33.
25 Peterson, p. 477.
26 White, p. 7.
27 Fiennes, p. 9. US Army and US Marine Corps, *Counterinsurgency Field Manual (Fm3-24)* (Chicago: University of Chicago, 2007), p. 22. Robert Grainger Ker Thompson, *Defeating Communist Insurgency: Experiences from Malaya and Vietnam* (London: Chatto & Windus, 1966), pp. 48–49.
28 TNA—FCO 8/41, 'Persian Gulf: Political Affairs (Ext:) Bilateral Effects On: Aden', Clark to Balfour-Paul, 7 Sep 1967.
29 Akehurst, p. 25.
30 Ladwig III, p. 67.
31 Akehurst, pp. 24–25.
32 Purdon, p. 294.
33 Graham, p. 321.
34 Hughes, p. 281. DeVore, p. 10.
35 Benest. Referring to Creasey and Fletcher, Bryan Ray states: 'They had been a great pair to have guided us through a crucial part of the Dhofar War, the country was lucky to have had them and so was SAF.' Bryan Ray, *Dangerous Frontiers: Campaigning in Somaliland and Oman* (Barnsley: Pen and Sword, 2008), p. 197.
36 Graham, p. 342.
37 Ibid.

NOTES

38 Ibid.
39 Ladwig III, p. 72.
40 Graham, p. 347.
41 DeVore, p. 163.
42 Graham, p. 328.
43 DeVore, p. 12. TNA—DEFE 24/575—'Oman'—CSAF's Assessment of the Military Situation in Dhofar as at 14 February 1972, 17 Feb 1972.
44 Graham, p. 367.
45 Ibid., pp. 370–71.
46 Hughes, p. 92.
47 Graham, p. 371.
48 Beckett and Pimlott, p. 64.
49 Peterson, p. 482.
50 Hughes, pp. 284–85.
51 Peterson, p. 342.
52 DeVore, p. 164.
53 Hughes, p. 103.
54 Graham, p. 362.
55 Ibid., p. 375.
56 DeVore, p. 166.
57 Ibid., p. 163.
58 Ibid.
59 The Sultan's Armed Forces Association Newsletter No. 16 (November 1975), 'Dhofar War—January to June 1975'.
60 Hughes, p. 285.
61 Perkins, p. 45.
62 Jeapes, p. 28.
63 Peterson, pp. 228–29.
64 TNA—FCO 8/1688—'Attachment of SAS Division of United Kingdom to Armed Forces of Oman', Letter Ackland to Parsons, 1 Feb 1971.
65 TNA—DEFE 25/186—'Muscat and Oman General' Psyops in Oman and Dhofar—Up Dating Stirep, Bond to VCDS, 19 Mar 1971.
66 DeVore, p. 152.
67 Allen and Rigsbee, p. 67.
68 Ladwig III, p. 76. Beckett and Pimlott, p. 23.
69 DeVore, p. 152. Billière, pp. 105–30.
70 Fiennes, pp. 30–31. DeVore, p. 14. TNA—DEFE 25/186—'Muscat and Oman General' Psyops in Oman and Dhofar—Up Dating Stirep, Bond to VCDS, 19 Mar 1971.
71 Ibid.
72 Gunther, p. 241.

THE DHOFAR WAR

73 Graham, p. 346.
74 Leaflets for propaganda purposes were produced locally in Dhofar or in Bahrain. TNA—DEFE 25/186—'Muscat and Oman General' Psyops in Oman and Dhofar—Up Dating Stirep, Bond to VCDS, 19 Mar 1971. UAE NA—FCO 8/1856, 'Military Assistance to Oman from UK'— Memorandum prepared by D. Hawley, British Ambassador, Muscat, 26 Feb 1972.
75 Tony Geraghty, *Who Dares Wins: The Story of the SAS 1950–1982* (London: Fontana/Collins, 1990), p. 100.
76 Paget, p. 102. Frank Kitson, *Bunch of Five* (London: Faber and Faber, 1977), p. 34.
77 Geraghty, pp. 100–01.
78 DeVore, p. 9.
79 Robert Jackson, *The Malayan Emergency and Indonesian Confrontation: The Commonwealth's Wars, 1948–1966* (Barnsley: Pen and Sword, 2008), p. 38.
80 Billière, p. 232.
81 Akehurst, p. 43.
82 Interview correspondence response, Neild, D., 14 May 2019.
83 Akehurst, p. 43.
84 Ladwig III, p. 73.
85 Akehurst, p. 42. DeVore, p. 20.
86 Graham, p. 347.
87 Ibid.
88 Richard J. Aldrich and Rory Cormac, *The Black Door: Spies, Secret Intelligence, and British Prime Ministers* (London: William Collins, 2016), p. 311.
89 Hughes, p. 92. Cormac, p. 193.
90 Alston and Laing, p. 252.
91 DeVore, p. 161.
92 Worrall, p. 286.
93 Jeapes, p. 204. DeVore, p. 162. M. Robb, The Anglo-Omani Society/Sultan's Armed Forces Association Lecture: 'Civil Aid in Dhofar: The Key to Peace', London, 15 Jun 2023.
94 Ibid.
95 Lewis, p. 40. Ladwig III, p. 70.
96 Peterson, pp. 5–6.
97 TNA—WO 106/6020—'Report on the Cyprus Emergency', Chapters 1 & 3, 31 Jul 1959.
98 Lewis, p. 35.
99 Purdon, p. 237.
100 TNA—FCO 8/1688—Attachment of SAS Division of United Kingdom to Armed Forces of Oman—Letter, Ackland to Parsons, 1 Feb 1971. Graham, pp. 346–47.
101 Clive A. Jones, 'Military Intelligence and the War in Dhofar: An Appraisal', *Small Wars & Insurgencies*, 25 (2014), 9.
102 Hughes, pp. 444–45.
103 Hughes, p. 293.

NOTES

104 TNA—DEFE 11/759—Creasey to Qaboos bin Said—'Initial Report on Operation JASON', 4 Jan 1973.
105 Ibid.
106 Jones, p. 19. McKeown, p. 77. The Sultan's Armed Forces Association Newsletter—Issue No.12 (July 1973), 'Oman Report—Northern Oman'.
107 Akehurst, p. 65.
108 Jeapes, p. 14.
109 Charters, p. 63. Paul *et al.*, p. xv.

5 Military Operations and Tactics

1 Graham, pp. 314–15.
2 Peterson, p. 480.
3 Purdon, pp. 188–90.
4 Peterson, p. 250.
5 Purdon, p. 286.
6 Hughes, p. 279. Hughes, p. 439.
7 Ladwig III, p. 68.
8 Hughes, p. 279.
9 Hughes, p. 94.
10 McKeown, p. 105.
11 Paget, p. 78.
12 TNA—WO 106/6020—'Report on the Cyprus Emergency', Chapter 1, 31 Jul 1959. Paget, p. 153.
13 TNA—CAB21/1681—'Cabinet Malaya Committee on Operation against Bandits etc. (General)'. Meeting Minutes 25 Sep 1950. Colin Mitchell, *Having Been a Soldier* (London: Hamish Hamilton, 1969), p. 150. Paget, pp. 90 & 107.
14 Frank Kitson, *Low Intensity Operations: Subversion, Insurgency and Peacekeeping* (London: Faber and Faber, 1991), p. 95.
15 Interview Correspondence Response, Neild, D., 14 May 2019.
16 Ladwig III, p. 67.
17 Akehurst, p. 25.
18 Ibid., pp. 24–25.
19 Ladwig III, p. 67.
20 Akehurst, pp. 24–25.
21 Peterson, p. 369.
22 Lewis, p. 32.
23 Walker, pp. 132–34. Ibid., p. 196.
24 Plekhanov, p. 126.

THE DHOFAR WAR

25 Sultanate of Oman NRAA—Records of Oman 1966–1971 (Cambridge Archive Editions, 2003) Vol. 4: Annual Review 1969 correspondence—'Annual Review 1969', D.G. Crawford, 30 Dec 1969.
26 Brig. Purdon highlights an Omani proverb told him by Sultan Said: 'If you are out walking and meet a Dhofari and a snake, tread on the Dhofari', Purdon, p. 244. Lewis, p. 40.
27 Ibid.
28 Ibid.
29 Purdon, pp. 292–3.
30 Ibid., p. 244. Lewis, p. 35.
31 LHCMA, KCL—THWAITES COLLECTION—Letters, Sultan Said to Thwaites, 8 Jan 1970 and 18 Jan 1970.
32 Hughes, p. 454.
33 Halliday, p. 348.
34 Peterson, p. 485.
35 Ladwig III, p. 76. Peterson, pp. 329–31.
36 Hughes, pp. 102–05.
37 DeVore, p. 20. Ladwig III, p. 72.
38 DeVore.
39 Peter Thwaites, *Muscat Command* (London: Leo Cooper, 1995), p. 40.
40 Hughes, p. 103. Akehurst, pp. 83–4.
41 AGDA FCO 8/2442, 'Iranian Military Assistance to Oman', Hawley, 4 Dec 1974. AGDA FCO 8/2458, 'Political Relations Between Oman and Iran', Gooch (Tehran) to UKMOD, 9 Jan 1975.
42 AGDA FCO 8/2442, 'Iranian Military Assistance to Oman', Callaghan to Tehran, 9 Aug 1974 & Hawley to MOD, 6 Dec 1974. AGDA FCO 8/1859, 'Military Assistance to Oman from Jordan and Iran', Clark (Muscat) to MODUK, 17 Aug 1972.
43 Gardiner, p. 154.
44 AGDA FCO 8/2442, 'Iranian Military Assistance to Oman', Azhari to Creasey, 30 Jul 1974.
45 AGDA FCO 8/2442, 'Iranian Military Assistance to Oman', Callaghan to Tehran, 13 Aug 1974, Parsons to Muscat, 10 Apr 1974,Creasey to Minister of Defence, 18 Aug 1974 & Parsons to Muscat/MODUK, 9 Dec 1974.
46 AGDA FCO 8/2442, 'Iranian Military Assistance to Oman', Creasey to Qaboos 'General Azhari's Visit 28–29 August', 25 Aug 1974.
47 Newsinger, p. 152.
48 Perkins, p. 39.
49 AGDA FCO 8/2442, 'Iranian Military Assistance to Oman', Azhari to Creasey, 13 Aug 1974 & CSAF Operational Instruction 6 of 1974, 29 Sep 1974. AGDA FCO 8/2241, 'Iranian Military Assistance to Oman', Review of the Situation, CSAF, 17 Mar 1974.
50 Peterson, p. 347. AGDA FCO 8/2458, 'Political Relations Between Oman and Iran', Hawley to Tehran, 7 Jan 1975.
51 Perkins, p. 40.

NOTES

52 AGDA FCO 8/2442, 'Iranian Military Assistance to Oman', Creasey to Azhari, 7 Aug 1974 & SAF Operational Instruction 6 of 1974, 29 Sep 1974.
53 AGDA FCO 8/2442, 'Iranian Military Assistance to Oman', Hawley to Wright, 30 Sep 1974.
54 DeVore, p. 20.
55 Ibid., p. 17.
56 Peterson, pp. 481–86. TNA—FCO 46/609—'Defence Planning of UK Armed Forces in Muscat and Oman', Annex A to COS 1166/6/3/70, 'The Employment of an SAS Squadron in Dhofar', 26 Feb 1970. TNA—FCO 8/2960, '"Soldier" Magazine Story on Royal Engineer Squadron in Oman + other Publication of the Dhofar War', (Secret) Memo, Douglas-Home to Secretary of State for Defence FCS/70/56, 'Special Air Service (SAS Assistance to the Sultanate of Oman)' (undated). Billière, p. 271.
57 TNA FCO 8/1688, 'Attachment of SAS Division of UK to Armed Forces of Oman', Ackland to Parsons, 1 Feb 1971.
58 TNA—FCO 46/609—'Defence Planning of UK Armed Forces in Muscat and Oman'—Annex to D/DS 6/7/155/13, 17 Aug 1970.
59 DeVore, pp. 151–2.
60 Graham, p. 347. Peterson, pp. 392–93.
61 Billière, p. 270.
62 Ibid. DeVore, p. 155.
63 Graham, p. 351.
64 DeVore, p. 155. Hughes, p. 283.
65 Akehurst, p. 43.
66 Graham, p. 347.
67 Peterson, pp. 267–68.
68 Ibid., pp. 300–02. MEC Graham Collection—Graham to Oldman, 29 Jul 1972.
69 Ladwig III, p. 75.
70 Graham, p. 347.
71 Peterson, pp. 328–30. Ibid., pp. 377–78.
72 Ibid.
73 Gardiner, pp. 78–80.
74 Peterson, p. 328.
75 Ibid., p. 329. Allen and Rigsbee, p. 74.
76 Hughes, pp. 444–45.
77 Jones, p. 643.
78 Ibid.
79 Peterson, p. 307.
80 Jones, p. 643.
81 Graham, p. 347.
82 Ibid. TNA—DEFE 24/575—'Oman'—CSAF's Assessment of the Military Situation in Dhofar as at 14 February 1972, 17 Feb 1972.

THE DHOFAR WAR

83 Fiennes, p. 13.
84 TNA—DEFE 24/575—'Oman'—CSAF's Assessment of the Military Situation in Dhofar as at 14 February 1972, 17 Feb 1972.
85 Hughes, p. 441.
86 White, p. 8. TNA—DEFE 11/854 'Oman'—Woodard to Head of DS11, 5 Mar 1975. DeVore, p. 11.
87 Graham, pp. 374–5. Peterson, p. 296. Ibid., pp. 301–02.
88 DeVore, p. 144. Graham, p. 374.
89 MEC—GRAHAM COLLECTION—Box 2/5, John Graham, Personal Diary Entry, 19 Jul 1972. DeVore, p. 157. Graham, p. 374.
90 Peterson, p. 302. Graham, p. 374.
91 MEC—GRAHAM COLLECTION—'Point Summary on Development of SAF for Lecture at Anglo-Omani Society, June 1996'. Billière, p. 276.
92 Ibid., p. 277.
93 Peterson, p. 300. MEC—GRAHAM COLLECTION—Graham to Oldman, 29 Jul 1972.
94 Newsinger, p. 152.
95 Hughes, p. 425. Geraghty, p. 164.
96 MEC—GRAHAM COLLECTION—Graham to Oldman, 29 Jul 1972.
97 Peterson, p. 296. Graham, pp. 374–75. Newsinger, p. 151.
98 Graham, pp. 374–75.
99 Peterson, p. 301.
100 MEC—GRAHAM COLLECTION—Graham to Oldman, 29 Jul 1972. Peterson, p. 302.
101 Ibid.
102 Jeapes, p. 158.
103 Ibid.
104 MEC—GRAHAM COLLECTION—'A Message from Brigadier J.D.C. Graham OBE Outgoing President [of SAF Association]', Sep 1972. Akehurst, p. 30. Alston and Laing, p. 295.
105 Peterson, p. 301.
106 MEC—GRAHAM COLLECTION—Graham to Oldman, 29 Jul 1972.
107 Hughes, p. 285.
108 Perkins, p. 44.
109 Peterson, p. 485.
110 Perkins, p. 45.
111 Ibid.
112 TNA FCO 8/2006, 'Annual Review of Oman 1972', Parsons to Le Quesne, 12 Feb 1973.
113 Graham, pp. 314–15.
114 Peterson, pp. 191–92.
115 Lewis, pp. 36–38.
116 Ibid. Peterson, pp. 198–99.

NOTES

117 Morris, p. 27. Hughes, p. 280.
118 Peterson, p. 477.
119 Worrall, pp. 54 & 280.
120 Lewis, p. 39.
121 Peterson, p. 206.
122 Lewis, p. 39.
123 Hughes, p. 280. DeVore, pp. 10–11.
124 DeVore, pp. 144–45.
125 TNA FCO 46/609, 'Defence Planning of UK Armed Forces in Muscat and Oman', Note by the Defence Operational Planning Staff, 30 Jul 1970. LHCMA, KCL—THWAITES COLLECTION—'Operation Lance', *Guards Magazine: Journal of the Household Division* (Summer 1970), p. 65.
126 Graham, p. 320.
127 Ibid., p. 346.
TNA—FCO 8/1688—Attachment of SAS Division of United Kingdom to Armed Forces of Oman—Letter Ackland to Parsons, 1 Feb 1971.
128 Billière, pp. 264–66. Worrall, p. 92. Athol Yates and Geraint Hughes, 'Operation Intradon in the Musandam, 1970–1971: What This Counterinsurgency Operation Says About British Military Operations in the Arabian Gulf', *Small Wars & Insurgencies* (2022), p. 17.
129 Ladwig III, p. 72.
130 DeVore, p. 163.
131 Jeapes, pp. 136–40.
132 Hughes, p. 283.
133 Graham, p. 360. Jeapes, p. 142.
134 DeVore, p. 12.
135 DeVore, p. 144.
136 Peterson, p. 296. Billière, p. 277.
137 Alston and Laing, p. 296. Beckett, p. 228.
138 DeVore, pp. 17 & 22.
139 Hazelton, p. 112. DeVore, pp. 165–66.
140 AGDA FCO 8/2442, 'Iranian Military Assistance to Oman', Azhari to Creasey, 13 Aug 1974 & CSAF Operational Instruction 6 of 1974, 29 Sep 1974.
141 Peterson, pp. 346–7. AGDA FCO 8/2458, 'Political Relations Between Oman and Iran', Hawley to FCO (priority Tehran), 7 Jan 1975.
142 DeVore, p. 20. Goode, p. 441.
143 Hughes, p. 454.
144 DeVore, p. 163. Ladwig III, p. 72.
145 Benest. TNA—FCO 46/835—'Armed Forces of United Kingdom in Muscat and Oman'—Memo, 'Assessment of the situation by Major-General Tim Creasey Commander Sultan's Armed Forces', 16 Oct 1972.

146 Graham, p. 315.
147 Ibid., pp. 355–56,Hughes, pp. 282–84. Ladwig III, pp. 73–74. Perkins, pp. 38, 40 & 43–44. TNA—FCO 46/835—'Armed Forces of United Kingdom in Muscat and Oman'—Memo, 'Assessment of the situation by Major General Tim Creasey Commander Sultan's Armed Forces', 16 Oct 1973. Akehurst, pp. 45 & 82–83.
148 Purdon, p. 235.
149 Ibid., pp. 186–88.
150 Graham, pp. 355–56.
151 Ibid., pp. 315, 356.
152 Hazelton, p. 81.
153 TNA CAB/129/96—'Security Measures in Kenya', Memorandum by the Secretary of State for the Colonies, 5 March 1959.
154 TNA AIR20/10377—(Chiefs of Staff Committee) Review of the Emergency in Malaya from June 1948 to August 1957.
155 Graham, p. 315.
156 Peterson, p. 480.
157 Ibid.
158 Graham, p. 315. Purdon, p. 195.
159 Hughes, p. 279.
160 Graham, p. 315.
161 Ibid.
162 Ibid., p. 343.
163 Ibid.
164 Goode, p. 451.
165 Hughes, pp. 104–05. Akehurst, pp. 82–85.
166 LHCMA, KCL—THWAITES COLLECTION—'Brief on Muscat and Oman', Rooke to CO of Sultan's Armed Forces, Jun 1965.
Graham, p. 315.
167 Ibid.
168 TNA—FCO 46/835—'Armed Forces of United Kingdom in Muscat and Oman'—Memo, 'Assessment of the Situation by Major-General Tim Creasey Commander Sultan's Armed Forces', 16 Oct 1972.
169 Peterson, pp. 356–57.
170 Perkins, p. 44.
171 McCloskey, p. 141.
172 Akehurst, p. 45.
173 Perkins, p. 40.
174 Hughes, pp. 92 & 104–5. Akehurst, pp. 82–83.
175 Ibid. Hughes, pp. 103–05.
176 Graham, p. 347.

NOTES

177 TNA—DEFE 24/575—'Oman'—CSAF's Assessment of the Military Situation in Dhofar as at 14 February 1972, 17 Feb 1972.
178 Graham, p. 343.

6 Non-Kinetic Military and Informal Support

1   Hughes, p. 454. DeVore, p. 17.
2   Anglim.
3   Peterson, p. 65.
4   Peterson, p. 102.
5   Ibid., p. 148.
6   Ibid.
7   Ibid.
8   Ladwig III, p. 76.
9   TNA—CAB 186/11—Joint Intelligence Committee (A) (JIC(A)): reports 1–16—JIC, 'The Outlook for Oman', 1 Mar 1972. C. Richarson, *Masirah: Tales from a Desert Island* (Durham: Pentland Press, 2001), p. 243.
10 Alston and Laing, pp. 135–36.
11 Peterson, pp. 392–93.
12 M. Robb, The Anglo-Omani Society/Sultan's Armed Forces Association Lecture: 'Civil Aid in Dhofar: The Key to Peace', London, 15 Jun 2023.
13 Ibid. Jeapes, pp. 231–32.
14 Alston and Laing, p. 135.
15 AGDA FCO 8/2220, 'Visits of Ministers or Parliament Between Oman and UK', Wright to Wier/Private Secretary, (attached briefing notes) 30 Oct 1974. DeVore, p. 161. Peterson, p. 420.
16 Beasant, pp. 195–96. Gunther, p. 272.
17 AGDA FCO 8/2005, 'Political Situation in Oman', Hawley to Wright, (attached memorandum) 11 Jul 1975.
18 DeVore, p. 161. Worrall, p. 191.
19 DeVore, p. 162.
20 Ibid.
21 Worrall, p. 173.
22 Hughes, p. 290. Worrall, pp. 172–73.
23 Worrall, pp. 176 & 181.
24 Alston and Laing, p. 255.
25 Allen and Rigsbee, p. 109.
26 Ibid.
27 Ibid., p. 104.

28 AGDA FCO 8/2465, 'Economic Situation in Oman', White to Brown, 11 May 1975, Armitage to FCO Telex, 'Oman's Economy', 13 May 1975, McCarthy to Clark, 18 May 1975, and Memo 'Oman Internal' (Treadwell), 11 Jun 1975. AGDA FCO 8/2215, 'Political Situation in Oman', Diplomatic Report 379/74, 'The anatomy of Oman' (D. Hawley), 31 Oct 1974.
29 Worrall, pp. 91 and 115.
30 Peterson, p. 80.
31 Alston and Laing, p. 272.
32 Ibid.
33 Ibid., p. 273.
34 Hughes, p. 290.
35 Alston and Laing, p. 274.
36 Ibid., pp. 255–56.
37 Ladwig III, p. 76.
38 Valeri, p. 68.
39 DeVore, p. 161.
40 Alan Hoskins, *A Contract Officer in the Oman* (Tunbridge Wells: Costello, 1988), p. 11. TNA—FCO 8/2235, 'UK Arms Sales to Oman', Scott to Jeffery, 29 May 1974 & local file number documents 170–74. Billière, p. 286. Allen and Rigsbee, pp. 76–77.
41 Takriti, pp. 171–73.
42 Graham, p. 371.
43 TNA—FCO 8/2687—Oman—Annual Review 1975, British Ambassador, Muscat (C. Treadwell) to J. Callahan (Prime Minister), 1 Jan 1976.
44 AGDA FCO 8/2442, 'Iranian Military Assistance to Oman', Hawley, 5 Dec 1974. Hawley to MODUK AIR 10 Oct 1974, Hawley to MODUK 15 Oct 1974, Hawley to MODUK 29 Oct 1974.
45 Anglim. Beasant, pp. 119–28.
46 Effectively the Omani 'Minister of Defence'.
47 Graham, p. 314.
48 Cobain. Alston and Laing, p. 219. Peterson, pp. 464–65, 483.
49 Lewis, p. 32.
50 Beasant, p. 123.
51 Alston and Laing, p. 255.
52 Beasant and Ling, p. 37.
53 Worrall, pp. 46–47.
54 Ibid.
55 Purdon, p. 218.
56 Johnny Cooper, *One of the Originals: The Story of a Founder Member of the SAS* (London: Pan Books Ltd, 1991), pp. 157–58. Ibid., p. 186.
57 Purdon, p. 188.
58 Ibid., pp. 188–89.

NOTES

59   Peterson, p. 104.
60   Hughes, p. 430. Ibid., p. 440.
61   Peterson, p. 250.
62   Hughes, p. 279. Hughes, p. 435. Graham, p. 314.
63   Peterson, p. 465. Allen and Rigsbee, pp. 74–76.
64   Peterson, p. 466.
65   Valeri, p. 158.
66   Michael Barber, 'Brigadier Tim Landon—Soldier of Fortune Who Helped Ease Oman into the Modern World', *The Guardian*. https://www.theguardian.com/news/2007/aug/28/guardianobituaries.military
67   AGDA FCO 8/2215, 'Political Situation in Oman', Hawley to Wright, 14 Nov 1974.
68   Fiennes, p. 144.
69   Beasant, p. 173. Ibid., p. 192. Vron Ware, *Return of a Native: Learning from the Land* (London: Repeater Books, 2022), p. 54.
70   Graham, pp. 322–23, 331. Fiennes, p. 144. Hughes, p. 438.
71   Sarika Breeze, 'His Quest for the Lost City of Uber and Other Omani Adventures (Sir Ranulph Fiennes for the Anglo-Omani Society)', (The Anglo-Omani Society, 2020).
72   AGDA FCO 8/2215, 'Political Situation in Oman', Hawley to Wright, 14 Nov 1974.
73   Ibid. AGDA FCO 8/2027, 'Diplomatic Representation of Oman in UK', Hawley to Wright, 7 Oct 1973. AGDA FCO 8/2244, 'Movements of Sultan Qaboos bin Said of Oman', Hawley to Wright, 29 Jun 1974. AGDA FCO 8/2236, 'UK Arms Sales to Oman', Tatham to MODUK, 6 Aug 1973. AGDA FCO 8/1961, 'UK Defence Relations in the Persian Gulf', Goulding to Wright, 9 Aug 1973.
74   AGDA FCO 8/2465, 'Economic Situation in Oman', Treadwell to Lucas, 4 May 1975.
75   AGDA FCO 8/2215, 'Political Situation in Oman', Hawley to Wright, 14 Nov 1974. Allen and Rigsbee, p. 36.
76   AGDA FCO 8/2470, 'Military Assistance from UK to Oman', Treadwell to MODUK, 15 Mar 1975. AGDA FCO 8/2241, 'Iranian Military Assistance to Oman', Hawley to FCO, 5 May 1974.
77   AGDA FCO 8/2215, 'Political Situation in Oman', Hawley to Wright, 14 Nov 1974. Beasant, p. 193.
78   AGDA FCO 8/2215, 'Political Situation in Oman', Hawley to Wright, 14 Nov 1974.
79   Valeri, pp. 158–59.
80   AGDA FCO 8/2215, 'Political Situation in Oman', Hawley to Wright, 14 Nov 1974.
81   Barber.
82   Beasant pp. 196–99
83   AGDA FCO 8/5516, 'Oman: Successor to General Sir Tim Creasey as Chief of Defence Staff', Butler to Ackland, 24 Feb 1984. Haskell to Leahy, 29 Feb 1984.
84   Beasant, p. 192.
85   Ibid., pp. 192–96.
86   Valeri, p. 159. Barber.

87 Valeri, p. 158.
88 AGDA FCO 8/2215, 'Political Situation in Oman', Hawley to Wright, 14 Nov 1974.
89 Ibid.
90 Barber.
91 AGDA FCO 8/2242, 'Iranian Military Assistance to Oman', Callaghan Priority Dispatch, 15 Oct 1974.
92 Beasant, p. 212.
93 Ibid., pp. 213–14.
94 Ibid., p. 213.
95 Graham, p. 315. AGDA FCO 8/2235, 'UK Arms Sales to Oman', Tatham to MODUK, 25 May 1974.
96 Mockaitis, p. 72. Beckett and Pimlott, p. 32. Halliday, p. 346. TNA—DEFE 11/656 'Oman'—COS Committee: Report on British Service Assistance to Oman, 7 Aug 1974.
97 Graham, p. 315.
98 Ibid.
99 Worrall, p. 292.
100 Graham, p. 371.
101 DeVore, p. 16. Geraghty, p. 176.
102 Geraghty, pp. 176–77. David Arkless, *The Secret War* (London: William Kinber & Co. Ltd., 1988), p. 92.
103 Sultanate of Oman NRAA—Records of Oman 1966–1971 (Cambridge Archive Editions, 2003) Vol. 4: Correspondence PRPG to British Consulate General, Muscat—Sultanate Balance Sheet—3rd Quarter 1969, 13 Oct 1969. Hoskins, p. 15.
104 Nikolas Gardner, 'The Harold Wilson Government, Airwork Services Limited, and the Saudi Arabian Air Defence Scheme, 1965–73', *Journal of Contemporary History*, 42 (2007), p. 345 and pp. 347–49.
105 The Saudi 'Magic Carpet' Air Defence Scheme, for example, of the 1960s/70s was worth tens of millions of pounds. Ibid., pp. 349–50.
106 MEC—GRAHAM COLLECTION—Notes on the Sultan's Armed Forces for Contract Officers' JDG—1970.
107 Graham, p. 314.
108 DeVore, p. 163.
109 Peterson, pp. 483–84. UAE NA—FCO 8/2021—Extracts from Correspondence: Muscat and Oman: Cooperation between armed forces of Oman and United Arab Emirates. Wright to Lloyd-Jones, 2 Aug 1973 & Pridham to FCO, 5 Aug 1973.
110 DeVore, p. 163. DeVore, p. 17.
111 AGDA FCO 8/2442, 'Iranian Military Assistance to Oman', Operational Order 5 of 1974, 5 Aug 1974.
112 AGDA FCO 8/2442, 'Iranian Military Assistance to Oman', Creasey to Azhari, 7 Aug 1974. Azhari to Creasey, 13 Aug 1974.

NOTES

113 AGDA FCO 8/2442, 'Iranian Military Assistance to Oman', Creasey to The Equerry to His Majesty the Sultan, Aug 1974.
114 Peterson, p. 484.
115 Hughes, p. 454.
116 Ladwig III, p. 72.
117 Akehurst, p. 30.
118 DeVore, p. 163.
119 Hughes, pp. 454–55.
120 Ladwig III, p. 72.
121 Graham, p. 343.
122 Ibid.
123 Graham, p. 343.
124 The Newsletter of the Sultan's Armed Forces Association—Issue No. 32 (December 1983), 'The Sultan's Armed Forces March 1970 to September 1972, Part 2: Autumn 1970–Spring 1971 (Major General J.D.C. Graham)'.
125 LHCMA, KCL—THWAITES COLLECTION—'Guide to Officer and Junior Leaders in Commanding Troops in Oman', 30 Jun 1965.
126 Fiennes, p. 87.
127 Peterson, p. 246. TNA FCO 8/1688, 'Attachment of SAS Division of United Kingdom to Armed Forces of Oman', Ackland to Parsons, 1 Feb 1971.
128 Hughes, p. 283.
129 Jeapes, p. 231.
130 Ibid.
131 Ibid.
132 Ibid., p. 162.
133 Hughes, p. 299.
134 Iran was the largest arms exporter to Oman in 1972 with double the UK value—'Sipri Arms Transfers Database'. https://www.sipri.org/
135 Alston and Laing, p. 249.
136 TNA FCO 8/1669—'Annual Review of Oman', Gow to Adler, 25 Apr 1970.
137 TNA FCO 8/1437—'British Assistance to the Sultan of Oman's Armed Forces', Charles Kendall and Partner's Ltd. to Adler, 21 Sep 1970, Nissen to Kendall, 15 Sep 1970, Charles Kendall & Partners to Nissen, 10 Sep 1970.
138 Hughes, p. 288.
139 Ibid.
140 Ibid.
141 DeVore, p. 157.
142 DeVore, p. 17.
143 Graham, p. 372.
144 Worrall, p. 287. Perkins, p. 147.

THE DHOFAR WAR

145 Worrall, p. 209. TNA—FCO 8/2687—Oman—Annual Review for 1975 (Calendar of Events 1975). Peterson, p. 441. USA National Archives Catalog Collection GRF-0314 Memorandum of Conversations—'January 9, 1975—Ford, Kissinger, Oman Sultan Qaboos bin Said'.
146 DeVore, p. 164. Perkins, pp. 132–33.
147 Hughes, pp. 101–02. Akehurst, p. 66.
148 Peterson, p. 329. Hughes, p. 101.
149 Hughes, p. 102.
150 Graham, p. 372.
151 Perkins, p. 44.
152 Allen and Rigsbee, p. 74. Peterson, p. 485.
153 AGDA FCO 8/2235, 'UK Arms Sales to Oman', Tatham to MODUK, 25 May 1974.
154 McCloskey, pp. 97–99.
155 Gardner, p. 345.
156 Ibid., p. 349. McCloskey, p. 98.
157 Gardiner, p. 350.
158 Purdon, p. 277.
159 Ladwig III, pp. 75–76.
160 DeVore, p. 20.
161 Worrall, p. 191.
162 TNA FCO 8/2006, 'Annual Review of Oman 1972', Parsons to Le Quesne, 12 Feb 1973.
163 Worrall, pp. 213–14.
164 AGDA FCO 8/2465, 'Economic Situation in Oman', FCO Memo 'Yahya Omar' (Treadwell), 8 Jun 1975. AGDA FCO 8/2235, 'UK Arms Sales to Oman', Shaker to Anderson, 11 Apr 1974. 'Oman—Rapier: Note of a Meeting Held on 23 April 1974', Apr 1974. AGDA FCO 8/2215, 'Political Situation in Oman' Memo, 'Call on Minister of Works' (Hawley), 12 Dec 1974, Clark to Hawley, 12 Dec 1974. Gardner, pp. 49–50.
165 Worrall, p. 214.
166 Gardner, pp. 55–6.
167 UAE NA—FCO 8/2020—'Summary of main points discussed in the meeting between DMO and CSAF 12 Jul 1973', Loose Minute: meeting between DMO and CSAF on 12 Jul 1973.
168 Gardner, p. 55.
169 Sultanate of Oman NRAA—Records of Oman 1966–1971 (Cambridge Archive Editions, 2003) Vol. 5: Letter, British Consulate General to Mr. M. Wier (Bahrain), 3 Aug 1970. Sultanate of Oman: Annual Review for 1970, D. Crawford (Consul General), 4 Jan 1971.
170 TNA—FCO 8/2687—Oman—Annual Review 1975, British Ambassador, Muscat (Treadwell) to Callahan (Prime Minister), 1 Jan 1976.
171 Allen and Rigsbee, pp. 75–77.
172 Ibid., p. 78. Peterson, p. 466.
173 SIPRI Arms Transfers Database: https://www.sipri.org/ [accessed 31 Apr 2023].

NOTES

7 Conclusion

1. Perkins, p. 39. DeVore, p. 163. Beckett, p. 218. Joshua Thiel, 'Coin Manpower Ratios: Debunking the 10 to 1 Ratio and Surges', *Small Wars Journal* (2011), pp. 1 & 7. Fiennes, p. 9. The US Army and Marine Corps Counterinsurgency Field Manual (FM-23), (Chicago: University of Chicago Press, 2007) p. 22. Thompson, pp. 48–49.
2. Jeapes, pp. 11–14, Devore, p. 2. Beckett, p. 230. Mockaitis, p. 93. Charters, p. 63.
3. Hughes, p. 423. DeVore, pp. 1, 12, 17. Newsinger, pp. 146–49. Hughes, pp. 298–300.
4. Plekhanov.
5. Paul *et al.* pp. xv and 1. Newsinger, pp. 134–5.
6. Charters, p. 63.
7. Beckett and Pimlott, p. 42.
8. DeVore, p. 22.
9. Paul *et al.*, pp. 284–86.
10. Abigail Watson, 'The Integrated Review: Lessons Learned from Remote Warfare' (London: Oxford Research Group, 2020), p. 4.
11. Cormac, p. 192.
12. Hughes, p. 454. DeVore, pp. 17 & 22. Newsinger, pp. 147 & 53.
13. DeVore, pp. 144–45. White, p. 8. Benest.
14. TNA—DEFE 11/854, 'Oman'—Woodard to Head of DS11, 5 Mar 1975.
15. Jeapes, p. 14.
16. Paul *et al.* p. xv.
17. Ladwig III, p. 63. Paul *et al.*, pp. 284–86.
18. Ladwig III, p. 63. Jeapes, pp. 11–14. Paul *et al.*, pp. 284–86.
19. Emily Knowles and Abigail Watson, 'Remote Warfare: Lessons Learned from Contemporary Theatres' (London: Oxford Research Group, 2018), pp. 2–5.
20. Peterson, p. 401.
21. Mockaitis, p. 72.
22. Peterson, p. 401.
23. The five as listed in the study out of seventy-one cases covered and twenty-one considered COIN 'wins', but the sixth considered as Brunei/early stages of Borneo campaign. Paul *et al.*, pp. xiv–xv.
24. Ministry of Defence (UK) Command Paper, 'Defence in a Competitive Age' (CP411) (HMSO, London: 2021). Ministry of Defence (UK), 'Integrated Operating Concept' (HMSO, London: 2021).
25. Ibid. Ministry of Defence (UK) Command Paper, 'Defence in a Competitive Age' (CP411) (HMSO, London: 2021), pp. 1–22.
26. Peterson, p. 234.
27. Oman News Agency (ONA), 'Oman Rennaisance March Presses Ahead with Full Confidence, Aptitude', https://www.omanobserver.om/article/8523/Main/oman-renaissance-march-presses-ahead-with-full-confidence-aptitude [accessed 22 Feb 2022].
28. Hawley, p. 59.

Bibliography

Oman News Agency (ONA), 'Oman Rennaisance March Presses Ahead with Full Confidence, Aptitude'. *Oman Observer*, 1 Nov 2020. https://www.omanobserver.om/article/8523/Main/oman-renaissance-march-presses-ahead-with-full-confidence-aptitude

John Akehurst, *We Won a War: The Campaign in Oman 1965–1975* (Salisbury: M. Russell, 1982).

Khalid Al Kharusi, 'The Dhofar War 1965–1975' (University of Central Lancashire, 2018).

Richard J. Aldrich, and Rory Cormac, *The Black Door: Spies, Secret Intelligence, and British Prime Ministers* (London: William Collins, 2016).

Calvin H. Allen, and W. Lynn Rigsbee, *Oman Under Qaboos: From Coup to Constitution, 1970–1996* (London: Frank Cass, 2002).

Robert Alston, and Stuart Laing, *Unshook to the End of Time: A History of Britain and Oman, 1650–1970* (London: Gilgamesh Publishing, 2012).

Simon Anglim, 'The Oman Djebel War, 1957–9', in https://thestrategybridge.org.

David Arkless, *The Secret War* (London: William Kinber & Co. Ltd., 1988).

US Army, and US Marine Corps, *Counterinsurgency Field Manual (Fm3-24)* (Chicago: University of Chicago, 2007).

Michael Barber, 'Brigadier Tim Landon—Soldier of Fortune Who Helped Ease Oman into the Modern World', *The Guardian*, 26 August 2007. https://www.theguardian.com/news/2007/aug/28/guardianobituaries.military

John Beasant, *Oman: The True-Life Drama and Intrigue of an Arab State* (New York: Random House, 2011).

John Beasant, and Christopher Ling, *Sultan in Arabia: A Private Life* (Edinburgh: Mainstream Publishing, 2004).

Ian Beckett, *The Roots of Counter-Insurgency; Armies and Guerilla Warfare, 1900–1945* (London: Blandford Press, 1988).

Ian F. Beckett, *Modern Insurgencies and Counter-Insurgencies: Guerrillas and Their Opponents since 1750* (London: Routledge, 2001).

Ian Beckett, and John Pimlott, *Counter Insurgency: Lessons from History* (Barnsley: Pen and Sword, 2011).

BIBLIOGRAPHY

David Benest, 'Ponder Anew: Brigadier John Graham and the Dhofar War 1970–1972', in *The Bridge* (2015). https://thestrategybridge.org/the-bridge/2016/1/1/ponder-anew-brigadier-john-graham-the-dhofar-war-19701972?rq=benest

Richard K. Betts, 'Is Strategy an Illusion?', *International Security*, 25 (2000), 5–50.

Peter de la Billière, *Looking for Trouble: SAS to Gulf Command* (London: Harper Collins, 1995).

Matthew Campbell, 'The Soldier Who Overthrew the Sultan of Oman in a Very British Coup', *The Sunday Times*, 22 Nov 2020.

David A. Charters, 'Counter-Insurgency Intelligence: The Evolution of British Theory and Practice', *Journal of Conflict Studies*, 29 (2009), 55–74.

Ian Cobain, 'Britain's Secret Wars', *The Guardian*, 8 September 2016.

The Gulf Committee, 'Dhofar: Britain's Colonial War in the Gulf' (London: The Gulf Committee, 1972).

Johnny Cooper, *One of the Originals: The Story of a Founder Member of the SAS* (London: Pan Books Ltd, 1991).

Rory Cormac, *Disrupt and Deny: Spies, Special Forces, and the Secret Pursuit of British Foreign Policy* (Oxford: Oxford University Press, 2018).

Michael Crawshaw, 'The Evolution of British COIN', ed. by Ministry of Defence Joint Doctrine Publication (JDP 3-40) (2012).

D. de C. Smiley, 'Muscat and Oman', *Royal United Services Institution Journal*, 105 (1960), 29–47.

Marc DeVore, 'The United Kingdom's Last Hot War of the Cold War: Oman, 1963–75', *Cold War History*, 11 (2011), 441–71.

Marc R. DeVore, 'A More Complex and Conventional Victory: Revisiting the Dhofar Counterinsurgency, 1963–1975', *Small Wars & Insurgencies*, 23 (2012), 144–73.

'Dhofar: Britain's Colonial War in the Gulf', ed. by The Gulf Committee (London: The Gulf Committee, January 1972).

Paul Dixon, '"Hearts and Minds"? British Counter-Insurgency from Malaya to Iraq', *Journal of Strategic Studies*, 32 (2009), 353–81.

Ranulph Fiennes, *Where Soldiers Fear to Tread* (London: New English Library, 1976).

David French, 'Nasty Not Nice: British Counter-Insurgency Doctrine and Practice, 1945–1967', *Small Wars & Insurgencies*, 23 (2012), 744–61.

Ian Gardiner, *In the Service of the Sultan: A First-Hand Account of the Dhofar Insurgency* (Barnsley: Pen and Sword, 2007).

Nikolas Gardner, 'The Harold Wilson Government, Airwork Services Limited, and the Saudi Arabian Air Defence Scheme, 1965–73', *Journal of Contemporary History*, 42 (2007), 345–63.

Nikolas Gardner, 'The Limits of the Sandhurst Connection: The Evolution of Oman's Foreign and Defense Policy, 1970–1977', *The Journal of the Middle East and Africa*, 6 (2015), 45–58.

Tony Geraghty, *Who Dares Wins: The Story of the SAS 1950–1982* (London: Fontana/Collins, 1990).

James F. Goode, 'Assisting Our Brothers, Defending Ourselves: The Iranian Intervention in Oman, 1972–75', *Iranian Studies*, 47 (2014), 441–62.

THE DHOFAR WAR

John Graham, *Ponder Anew: Reflections on the 20th Century* (Kent: Spellmount, 1999).

Michael J. Gunther, 'Combined Omani-British Strategy During the Dhofar Rebellion (1963–1982)' (King's College London, 2019).

Fred Halliday, *Arabia Without Sultans* (Harmondsworth: Penguin, 1974).

Donald Hawley, *Oman and Its Renaissance*, ed. by Foreign Great Britain and Library Commonwealth Office. Revised edn, *Oman and Its Renaissance* (London/New Jersey: Stacey International, 1990).

Jacqueline Hazelton, 'The "Hearts and Minds" Fallacy: Violence, Coercion, and Success in Counterinsurgency Warfare', *International Security*, 42 (2017), 80.

Alan Hoskins, *A Contract Officer in the Oman* (Tunbridge Wells: Costello, 1988).

Geraint Hughes, '"Amateurs Who Play in League Division One"? Anglo-Iranian Military Relations During the Dhofar War in Oman', *British Journal for Military History*, 4 (2017).

Geraint Hughes, 'Demythologising Dhofar: British Policy, Military Strategy, and Counter-Insurgency in Oman, 1963–1976', *Journal of Military History*, 79 (2015).

Geraint Hughes, 'A "Model Campaign" Reappraised: The Counter-Insurgency War in Dhofar, Oman, 1965–1975', *Journal of Strategic Studies*, 32 (2009), 271–305.

Geraint Hughes, 'A Proxy War in Arabia: The Dhofar Insurgency and Cross-Border Raids into South Yemen', *The Middle East Journal*, 69 (2015), 91–104.

Neil Innes, *Minister in Oman: A Personal Narrative* (Cambridge: The Oleander Press Ltd, 1987).

Robert Jackson, *The Malayan Emergency and Indonesian Confrontation: The Commonwealth's Wars, 1948–1966* (Barnsley: Pen and Sword, 2008).

Tony Jeapes, *SAS Operation Oman* (London: HarperCollins, 1980).

Clive Jones, *Britain and the Yemen Civil War, 1962–1965: Ministers, Mercenaries and Mandarins—Foreign Policy and the Limits of Covert Action* (Eastbourne/Portland, OR: Sussex Academic Press, 2010).

Clive A. Jones, 'Military Intelligence and the War in Dhofar: An Appraisal', *Small Wars & Insurgencies*, 25 (2014), 628–46.

Jeremy Jones, and Nicholas Ridout, *Oman, Culture and Diplomacy* (Edinburgh: Edinburgh University Press, 2013).

David Kilcullen, *Counterinsurgency* (Oxford: Oxford University Press, 2010).

Frank Kitson, *Bunch of Five* (London: Faber and Faber, 1977).

Frank Kitson, *Low Intensity Operations: Subversion, Insurgency and Peacekeeping* (London: Faber and Faber, 1991).

Emily Knowles, and Abigail Watson, 'Remote Warfare: Lessons Learned from Contemporary Theatres' (London: Oxford Research Group, 2018).

Walter C. Ladwig III, 'Supporting Allies in Counterinsurgency: Britain and the Dhofar Rebellion', *Small Wars & Insurgencies*, 19 (2008), 62–88.

BIBLIOGRAPHY

Tony Lewis, 'The Story of the Sultan of Oman's Armed Forces 1964–67', *The Journal of the Sultan's Armed Forces Association*, 7 (1988), 31–40.

Daniel Marston, and Carter Malkasian, *Counterinsurgency in Modern Warfare* (London: Bloomsbury, 2011).

Keith McCloskey, *Airwork: A History* (Stroud: The History Press, 2012).

John McKeown, 'The Dhofar War and Its Significance' (Cambridge, MA, 1981).

Colin Mitchell, *Having Been a Soldier* (London: Hamish Hamilton, 1969).

Thomas R. Mockaitis, *British Counterinsurgency in the Post-Imperial Era* (Manchester: Manchester University Press, 1995).

S. Monick, 'Victory in Hades: The Forgotten Wars of the Oman 1957–1959 and 1970–1976. Part 2: The Dhofar Campaign 1970–1976', *Scientia Militaria: South African Journal of Military Studies*, 12 (1982), 1–26.

Jan Morris, *Sultan in Oman* (London: Arrow Books Ltd, 1990).

David Neild, *A Soldier in Arabia* (Surbiton: Medina Publishing Ltd, 2015).

John Newsinger, *British Counterinsurgency*, 2nd edn (Basingstoke, Hampshire: Palgrave Macmillan, 2015).

Mackubin Owens, 'Strategy and the Strategic Way of Thinking', *Naval War College Review*, 60 (2007), 111–24.

Francis Owtram, 'Oman and the West: State Formation in Oman since 1920' (University of London, 1999).

Julian Paget, *Counter-Insurgency Campaigning* (London: Faber and Faber, 1967).

Anthony Parsons, *They Say the Lion: Britain's Legacy to the Arabs—A Personal Memoir* (London: Random House, 1986).

Christopher Paul, Colin P. Clarke, Beth Grill, and Molly Dunigan, 'Paths to Victory: Detailed Insurgency Case Studies' (Rand National Defense Research Inst Santa Monica CA, 2013).

K. Perkins, 'Oman 1975: The Year of Decision', *The RUSI Journal*, 124 (1979), 38.

Ken Perkins, *A Fortunate Soldier* (London: Brassey's Defence Pubishers Ltd, 1988).

Ken Perkins, *Khalida* (London: Quartet Books, 1991).

J.E. Peterson, 'The Experience of British Counter-Insurgency Campaigns and Implications for Iraq', in *Arabian Peninsula Background Note—APBN-009* (2009).

John Peterson, *Oman's Insurgencies: The Sultanate's Struggle for Supremacy* (London: Saqi, 2007).

John E. Peterson, 'Guerrilla Warfare and Ideological Confrontation in the Arabian Peninsula: The Rebellion in Dhufar', *World Affairs*, 139 (1977), 278–95.

Wendell Phillips, *Oman: A History* (Beirut: Librarie du Lebanon, 1971).

John Pimlott, *British Military Operations 1945–1985* (London: Bison Books, 1984).

Sergey Plekhanov, *A Reformer on the Throne: Sultan Qaboos Bin Said Al Said* (London: Trident Press Ltd, 2004).

Douglas Porch, *Counterinsurgency: Exposing the Myths of the New Way of War* (Cambridge: Cambridge University Press, 2013).

Corran Purdon, *List the Bugle: Reminiscences of an Irish Soldier* (Vancouver: Greystone Books, 1993).

Bryan Ray, *Dangerous Frontiers: Campaigning in Somaliland and Oman* (Barnsley: Pen and Sword, 2008).

Colin Richardson, *Masirah: Tales from a Desert Island* (Durham: The Pentland Press 2001).

Ash Rossiter, 'Britain and the Development of Professional Security Forces in the Gulf Arab States 1921–71: Local Forces and Informal Empire' (University of Exeter, 2014).

Pauline Searle, *Dawn Over Oman* (London: George Allen & Unwin, 1979).

'Sir Donald Hawley (Obituary)', in *The Telegraph*, 11 Feb 2008.

Ian Skeet, *Muscat and Oman: The End of an Era* (London: Faber and Faber, 1974).

David Smiley, *Arabian Assignment* (London: Leo Cooper, 1975).

Hew Strachan, 'British Counter-Insurgency from Malaya to Iraq', *The RUSI Journal*, 152 (2007), 8–11.

Abdel Razzaq Takriti, 'The 1970 Coup in Oman Reconsidered', *Journal of Arabian Studies*, 3 (2013), 155–73.

Abdel Razzaq Takriti, *Monsoon Revolution: Republicans, Sultans, and Empires in Oman, 1965–1976* (Oxford: Oxford University Press, 2013).

Joshua Thiel, 'COIN Manpower Ratios: Debunking the 10 to 1 Ratio and Surges', *Small Wars Journal* (2011).

Robert Grainger Ker Thompson, *Defeating Communist Insurgency: Experiences from Malaya and Vietnam* (London: Chatto & Windus, 1966).

Peter Thwaites, *Muscat Command* (London: Leo Cooper, 1995).

Marc Valeri, *Oman: Politics and Society in the Qaboos State* (London: C. Hurst & Co., 2017).

Jonathan Walker, *Aden Insurgency: The Savage War in Yeman 1962–67* (Barnsley: Pen and Sword, 2014).

Vron Ware, *Return of a Native: Learning from the Land* (London: Repeater Books, 2022).

Abigail Watson, 'The Integrated Review: Lessons Learned from Remote Warfare' (London: Oxford Research Group, 2020).

Jim White, 'Oman 1965–1976: From Certain Defeat to Decisive Victory', *Small Wars Journal*, 1 (2008).

James Worrall, *Statebuilding and Counterinsurgency in Oman: Political, Military and Diplomatic Relations at the End of Empire*, Library of Modern Middle East Studies (London: I.B.Tauris, 2014).

Athol Yates, and Geraint Hughes, 'Operation Intradon in the Musandam, 1970–1971: What This Counterinsurgency Operation Says About British Military Operations in the Arabian Gulf', *Small Wars & Insurgencies* (2022), 1–23.

BIBLIOGRAPHY

Archival Resources

Air Ministry Records (AIR)
Cabinet Office Records (CAB)
Foreign and Commonwealth Office Records (FCO)
Foreign Office Records (FO)
Granada TV 'End of Empire'—Transcripts Archive Collection
Liddell Hart Centre for Military Archives (LHCMA), King's College London—Thwaites Collection
Middle East Centre (MEC), St Anthony's College, Oxford—Graham Collection
Ministry of Defence Records (DEFE)
Prime Minister's Office Records (PREM)
The National Archives (TNA), Kew, London
War Office Records (WO)

Sultanate of Oman, National Records and Archives Authority, Muscat, Oman
United Arab Emirates National Archives (NA), Abu Dhabi, UAE
Arabian Gulf Digital Archive (AGDA) (online access)
USA National Archives Catalog Collection (online access)

Regimental Publications

The Sultan's Armed Forces Association Newsletter
The Journal of the Sultan's Armed Forces Association
The Guards Magazine: Journal of the Household Division

Podcasts

Mike Thomson, 23-11-2009' in *BBC Sounds (Radio 4)*, 23 Nov 2009. https://www.bbc.co.uk/sounds/play/b00ny7nb

Sarika Breeze, 'His Quest for the Lost City of Uber and Other Omani Adventures (Sir Ranulph Fiennes for the Anglo-Omani Society)', (The Anglo-Omani Society, 2020). https://www.britishomani.org/news/bos/podcast-transcript-sir-ranulph-fiennes

Databases

Sipri Arms Transfers Database. https://www.sipri.org/

THE DHOFAR WAR

Lectures

Martin Robb, The Anglo-Omani Society/Sultan's Armed Forces Association Lecture: 'Civil Aid in Dhofar: The Key to Peace', London, 15 Jun 2023

Interviews

David Neild (Former TOS officer, founding Commanding Officer of Ras Al Khaimah Mobile Force (1969) and Sharjah National Guard (1972)

Ray Goodall (former RAF Group Captain with extensive experience of operating through RAF Masirah 1975–1977)

Index

1798 Treaty (and 1800 reaffirmation) 44
1839 Treaty of Commerce 44
1861 Canning Award (Zanzibar
    Subsidy) 44
1958 'Exchange of Letters' agreements
    143, 146–7
1970 coup 24–5
1973 Yom Kippur War 180
1973–1974 Middle Eastern Oil
    Crisis 148
1974 Sherishitti Caves operation 166

Aden COIN campaign 90
Akehurst, John, Brig. 2, 28, 69, 76, 83, 99,
    101, 111, 119, 147, 157
Al Ghassani, Mohammed 23
al Hinai, Talib bin Ali 18
al Nabhani, Suleiman bin Himyar 18
Al Said dynasty 46
Arthur, Geoffrey, Sir 154
Ashworth, Anthony 74, 162
Augusta Bell 205 helicopters
    76, 102, 172

Balfour, Hugh, Rear-Ad. 158, 181
Barouni, Omer 37, 180
Batinah Force (BF) 19
Battle of Mirbat 111, 115–18, 135
BATT 'Radio Detachment'
    interrogation 113
Baxter, David, Capt. 168

Beckett, Ian 63
Bell, Graham, Sir 162
Benest, David 79
Bennett, Erik, Sir 39, 158, 181
bin Nufl, Musallam 19–20, 77, 89
'block and clear' strategy 129
'blocking line' strategy 172
Borneo campaign 87
Boustead, Hugh, Sir 92, 155–6
Braddell-Smith, Johnny, Maj. 140
Braik, HE Sheikh 147
British Army Training Team (BATT) 27
British Lee Enfield bolt-action rifles 102
British–Omani treaties and agreements
    42–68, 44
    1646 and 1659 Rainsford Treaties 44
    1839 Treaty of Commerce 44
    1861 Canning Award
        (Zanzibar Subsidy) 44
    1891, 1939, and 1951 Treaties of
        Friendship, Commerce and
        Navigation 44
    1920 Treaty of Sib (or Seeb) 44
    1958 Exchange of Letters 44
    1960 Exchange of Letters
        'upgrade' 45
    archival documents 50
    stability, status quo, and state-building
        42–68
Brook, Patrick, Maj. 140
Brown, Bob, Lt. Col. 94, 105, 147

Callaghan, James 162
Central Treaty Organization
    (CENTO) 35
Chauncy, Leslie, Maj. 46, 155
Chinook helicopters 103, 175
Civil Action Teams (CATs) 61
COIN (counterinsurgency) campaigns
    1, 84
  Aden COIN campaign 90
  Britain in Dhofar COIN
    campaign 31–2
  Britain's economic problem 32
  Cold War-era COIN campaigns 41
  Communist encroachment on
    Arabian Peninsula,
    prevention 33
  'Question of Oman' issue 37, 39, 41
  Mau Mau COIN campaign 89, 135
  Omani COIN forces 27
  'open hand of friendship' COIN
    element 61
  UK COIN-style insurgent amnesty
    programme 93
Commander Sultan's Armed Forces
    (CSAF) 8
  COIN and warfare experience of
    CSAFs 72
Cormac, Rory 49
Crawford, Stewart, Sir 154
Creasey, Tim, Sir 39, 65, 72, 82, 109, 129,
    138, 158, 161

Damavand Line 27, 84, 108, 119, 131
de la Billière, Peter 73, 109, 116
DeVore, Marc 47
Dhofar Development Committee
    (DDC) 147
Dhofar province, operating sectors xvi
Dhofar War
  arms exports to Sultanate of
    Oman during 171
  events timeline 21–2
  historical reality of 2

left-leaning view 2
literature concerning 1
Omani COIN forces 27
Operation AQOOBA 27
Operation SIMBA 25
Operations JAGUAR 25
Operations LEOPARD 25
origins 17–19
  Imamate versus Sultanate power
    struggle 18
  insurgency begins 19–24
  Zakat tax on agricultural
    produce 18
orthodox historical view 1–2
Qaboos entry and 24–8
revisionist scholars' view 2
Dhufar Benevolent Society (DBS) 19
Dhufari Charitable Association (DCA) 19
Dhufar Soldiers Association (DSO) 19
Djebel War 18, 71, 73, 103

Entwistle, Brian, Sqn. Ldr. 98
'Exchange of Letters' agreements 179

Field Surgical Team (FST) 60, 114
'Five-Point Plan' 24, 87
Fletcher, Jack, Brig. 56, 83–4, 99, 157
'Flying Doctor' service 92

Gardner, Ian, Capt. 101
Ghalla-based SAF soldier training 167
Goode, James 49
Goodfellow, Bill, Flt. Lt. 62
Graham, John, Brig. 10, 13, 18, 21–2, 23,
    25, 27, 48, 51, 53, 55–6, 57, 65, 72,
    77, 78–82, 84, 85, 91, 114, 116, 117,
    118, 126, 163, 175
Ground attack BAC167 Strikemaster
    aircraft 76, 77, 102, 113, 177

Habrut Fort incident (Operation
    AQOOBA) 13
Harvey, Mike, Col. 12, 24, 99, 129, 136

INDEX

Hawker Hunter jet aircraft 36, 106, 113
Hawley, Donald, Sir 14, 59
'hearts and minds' approach 5, 12, 24, 48, 63, 73, 80, 86, 88, 92, 110, 126, 135, 147
Hornbeam Line 26, 73, 83, 106, 129, 172
Hughes, Francis 58, 151
Hughes, Geraint 34

Imperial Iranian Battle Group (IIBG) 106, 119
Integrated Operating Concept (IoC) 194
Interim Advisory Council (IAC) 9

Jeapes, Tony 2, 147
Jebel Akhdar rebellion 9, 1, 87

Katyusha rockets 102
Kealy, Mike, Capt. 116
'Keeni-Meeni' operations 90
Kendall, Charles 170–1
Kenyan Mau Mau campaign 64
Kitson, Frank, Capt. 90

Landon, Timothy 50, 57, 59, 158–61, 162
Leopard Line 25, 129
Lewis, Tony, Col. 8, 20, 21, 72, 75–7, 94, 98, 155
Loan Service Personnel (LSP) 19
Lobb, Mike, Capt. 140
Luce, William, Sir 154

MacLean, Jim 153, 155
Mahra operation 92
Marxist People's Republic of Southern Yemen (PRSY) 21
Mason, Peter 58, 151
Mau Mau COIN campaign 89, 135
Maxwell, Colin, Col. 19, 70, 98, 137
McKeown, John 18, 99
McLean, Colin, Lt. 147
military operations and tactics 97–141

Adeni National Liberation Front (NLF)-style assassinations 113
Adoo development 101
Battle of Mirbat 115–16
British in command of SOAF 99
British influence on 98–9
Egyptian-trained insurgents 101
Field Surgical Teams (FST) 114
Firqa units rise 110–11
Imperial Iranian Armed Forces 107–8
Operational TENABLE 112–13
SAF soldiers equipped 102, 110, 119
Sarfait operation 114–15
see also operations, war phase
military strategy 69–96
Britain's main latent influence over 71
COIN and warfare experience of CSAFs 72
containing the threat 74–8
cross-border insurgency 92
goals 70–4
'Five-Point Plan' 87
Operation HORNBEAM 83
SAF capability 80–1
stabilize, expand, and defeat 78–96
Mirbat action 115–19
Monsoon Revolution: Republicans, Sultans, and Empires in Oman (Takriti) 3
Movement of Arab Nationalists (MAN) 19
Muscat and Oman Field Force (MOFF) 19, 151
Muscat Infantry (MI) 19
Muscat Regiment (MR) 20

National Democratic Front for the Liberation of Oman and the Arabian Gulf (NDFLOAG) 23, 95
Nimrod nuclear submarine 36
non-kinetic military and informal support 142–83
aircraft maintenance and combat preparation 177–8

Britain's financial influence over
  Oman 148
Britain's personnel contribution 157–8
British contribution towards civil
  development 147
economic/finance factor 144
limiting support and maximizing
  ongoing influence 178–83
non-British materials supply 173
personnel provision factor 144
provision 143–78
secondary benefits 149
technical/maintenance support
  factor 145
training 145, 167
under Qaboo's rule 151–2
war materials supply 172–5
war supplies/ logistics factor 145
Northern Frontier Regiment (NFR) 20
Nufl, Musallam bin 89

Oldman, Hugh, Col. 19, 57–8, 60, 72,
  80, 154, 159
Oman and Gulf region (pre-1970 coup) xv
Oman during Dhofar War, British
  influence in 154
Omani COIN forces 27
Oman Intelligence Service (OIS) 62
Oman Research Department (ORD) 62
Oman Revolutionary Movement
  (ORM) 19
*Oman's Insurgencies: The Sultanate's Struggle
  for Supremacy* (Peterson) 2
Omer, Yahya 37, 180
'open hand of friendship' COIN
  element 61
Operation AQOOBA 13, 27, 53–4, 69, 81,
  104, 153, 163
Operation CAVIAR 56
Operation DHIB 92
Operation HADAF 119, 131
Operation HILWAH 131
Operation HIMAAR 138–9

Operation HORNBEAM 83
Operation INTRADON 126
Operation JAGUAR 81, 111, 128–9
Operation JASON 94–5, 113
Operation LANCE 23
Operation LEOPARD 81
Operation SIMBA 25, 81, 111, 114
Operation STORM 52, 87
Operation TENABLE 65, 112–13
Operations JAGUAR 25
Operations LEOPARD 25
operations, war phase 121–41
  'block and clear' strategy 129
  defensive 126–7
  Firqa establishment issue 128
  non-UK foreign troops
    contribution 132–3
  offensive 122–6
  Phase 1 (1964–1970) 121–2, 123
  Phase 2 (Jul 1970–Sept 1971) 123
  Phase 3 (Oct 1971–end 1974) 123–4
  Phase 4 (Jan–Dec 1975) 124
  SAF numbers increased 127–8
  UK-deployed forces increased 127
  Watts 'Five-Point Plan' 130

People's Democratic Republic of Yemen
  (PDRY) 21
Perkins, Ken, Maj-Gen. 22, 28, 50, 72, 86,
  108, 119, 176, 181
PFLOAG order of battle (ORBAT) 86–7
politics and diplomacy, Dhofar War 29–68
  1965–1971 29
  Britain in Dhofar COIN campaign 31–2
  Britain's economic problem 32
  Cold War-era COIN campaigns 41
  Communist encroachment on
    Arabian Peninsula,
    prevention 33
  'Question of Oman' issue 37, 39, 41
  Cold War geopolitical situation 30
  from oil to international reputation
    30–42

INDEX

Oman-centric and British-related
aims 42–68
overarching and regional strategic
aims 30–42
Popular Front for the Liberation of
Oman (PFLO) 4
Popular Front for the Liberation of the
Occupied Arabian Gulf
(PFLOAG) 4
Purdon, Corran, Brig. 18, 70, 72, 76–7, 94,
98, 105, 126, 156

Qaboos (Sultan) 9, 14, 34, 46–7, 57,
69, 104
'Q' unit detachments 90

Radfan/Aden conflict 73
Reminiscences of an Irish Soldier 98
Robb, Martin, Lt. Col. 61, 147
Royal Fleet Auxiliary (RFA) ships 172

Sarfait operation 114–15
SAS Operation Oman (Jeapes) 2
Secret Intelligence Service (SIS) 62
'sliding scale of influence' framework
8, 97, 167
accelerated decline (late 1972 onwards)
phase 11, 13
post-1970 coup (to 1972) phase 10
pre-1970 coup phase 10
war phases 10, 14
Smiley, David, Col. 19, 45, 70–1, 72, 156
Spagin recoilless rifles 102
Special Air Service (SAS) Regiment 12
*Statebuilding and Counterinsurgency in
Oman: Political, Military and
Diplomatic Relations at the End of
Empire* (Worrall) 3
'state power' approach 64
Stoker, Bill, Sqn. Ldr. 116
Sultan of Oman's Air Force (SOAF) 16
Sultan Qaboos 3
Sultan's Armed Forces (SAF) 3
surface-to-air missiles (SAM) 102
Surrendered Enemy Personnel (SEP) 49

Taimur, Said bin (Sultan) 17
Taimur, Tariq bin 60
Takriti, Abdel 3, 18
Taylor Woodrow 39, 181
Templar, Gerald, Gen. Sir 5, 45
Thwaites, Peter, Brig. 39, 51, 158
Turnhill, Teddy, Lt. Col. 50, 99, 159

UK COIN-style insurgent amnesty
programme 93
Union de Banques Arabes et Françaises
(UBAF) 160

Victor V-Bombers 36

Waterfield, Pat, Brig. 19, 98, 154, 156
Watts 'Five-Point Plan' 87–9, 93, 130
Watts, John, Lt. Col. 24, 73, 87, 109, 158
'Westphalian order' 48
*We Won a War: The Campaign in Oman
1965–75* 2
Wilson, Harold 32, 47, 66, 91
Worrall, James 3, 59

Zanzibar Subsidy payment 148
Zulu Wars 117

235

www.ingramcontent.com/pod-product-compliance
Lightning Source LLC
Chambersburg PA
CBHW020646300426
44112CB00007B/263